The Language of Vinyl

The Language of Vinyl

Record Industry Terms and Phrases of the Golden Era

RANDY McNUTT

McFarland & Company, Inc., Publishers
Jefferson, North Carolina

All images are from the author's collection.

Library of Congress Cataloguing-in-Publication Data

Names: McNutt, Randy, author.
Title: The language of vinyl : record industry terms and phrases of the golden era / Randy McNutt.
Description: Jefferson, North Carolina : McFarland & Company, 2021. | Includes bibliographical references and index.
Identifiers: LCCN 2021022833 | ISBN 9781476685724 (paperback : acid free paper) ∞
ISBN 9781476643656 (ebook)
Subjects: LCSH: Sound recording industry—Dictionaries. | BISAC: MUSIC / History & Criticism
Classification: LCC ML102.S67 M36 2021 | DDC 780.26/603—dc23
LC record available at https://lccn.loc.gov/2021022833

British Library cataloguing data are available
ISBN (print) 978-1-4766-8572-4
ISBN (ebook) 978-1-4766-4365-6

© 2021 Randy McNutt. All rights reserved

No part of this book may be reproduced or transmitted in any form or by any means, electronic or mechanical, including photocopying or recording, or by any information storage and retrieval system, without permission in writing from the publisher.

Front cover photograph by Annette Shaff (Shutterstock)

Printed in the United States of America

*McFarland & Company, Inc., Publishers
Box 611, Jefferson, North Carolina 28640
www.mcfarlandpub.com*

For Shad O'Shea
Friend, Character, Record Man

Table of Contents

Preface 1

The Dictionary 5

Bibliography 249

Index 255

Preface

When I first heard a recording engineer utter the term "butt splice," I cringed. Then someone said "iron mother," and I thought of *The Pit and the Pendulum*. I felt better when another record man said he had a problem with his biscuit. At that time, I had been producing records for a few years, but I had never heard these terms spoken in the studio or in a record label office. Later, I learned that they were a part of a fading vocabulary that I had not been taught—yet. Today, this lost language of the vinyl-era music business is obscured by digital mumbo-jumbo. At one time, however, the old language was spoken by big-name recording engineers, rural jukebox operators, and independent label owners like Johnny Vincent at Ace Records in Jackson, Mississippi, Stan Lewis at Paula Records in Shreveport, Louisiana, and Harry Carlson at Fraternity Records in Cincinnati. Once they got wound up, they spewed out all sorts of these alien words. Being a generation younger, I felt like an interstellar traveler who had just arrived on a new planet.

In this book you will learn many odd words and phrases related, directly and indirectly, to the record industry's golden age of vinyl, from the 1950s through the 1970s.

A gold mine of definitions came from Shad O'Shea (born Howard Lovdal), my late friend and mentor. He produced hundreds of records over fifty years in the radio and music businesses. He understood the lost language and legends and he passed them on to me. Shad knew everyone because he leased masters to big labels, small labels, and labels that operated on a telephone and a prayer. A wall in the hallway of his recording studio featured fifty to sixty singles released on important labels, all produced by Shad himself or issued by him on one of his own labels. At twenty-two years old, I was impressed by anyone who had leased a master to any kind of label. Imagine what an entire wall did for me.

These music-business catchwords come from my own experiences as a producer and writer, as well as from the mouths of professionals like Shad.

These people were a hardy stock of mostly men who spoke the exotic language "recordese." Additional words were discovered by digging through newspapers, magazines, album notes, and books. Friendly disc jockeys also helped. Some antiquated words and phrases used in the early 1900s—"cut a record," for example—continue in use. A number of others that linger have morphed into new meanings. All this reminds me of a story I once wrote about the efforts of educators at Miami University in Oxford, Ohio, to save and catalog pieces of the Miami tribe's lost language. Few people, including descendants of the Native American tribe, could speak it. So it is with many of the words I have gathered.

Few people associated with the old record business ever bothered to save their niches' peculiar language. They were too busy earning a living to keep track of their colorful language, lore, characters, and stories. But I cared about retrieving this history before the original practitioners were all gone. I started working sporadically on this project early enough to meet some 1950s industry veterans at the end of their long lives and prolific careers. My interviews with them turned into big adventures.

Some of my most memorable conversations were with Shad when he spoke in the old language. His knowledge dated to 1959, when he worked at WNOE in New Orleans, where he cut his first record. By 1963, he was on the air at WCPO radio in Cincinnati, where he founded a regional label called Counterpart Records and its publishing company, Counterpart Music (BMI). Later came Counterpart Creative Studios. Shad recorded garage bands, country acts, and gospel, but his real love was the novelty record. It became his funny forum. He wrote, produced, and recorded many novelties, using his smooth, deep disc jockey voice. One of his forgotten gems is "Bare She Is," about a real Miss America who lost her crown over some nude photos that surfaced about the time she won the title.

In every way, Shad was a real character. The record industry used to be filled with guys like him, but no longer. They retired, died, or burned out at 45 rpm. With them went their language and stories. I hope you will smile when you read about the days when trade magazines used outlandish euphemisms and titles, just for the sake of sounding impressive. "Warbler" comes to mind as one of the worst descriptions of a singer in the 1940s and early 1950s. Imagine calling Elvis Presley a warbler.

Some terms in this book will give you a feel for what trade reporting was like in the days when jukebox guys with shellac in their veins ruled the recording world, curious producers traveled the back roads, and vinyl was beginning to take root. Let the book transport you back to the time when disc jockeys loved the records they played, the music industry wasn't so predictable, musicians (not machines) played on recording sessions, and singers had to be able to "carry a tune" if they wanted to record. This was also a time when small labels with a little money could discover talented vocalists, record them, and occasionally place their records in the top ten locally, regionally, and nationally.

Shad's world was local, regional, and national. He lived every producer's dream. He met and became friends with many indie producers. He leased a ton of masters. He operated his own studio and discovered talent. He wrote and recorded his own material.

I wish he could be here to see his name on the dedication page. He would say what he always said to me: "If God offered me another ten years of life in exchange for the life I lived in the record business, I would have to say no. The business was fun back then. I didn't have a lot of hits, but I had a good time."

Shad O'Shea, R.I.P.

The Dictionary

A

Acetate

Synthetic plastic made from cellulose nitrate lacquer. It was applied to discs that could tolerate several plays before beginning to wear. The acetate, invented in 1934 by Cecil Watts, was used primarily to record masters in the pre-tape days. Because of its low surface noise, the acetate disc was the chief recording medium for years. Many hits from the 1940s and 1950s were cut directly onto blank acetate discs. If you wanted to record something right away, you did it on "an acetate," as they were known in the trade. But the discs had other purposes, too. Label executives used to say, "Send me an acetate," meaning a demo. This practice continued for a surprisingly long time. Meanwhile, acetates were used for something even more important. When audio engineers mastered recordings—from the birth of vinyl in the 1940s to its "death" in the late 1990s—they used acetates. Singer-songwriter Dan Penn, who did a lot of his early work at Fame Recording in Muscle Shoals, in northern Alabama, said he and a few other guys were working in the studio one night when Tommy Roe, who regularly recorded there, came in after finishing a tour of England. He was clutching an acetate. "He said, 'Boys, I've got something here that's going to change the world.' We said, 'Put it on! Put it on!' So he put it on a little turntable over in a corner, and we heard this 'I Want to Hold Your Hand.' It sounded so *bad*. He said, 'Well, what do you think?' I said, 'Tommy, if that's going to change the world, I don't know if I want to live in it!'" (See **Wax**.)

Advertising Discs

Promoted products, including movies. The records were issued as 45s and LPs. To promote films, movie distribution firms used to buy thirty- and sixty-second ad spots on radio stations, which played the special advertising records. Many were used to plug forgettable exploitation films, but other advertising records were not so blatant.

Advertising Promotion

Independent labels showed off their latest singles in full-, half-, and quarter-page advertisements. They called it advertising promotion. From the late 1940s through the '50s and '60s, this opportunity was vital to the success of many labels, including King, Imperial, DeLuxe, and others. In those days, advertising was more affordable. Singles ads allowed national and regional indie labels, and even jukebox and record-accessory firms, to reach radio personnel and record store owners directly. One of the more interesting full-page ads featured Terry Knight, manager and producer of Grand Funk Railroad, giving the finger to the record business as a Christmas gift. As the record industry became more sophisticated in the late 1970s, however, and several trade publications went out of business, indie labels could no longer afford to showcase their latest singles—even if many of them were breaking in several markets—to the nation's DJs. Welcome to the big, glitzy, costly record business.

Al Hirt Bill

Legislation aimed at protecting celebrities, including famous musicians in New Orleans. In July of 1970, by a vote of thirty-three to two, the Louisiana State Senate approved the "Al Hirt Bill," making it a criminal offense to throw an object at participants in a parade. The legislation was inspired by an incident in the New Orleans' French Quarter. The famous trumpet player suffered injuries when someone threw a brick at him as he was riding in the Mardi Gras parade. Soon after, he was recuperating and getting ready to promote his new GWP Records album, *Al Hirt Country*, his first collection of country and pop songs, which had been recorded in Nashville. But he would have to wait until his lip healed. Officials expected their bill to inspire similar laws, but that didn't happen. Perhaps throwing objects was already a criminal offense. This wasn't Hirt's only trouble in the Quarter. A few years earlier, thieves broke into his car and stole two trumpets valued at $900. They featured his name engraved on them, and medallions with his likeness.

Alan Freed Incident

The famous DJ was charged with inciting a riot at a rock 'n' roll show. Alan Freed is widely known as the 1950s DJ who helped launch rock 'n' roll to a large audience of young radio listeners. He also was known for owning his share of songs, publishing rights, and other perks. When you get as big as Freed was in 1958, your walkout gets its own name—"the Alan Freed Incident." That's what people in the radio and record business came to call it after Freed abruptly resigned from the staff of WINS in New York on May 3 of that year, while he was on the road promoting his rock tours. *Billboard* called it by that name, too. Complicating things was his indictment on a charge of "inciting to riot." The teen ruckus occurred in Boston that day, where Freed was staging a rock concert. The newspapers called it "the Second Boston Tea Party." Freed quit soon after because, as he put it, WINS "failed to stand behind policies and principles." This reportedly surprised the station, which claimed it hadn't fired Freed. Station executives said they treated the incident as something that occurred outside the scope of Freed's station duties. However, they couldn't have been pleased with his outside activities. In addition to the Boston show, he had scheduled additional events in Montreal, Hershey, Pennsylvania, and other cities. (See **Personality DJ** and **Payola**.)

Album

Originated from the similarity to a photograph album—that is, a number of pieces in one book into which the buyer could slip 78-rpm discs. In the United States, the preferred name for a group of recorded songs is the album. When the 12-inch long-playing vinyl disc arrived in 1948, people began calling it the album (many English people preferred the official name, the LP, for long-playing). The name continued to evolve when multiple songs were placed on one disc. The name album is still with us, being used to describe multiple-song compact discs, cassette tapes, digital releases, and other successors to the LP.

Album Cover

Also called a jacket. The album cover became a time-honored means of protecting and covering the twelve-inch vinyl LP. In the album's early days, the late 1940s and early 1950s, record labels considered the cover more functional than anything else. As the '50s wore on, however, record executives began to sell the entire package—the music as well as an attractive cover. It still provides an aesthetic thrill to millions of vinyl fans. (See **Album Cover Art**.)

Album Cover Art

Graphic artists' work on LP covers. When the compact disc arrived in the 1980s and production of LPs declined, buyers lamented the loss of a larger canvass. It was the disappearance of album-cover art. Some artists have compared it to that of colorful old film posters. It's back now, to a lesser degree of distribution. Because of the twelve-by-twelve-inch format, artists could work more freely than on the smaller-format CD inserts. In its heyday in the 1970s, album-cover art became the second most important question that record companies debated (the music being the other). More recognizable examples include The Beatles' *Yesterday ... and Today*, which featured the famous "butcher cover," pulled by the label because of its offensiveness; the *Abraxas* cover for Santana; and The Bee Gees' red felt cover for the original *Odessa*. Now that albums are coming back into record shops, album cover art is back in style.

Allied Record Company

Independent record-pressing company that stood out in the business through the years. A music trade magazine once described Allied Records successes as "a history of firsts." America's prototypical pressing company was the first to press LPs in L.A. It was the link between the past, present, and future of record manufacturing. But Allied didn't stop there. According to *Record World*, in the 1960s Allied became the first company to provide national distribution to independent labels. By then it had come a long way since its founding in 1933, when Allied pressed 78-rpm records and manufactured transcription discs. After vinyl LPs and 45s arrived in the late 1940s, Allied started making those records too, and became "one of the most creative companies in the record industry," according to a *Record World* story in 1969. By then the company, located at 2437 E. 57th Street in Los Angeles, offered custom pressing, plating, mastering, label and album printing, shipping, warehousing and, as an advertisement put it, "All Sizes—All Speeds." As a pressing firm, Allied received many patents, including some in the economical injection molding process. Other achievements came over the years, including development of the first tape duplicator for broadcasting. By the 1960s Allied reigned as one of the nation's largest and most respected custom pressing plants in the nation, manufacturing discs for big labels such as RCA Victor, Disney, Mercury, Pickwick, Columbia, and Tower. It operated facilities for pressing, offset printing, quality control, sleeve imprinting, shipping, and packaging. In 1979, WEA (Warner-Elektra-Asylum) purchased Allied. Another important name in America's music history vanished.

Allocations

Sending records to distributors. How many? That was the question. At trade conferences starting in 1963, record labels finally decided to do something about a long-time problem. They called the increasingly troublesome issue "allocations." The term referred to "the practice of assigning a specific number of each new LP to each distributor," as *Cashbox* explained it. "Sooner or later, an end to allocation must come. If it does end, there will definitely be less 'schlocking' of merchandise. Cut-outs will be decreased. Trans-shipping will be lessened." In other words, a record company would no longer set aside a finite number of albums for each of its distributors, which could total in the dozens and, in some cases, hundreds. The practice was cumbersome for bookkeepers and labor-intensive for the employees who had to gather a varied number of copies of each new album and ship them to distributors across the nation and even the world. Inevitably, many of these records would end up being returned due to defects or slow sales. The record labels had to eat the cost of shipping plus storing of returned albums, which ultimately were sold to cut-out companies that sold only returned records. Throughout the mid–1960s, record companies continued to debate whether to end allocations. Some labels were particularly successful in eliminating the practice. Others felt stuck with it. Now, it is all a moot point.

All-Request Radio

Simmered in small markets, waiting to boil over to the mainstream. By the mid–1960s, the all-request radio format (ARRF) was "mushrooming," in *Billboard's* words, into a few major markets—enough to force record companies' promoters to pay serious attention. For ten years ARRF had been simmering in small markets. Participating stations sometimes allowed the listener to request a song on the air, while other stations did not. Some stations began using one-half request programming and one-half regular programming. Many took the requests off the air and then played callers' requests back on live DJ broadcasts. This new format affected record labels—who were used to promoting their products directly to local or regional program directors, as well as other stations that now had to compete against stations that allowed the audience to dictate which records to play. By 1966, a breakout year for ARRF, stations going all-request included JRLA in Los Angeles, KDEO, San Diego, WYSL, Buffalo, and KROY, Sacramento. In time, however, the format slowly declined. Major top forty stations did not participate.

American Folk Records

Through the early 1950s, the umbrella term folk music referred to hillbilly, spiritual, and cowboy songs. In the '40s, *Billboard* even ran a column called American Folk Music. Using that loose definition, recordings by singers such as Jimmie Osborne and even Roy Rogers could be categorized as folk. As country music developed, cowboy songs lost popularity. Folk music began to take on more specific interpretation. With the coming of folk acts, including Joan Baez, Peter, Paul and Mary, and the New Christy Minstrels, the category called folk became far less inclusive. It became easier to know a folk record when you heard it. (See **Folk Music Hits**.)

American Record Manufacturers and Distributors Association

Record-business trade association hit its peak in the 1960s, when such industry heavyweights as Ahmet Ertegun of Atlantic Records and Art Talmadge of United Artists Records served as presidents. The group worked to solve distribution issues. The American Record Manufacturers and Distributors Association (ARMADA) served its constituency well when the record business was vinyl-focused. In 1961, *Music Vendor* described ARMADA as "a name referred to with increasing respect during the last two years." Under Talmadge's guidance in 1960, the magazine said, the group improved and he was "rapidly shaping the young organization into a powerful force."

AMI i-200

Iconic jukebox. Kids would drop a dime in the box and swap stories about seeing UFOs up above Kiss-and-Tell Hill. AMI, Inc., the jukebox manufacturer from Grand Rapids, Michigan, promoted its new i-200 model in 1958, just in time to further the development of early rock 'n' roll. As the advertisement went, "The i's have it! In fact the new Series i-200 has everything you want … attractive styling, ease of operation, superb sound and easy maintenance, fast service." The 200 looks like jukeboxes that show up in old sci-fi movies.

Ampex

Famous early name in professional recording tape and machines—and still a highly recognized one. Ampex was a major force in the industry when the competition was limited in the 1950s through the 1970s. Some of the most important records of all time, including the Sun recordings in Memphis, were cut on Ampex mono tape machines, including the 200 and 300 series models. In the late 1960s, Ampex even started its own label, Ampex Records. It achieved limited success but did break Runt's (Todd Rundgren's) "We Gotta Get You a Woman." The company continues to operate in Redwood City, California. It is a major part of music history.

Answer Record

A song that answered another. In the new era of the 45-rpm single, the answer record first developed in R&B. Producers and labels ran wild with it, sometimes using melodies and even lyrics from the originals. This Wild West approach ended after copyright lawsuits were filed over the answer records that came after the release of "(You Ain't Nothin' but a) Hound Dog" by Big Mama Thornton. After a brief hiatus, the answer record revived itself with the arrival of rock 'n' roll. The safest answer records did not borrow the tune or words from other works. In 1960, "the new entertainment gambit," as *Music Vendor* magazine called it, had only begun. It lasted throughout the '60s. An editorial in *Cash Box* claimed that 1960 "was the year of the answer record. It was the year for novelty singles." (The answer disc is practically unheard of these days.) The term "answer" was not invented by record collectors after the fact. It was used in the record industry in the years when the answer record was at its peak. Though never a major force on the pop charts, answer discs did have their successes and supporters in the business because many were low-budget efforts. Though the answer record is simple in concept, it is varied in character. An answer record often followed an original hit, referred to as the *parent song*. The response answered the message and theme of the original. Often a male vocalist sang the original; a female sang the response. In the early 1960s, *Music Vendor* advised jukebox operators to keep in mind an obvious point: An answer song is more effective if listeners heard the original hit song, so both versions should be placed on jukeboxes. Many times, labels answered other labels' songs. For example, the first two versions of "Tell Laura I Love Her" were country-style records. The big pop hit, by Ray Peterson on RCA, came later, in 1960. Marilyn Michaels answered him with "Tell Tommy I Miss Him." Some risky producers borrowed similar melodies and themes. By today's perspective, the answer record's definition is murky. What is an answer, a semi-answer, and a novelty? After studying answer records for years, Indianapolis music historian Larry Stidom defined what is and is not an answer: (1) DIRECT REPLY: The most obvious. "Yes, I'm Lonesome Tonight" is a reply to "Are You Lonesome Tonight?" (2) RESPONSE: "I'll Count You In" is a response to "Count Me In." (3) MALE/FEMALE: Lots of confusion here. Many songs have been recorded by male and female artists with few lyric changes, except to suit the proper gender. "The Girls in My Little Boy's Life" is an answer; "Image of a Boy" by Meredith McRae isn't, as it is basically the same song as "Image of a Girl." (4) INSPIRATION: Spoofs, follow-ups, and records with similar titles are not strictly considered answers. "Homer and Jethro, Weird Al Yankovic, and Ben Colder do not answer songs," Stidom said.

12 Answer Record

Dodie Stevens did more than answer Elvis Presley's "Are You Lonesome Tonight?" She plaintively asked him the same question. As soon as Presley cut the old song, Stevens recorded her answer for Dot Records. RCA Victor released Presley's version on November 1, 1960, and soon it hit number one. Stevens' version, like so many answer records, rose slowly on the charts, peaking at number sixty, a respectable showing for an answer disc. Stevens' vocal was more interesting than her record. She was only fourteen years old when she cut it, but her voice was going on forty. The Chicago-born singer based in California had established herself in 1959 when, at thirteen, she received a gold record for "Pink Shoe Laces." Stevens' "Lonesome" ended her presence on the national charts, but not her singing career.

"They poke fun at them. 'A Girl Named Johnny Cash' has nothing to do with 'A Boy Named Sue,' but it is still an answer." As the answer record became more accepted by radio, other labels and publishers found ways to participate without violating copyright law (a sticky issue). Teenagers enjoyed the new records. Some did no more than rehash the title for the opposite sex. An example is "He'll Have to Stay," which was Jeanne Black's reply to Jim Reeves' "He'll Have to Go." Most answer records weren't big hits, although some sold moderately. When Roger Miller hit with "Dang Me" in the 1960s, country singer Ruby Wright answered with "Dern Ya." In those days, when independent labels successfully courted radio stations, record companies didn't mind spending a little money to release a single that sold only 5,000 to 25,000 copies. King Records released "I Can't Help You, I'm Falling Too" by Tina and Merle, as an answer to Hank Locklin's RCA country hit, "Please Help Me, I'm Falling." (RCA Victor decided to outdo the competition by answering its own hit with "I'm Glad That You're Falling" by Skeeter Davis.) In addition, Betty Madigan replied to Locklin with a single on United Artists Records called "I'm Glad That I'm Falling Too." Some other now-obscure answer records were "Housewife from L.A." ("Okie from Muskogee") by Joni Credit; "An Open Letter to Dad" ("An Open Letter to My Teen-Age Son") by Chris Howard; and "The Boy from Ipanema" ("The Girl from Ipanema") by Julie London. Even some big-name vocalists and songwriters recorded answer records. As the '60s turned into the early '70s, the answer record began to fade. Then veteran vocalist Connie Francis, who had her first hit in 1958 on MGM Records, attempted a comeback in 1973 with an answer to "Tie a Yellow Ribbon 'Round the Old Oak Tree." Her version was "Should I Tie a Yellow Ribbon 'Round the Old Oak Tree?" It was written and produced by Irvin Levine and L. Russell Brown, who had composed Tony Orlando and Dawn's number one hit of February of that year. Only three months later, Levine and Brown were at it again, producing the Francis version for an aggressive new label named GFS Records out of New York. GFS believed in the record so much that it bought a full-page ad in *Cash Box* and other trade publications, showing the world that Connie still looked good. Never mind that the answer disc was no longer considered cool, and that she hadn't had a halfway solid chart hit since 1964. Francis was off and running with her answer record. (Perhaps because of the title's length and the original's overwhelming recognition, *Cash Box* referred to her record simply as "The Answer.") The music industry watched with curiosity, and wondered: Could Francis and the answer record both make comebacks? Possibly. She still had that "star power glow" about her, and her reviews were good. *Cash Box* noted: "For those of you who were wondering about the continuing episode of 'Tie a Yellow Ribbon…,' here's the answer from a woman's point of view as superbly performed by Connie Francis. Don't discount this one as a future hit. It certainly could happen all over again." Sadly, it didn't. Despite its fanfare, her record—and the answer record in general—hit bottom. Today, they are a relic of the old record industry.

Arranger

The one who creates the musical accompaniment. As most of the record jobs listed in this book, arrangers still work, and they will always be needed in some form. Unfortunately, they are not used nearly as often as they were in the 1950s and 1960s, when arranging work reached its heyday. At the time, singles and LPs were released so frequently that arrangers had plenty of work. Another reason was the use of strings. Labels spent a lot of money (for the day) to pay string and horn players and background vocalists, even on singles. As a result, arranging thrived. Then times changed. In the heyday of the vinyl single, 1955–1980, a few musical arrangers became nearly as influential as prominent record producers. They certainly were as important to the music, if not more. Unfortunately for behind-the-scene arrangers, the producers got most of the credit for the success of records. If given a chance, however, the more popular of the arrangers wielded nearly as much influence as producers in shaping the finished product. Arrangers even landed their own label deals—and sometimes hits (Jack Nitzsche, "The Lonely Surfer.") In the disco period of the 1970s, arranger-writer Van McCoy found success with his own singles and albums. Often arrangers were credited on the record with the producer. But as more electronic instruments came into wider use in the late 1980s, the role of the arranger became less public and more subdued. Complicated string arrangements became passe for a lot of Top 40 songs. Suddenly, many arrangers were forced to learn how to program music and use computers and synthesizers. A new wave of electronic-savvy studio operatives arrived. Although still vital, arrangers seem to have moved into the shadows of the studio, doing what they have always done: writing charts and arranging strings and horns, rhythm tracks, and vocals, and serving as the producer's top adviser. Some of the more well-known Top 40-style arrangers from the 1950s through the 1970s included Stan Applebaum, who arranged for Ben E. King and The Drifters and other big groups; Bergen White of Nashville, who arranged for hundreds of big-name singers (including Tony Joe White and Elvis Presley); Jimmy "The Wiz" Wisner, who arranged the records for Tommy James and the Shondells and many Los Angeles and New York acts; Charles Calello, a New York–based arranger who became known for his work with the Four Seasons; Jimmie Haskell, who was considered one of the top rock arrangers; Artie Butler, who worked mostly out of New York;

and Nitsche, who became famous in the business by arranging the "Wall of Sound" music for producer Phil Spector.

Artists and Repertoire (A&R)

The department that finds new artists and matches them with appropriate songs. The term is more widely recognized than ever by the public, although the department's goals have changed. In the 1930s, record labels gave various titles to the talent recruiter: recording director, recording supervisor, manager of recording laboratories, and musical director. Unlike today's highly structured departments, with their subtitles and subdivisions, early A&R departments consisted of one or two people to a dozen, usually males, who found songs and, by the 1960s, listened to tapes pitched by independent producers. The larger the label, the larger the department. Independent commercial labels had to get by with limited personnel. The larger labels, such as Columbia and Capitol in the 1960s, had enough representatives to send them out to hear new acts on the road. Most of the smaller indies had to rely on tips by local distributors and disc jockeys. Larger indies, such as King Records, had a small staff of A&R members who also recorded as artists and wrote songs. In the early days of America's A&R departments, Jack Kapp became a legend in New York. He defined A&R duties: knowledge of music, recording, merchandising, sales, and artist relations. Kapp, the son of a record salesman, worked for Columbia as a young man. In his spare time he operated a record mail-order company with his brother, David. In 1925, Brunswick-Balke-Collender hired him to operate its Vocalion race division. He also signed Al Jolson, Bing Crosby, and other pop singers. In the 1930s, he led the Decca label in America. When he died in 1949, at forty-seven years old, he was the most well-known A&R man in the country. In the modern era, the record business has seen other hands-on record chiefs such as Billy Sherrill, who ran Columbia's Nashville office; Chet Atkins, the premier guitarist in charge of RCA's Nashville office; Jimmy Bowen, an industry label chief and producer who has operated a number of financially successful record labels; and Clive Davis, the Columbia chief who later headed Arista Records. At the turn of the twenty-first century, as more majors were absorbed by international conglomerates, A&R departments were hiring younger people knowledgeable in particular sub-genres of music—hip-hop, for instance. Immediate results are expected. In 2008, music writer Megan Perry observed that the majors were often accused of using the indies as "low-risk farm teams," while often failing to allow artists to fully develop. The days of the supportive—and patient—A&R rep have all but ended.

A-Side

The preferred side of a record. In the early 1900s, some record companies started labeling their double-sided records. They didn't get fancy. The best side was side A; the other, side B. By the 1920s, the practice had caught on extensively. On the Banner label out of New York, "Hear Dem Bells" by Dalhart and Robison was proclaimed 2181-A in large letters, beating out the humble "Shine on Harvest Moon" as 2181-B. At first, the A side wasn't necessarily the label's favorite. By the 1950s, however, this wasn't the case. The A-side became the company's side to be promoted and played by radio stations. Through the years, the practice of using an A-side continued, and by the 1970s most records carried the A and B designations. (See **Double A**.)

Audition Disc

Blank transcription records used by radio stations and studios to record their own programs. The discs, 78-rpm acetates, were popular for this use in the 1930s, '40s, and early '50s. They were made for non-retail use. Standard Radio Transcription Services, Inc., was one of many companies that made them. Later, in the 1960s, the meaning of audition disc evolved. Some record companies used the term to describe their vinyl promotional copies sent to radio stations. The term audition disc or tape would also be used to showcase the talent of voiceover artists, singers, and musicians. (See **Transcription**.)

Auditioner

Phonograph consisting of a rectangular console with a high back and a series of push buttons. About 1950, Allied Radio Corporation of Chicago offered the new phonograph in hopes that it might catch the wave of sales of the new vinyl discs. In a recessed area on the console's surface were two dual-speed professional turntables with four pickups—two for each table. The Auditioner could be used for professionals or serious amateurs. According to the company, the machine was perfect for playing new LPs. Supposedly, owners could choose from among 371,293 possible combinations of amplifiers, tuners, pickups, speakers, etc. The Auditioner was an ancestor of modern nightclub phonograph equipment.

Auravision

In 1955, Columbia Transcriptions, a department of Columbia Records, developed a sound-with-printed-matter sales tool. Auravision discs were developed for direct-mail campaigns, Christmas cards, magazine inserts, and charity premiums. "More than a quarter million self-mailing

Auravision [free demonstration] records have been ordered by Philco," *Billboard* magazine reported, "for its Reverbaphonic Sound phonographs." Philco wanted the demonstration record to showcase the quality of their new phonograph compared to consumers' home record players. Philco must have had so much confidence in their sound that they were willing to put it out on a flimsy disc so people could compare the sound to a competitor's.

Automatic Drinking Machine

A record-hole punching machine and one of most interesting old record business terms. Off-center punching was a big problem with pressing singles. In 1972, the new "automatic drinking machine" became the first of its kind in the country. Developed by Allied and the New Jersey Labeling Machine Company, the automatic drinking machine supposedly eliminated "any off-center hole problems that might be encountered with a seven-inch product," according to *Billboard* magazine and Jack Wegner, manufacturing chief of Allied. Why was this so important? Off-center hole-punching was a problem. Unfortunately, it continued to be big trouble.

B

Background Vocals

Studio background vocal singers. They were often female, and a staple of recordings into the 1970s. They knew *how* and *when* to sing. Though such vocals have gone out of fashion on many modern recordings, backup singers remain a natural part of on-stage performances. Black female backups seem to have weathered the change in tastes a bit better, although even they are not as popular as the Sweet Inspirations were in the heyday of the backgrounders. In pop music, background session vocals can sound outdated unless used sparingly and minus the "oohs and ahhs." In the 1960s, the Anita Kerr Singers made a good living backing up many pop and country singers in the studio. Anita Kerr cut plenty of records herself. In those days, records were practically swimming in backgrounds of smooth-sounding vocals. When coupled with big echo, the background vocals added a certain flavor and power to a record. In the big cities, soprano session singers remained on call to hit what most humans would consider nearly unattainable high notes. Certainly in Nashville, L.A., and New York, session background groups stayed busy. Listen to Bobby Darin's "Things," a major hit in 1962, and Bobby Vee's "Rubber Ball," another big one in 1961, and you will hear the old-fashioned female background vocals that are now passe.

At their zenith in the late 1950s and early '60s, background vocal tracks were popular on records such as "Midnight Mary" by Joey Powers and on Elvis Presley's records. The Stamps, a white male Southern gospel group, performed with the King, both in concert *and* in the studio. In 1969, Elvis updated his sound by recording at Chip Moman's American Sound Studios in Memphis. He was accompanied by two of the top background session singers in the country, the sisters Mary and Ginger Holladay. They sang with Elvis on "Suspicious Minds" and "In the Ghetto" as well as on hits by B.J. Thomas and many other acts at American Sound into the '70s. The background vocals on "Suspicious Minds" helped take Elvis to a place he had never been. Supported by some right-on Memphis horns, and Tommy Cogbill's punching bass lines, "Suspicious Minds" became a premier single.

Bake

A method for rescuing old audio recording tape. When magnetic recording tape sits around for years, it can deteriorate. This could ruin valuable reels of tape. To counteract the problem, audio engineers "bake" the tapes to dry out a sticky compound that lies on the surface. Engineers bake the tapes at 130 degrees Fahrenheit. Interestingly, the older the tape, the less likely it is to stick. This is because tape companies changed the formula they used in the manufacturing process. While tapes from the late 1970s and '80s have a reputation for falling apart when played today, tapes from the 1950s still remain intact. Though baking won't always rescue old masters, the process is successful enough to attract a growing number of proponents.

Bakelite Phonographs

Table-top phonographs made of a sturdy material popular in the 1940s and early 1950s. The old Bakelites were often dark brown with one speaker up front. The name was trademarked. Its early plastic compound dated back to the early 1900s, and was used for a number of products, including jewelry, radios, and kitchenware. Bakelite record players look bulky and semi-art deco, but then they looked modern. The more sophisticated and larger Bakelite tabletop models were used by some record-business operatives as well as the general consumer. A number of companies made the table-toppers, especially RCA Victor. When RCA Victor unveiled its new 45-rpm single in 1949, the company knew it would need a new phonograph to showcase the firm's new seven-inch records. So RCA introduced a number of new record players. Bakelite was named for its inventor, a Belgian American named Leo Hendrik Baekeland. He created a synthetic resin, which replaced shellac and some hard rubber used in manufacturing. The material contained phenol and formaldehyde polymers. Most people referred to the smaller players as table-top models, but some other, larger phonographs could also fit on tables. RCA made the Bakelite players in various forms and limited colors from 1949 to around 1957, when they were phased out in favor of the new plastic phonographs that looked sharper and weighed less. A few years into the 45 player's life, RCA Victor came up with a cream-colored Disney model and soon other special ones also arrived. Younger people preferred the 45 players. By the coming of new aesthetic standards in the '60s, the old Bakelites looked clunky, chunky, and funky—perfect today for playing "Rock Around the Clock" and other old black-label Deccas by Bill Haley and the Comets.

Bakersfield Sound

Bakersfield, California's country music. In this homogenous age, we rarely hear of any cities and towns boasting about their own sound anymore. But in the 1960s and '70s, this wasn't the case. Bakersfield, California, had its own country sound then. As the *Bakersfield Californian* once described it in a headline: "The Bakersfield Sound: Raw, Real and not Nashville." That sums it up. Unlike the sounds of other regional music cities, Bakersfield's "sound" did not represent an identifiable approach to music in the studio, as did the Memphis Sound. Bakersfield's was a collective effort by everyone in the city's country-music orbit. The city was not known for any other kind of music, at least nationally. Some called it renegade music, but it wasn't about long hair and rebellion. It was more of a tradition in sound, the music of Buck Owens, Merle Haggard, Don Rich, and others. The sounds were peculiarly their own, but they all fell under the category of the Bakersfield Sound—and the mystique of the Telecaster guitar.

Ball

The stylus used on records pressed with the hill-and-dale method from about 1915 and on to the 1920s. (See **Hill-And-Dale Method.**)

Band

A song recorded on vinyl. In the early days, people in the business used the word band to describe a cut on an album. These days it is synonymous with a cut and a track. Any of these names get across the idea.

Banding

Separation of programs into sections on a vinyl disc. Each section stands out, connected by spirals.

Bans

Musician union strikes in the 1940s and '50s. In the 1940s, the American Federation of Musicians (AFM) struck the music business, causing all sorts of mischief. The strikes, 1942 to 1944, and again in 1948, were referred to as "bans," and specifically during the war years as the Petrillo Ban. The strikes were the brainchild of James C. Petrillo, the union's Chicago-based president. During his strikes, the trade union prohibited members from playing on recording sessions, which forced record labels to cut as many sides as possible before each strike began. Even with their war chest of masters, eventually the labels ran low on sides to release as 78-rpm discs. Some labels were reduced to leasing masters from European sources. Petrillo had different complaints for each strike, but they all involved better pay for musicians' work on records and in television. The strikes were the only major ones that nearly shut down the record business.

Battle of the Bands

Entertainment for teens and a good way for A&R men to scoop up talented garage bands. The battle of the bands was a 1960s concept that flourished when the Beatles set off a chain reaction of garage-band imitators. Usually, local promoters or radio stations arranged battle-of-the-band contests in VFW halls, in parking lots of shopping centers, and even in theaters. Contestants were often high school bands. Promoters selected from three to a half a dozen groups and let them play. Audience reaction counted, but the real decision came from local DJs or someone involved in the town's music business. Sometimes, A&R operatives were in the audience, as well as promoters with connections to A&R men. In the late 1960s, in Columbus, Ohio, a group named the Rebounds won a battle of the bands competition. The group received a recording contract with Tower Records. They cut "(I'm Not Your) Stepping Stone." Tower released it, and the single began receiving strong airplay in several cities. Unfortunately, the Monkees also cut the Tommy Boyce and Bobby Hart song. Sensing defeat, Tower shut down promotion of the Rebounds' record. The Monkees were the monster group of the day. The Rebounds did not rebound from the setback.

Bed

Instrumentation that plays under a performer's voice.

Bel Canto

Innovative independent label in Los Angeles and Columbus, Ohio, in the 1950s. The little jazz and tape label is hardly remembered, despite having been responsible for a major recording achievement. For during the week of June 23, 1958, Bel Canto released the first commercially available stereo 45-rpm record. Actually, it released four of them—all by Larry Fotine, an American jazz pianist and songwriter. Bel Canto may have also released the first commercially available stereo album late in December 1957. Bel Canto Magnetic Tapes was founded in October 1955, by Nate Duroff and Nate Rothstein, co-owners of Monarch Record Manufacturing Corporation. Bel Canto was one of the earliest companies to produce pre-recorded tapes. It gained a reputation for selling high-quality tapes, in part because they were duplicated in real time. Russ Molloy, formerly of Bowery Records, served as general sales manager and executive director. "Beginning with 'five duplicator slaves and a desk,' Molloy built Bel Canto into an organization that marketed its recorded tapes in all fifty states and many foreign countries," said David Meyers, a Columbus historian. Bel Canto was also the first company to publish a wide catalog of popular albums on tape. The label moved to Columbus some years later, when it was purchased and absorbed into larger companies. But in the 1950s, Bel Canto was a little label ahead of its time.

Big Groove

Slang for the larger grooves on 78-rpm discs from the late 1800s and early 1900s.

Big Ten-Incher

A 78-rpm disc. It made its way into a Bull Moose Jackson song title in 1952, "Big Ten-Inch Record," on the King label.

Bio Disc

An artist's life story on a record's label, front and back side. The innovative independent King Records of Cincinnati pressed many bio discs—white label promotional copies with a brief biography of the artist printed in tiny type on both sides of the paper label. Bios appeared only on promotional copies to radio stations. Today, those old bio discs are considered fascinating collectibles. King used bio discs more than any other label.

Biscuit

Press operators used either shellac or a soft vinyl material, both known as hot blanks or biscuits, to form a record. The word is older analog pressing terminology.

22   Blockbuster

Every label needed a blockbuster, and 20th Century–Fox Records was no different. This mid–1960s advertisement shows the faith the label had in former Motown Records star Mary Wells, who recently released an album for her new label. The company's new albums included the soundtrack to *Zorba the Greek*, *Al Martino Sings*, *The Best of Shirley Temple, Vol. II*, *The Harry Simeone Chorale: Climb Ev'ry Mountain*, and *Joya Sherrill Sings Duke*. This was not the only label bold enough to predict blockbuster status for its new records. Though the label's A&R department predicted blockbuster action for Wells' new single "Never, Never Leave Me," she did not come close to achieving the success she had with her Motown hit "My Guy."

Blockbuster

Used interchangeably with smash hit and monster. If you had a blockbuster, you were in the green. Every producer fantasized about his or her own blockbuster.

Bogus platters

Bootlegged discs. Also known in the trade as "boots" in the 1960s.

Bootleggers

Popular record industry term for illegal tape duplicators of all kinds, from the 1960s through the 1980s. Bootleggers most often copied music from the radio and concert performances. They duplicated their tapes and sold them to consumers. The trades also used the word to describe duplicators of audio cassettes. Though the term was sometimes applied to illegal vinyl duplicators as well, mainly bootlegging was used to describe tape renegades. (See **Tape Pirates**.)

B.P

Radio slang, meaning before payola. Things changed when the public realized that some DJs had been accepting money in exchange for playing records in the late 1950s and early '60s. To DJs involved in this activity, B.P. must have meant the good old days.

Branch Operation

A company-owned distribution center for a major label or even a large independent. At one time, the majors used independent distributors, which helped turn the growing labels into majors. Later, after their budgets increased, the big companies decided they could do business more effectively and efficiently by opening their own distributorships. Syd Nathan, founder of the independent King Records in Cincinnati, opened about thirty-three branches across the country. By the mid–1960s, however, changing times caught up with him. The branches had become cumbersome and too costly to operate. By then, only the big labels could afford them. But Nathan is considered an independent-label genius for he decided to spend a lot of his company's money to open King's branches. King was the only independent label to open a large branch operation. Nathan went from handling shellac 78s to vinyl 45s and LPs.

Break

Island of instrumentation in the middle of a vocal record. It broke up a constant barrage of singing, giving the listener an unexpected change before the singing began again. On rock records, most breaks were done with guitars. On more pop-oriented records, the break was often done with horns and strings. Today, breaks have gone out of fashion in many record-production quarters.

Break a Record

Radio stations playing a new record.to listeners. The term "break a record" was used widely by radio and record-label employees and trade writers. "Break a record" should not be taken literally. Derivatives included "breaking nationally" and "regional breakout." Though it's not clear when the term "break a record" came into use, it most likely began in the 1950s and gained notoriety in the '60s. In time, it became accepted record-business slang, and it is still used today to describe a record being "broken." Today, however, a recording can be introduced on television and on the Internet, among other sources. The meaning of the term has been diluted. As top L.A. DJ Gary Owens told *Billboard* in the late 1970s, "You don't break records like you did in the '60s. The difference now is there's so much ... music." In the '60s, he said, DJs in cities across the Midwest and other areas would jump on a record if Alan Freed did. "Today, everyone gets the record at the same time."

Break-In Record

Excerpts from popular records spliced together into a new record, with its own spoken story line. This was an early version of today's sampling. The break-in (or cut-in) record arrived in the mid–1950s, when producers coupled narrative with brief excerpts from popular records. The break-in told a story. In the late 1950s, "The Flying Saucer" by Buchanan and Goodman faked a radio broadcast interrupted by reports of flying saucer sightings. The repeated use of brief parts of current hits prompted lawsuits, but generally the courts ruled that break-ins did not violate copyrights. This opened the door to modern sampling by many rap and rock groups. Surprisingly, a number of break-in discs became hits over the next twenty years. Dickie Goodman became the king of the break-in. His chart records with Bill Buchanan also included "Buchanan and Goodman on Trial." Goodman recorded break-ins throughout his career, even when they were no longer fashionable. (See **Cut-In Record**.)

Breakout

A record that is coming on strong. *Billboard* and other trades—even record industry people—referred to hot records as breakouts. You were either breaking out regionally or nationally. Breaking out meant your record was hot.

Brill Building

One of New York's most important addresses in the days of early rock. Soon after the Brill Building opened for business at 1619 Broadway in New York, in 1931, it became one of a number of focal points of Tin Pan Alley's sheet-music publishing world. Its first tenant was Southern Music. Harms Brothers also arrived. When rock 'n' roll hit big in the mid–1950s, the reeling sheet-music companies began to leave the Brill. They were replaced by other firms that catered to the new popular music. The Brill's hallways soon echoed with iconic songs written by various staff writers such as Carole King and Gerry Goffin, Barry Mann and Cynthia Weil, Burt Bacharach and Hal David, Neil Sedaka, and many other incredibly talented people. And there were record labels—even a studio. Another building, at 1650 Broadway, also became a center for the new music. The 1600 block became a rock 'n' roll version of Tin Pan Alley, in a central part of the city's music business. The Brill represented creativity under one roof. No block of any city is so well-known and concentrated with important music people. Many songwriters work from home now. The Brill's concept as a music factory is no more. (See **Tin Pan Alley** and **Sixteen-Fifty Broadway**.)

British Invasion

An unprecedented attack on the United States record market by a foreign invader. In 1963, record sales failed to meet expectations during a time of national prosperity. Though the industry's total sales—$698 million—provided a small increase over 1962's, industry analysts were disappointed. The suddenly, just as 1964 arrived, the Beatles hit everywhere with the force of a hurricane. The public, especially teenagers, went berserk. Adults followed when they heard "Michele." Thanks in large part to the Beatles, America's record sales increased from $758 million in 1964 to over $1.1 million in 1968. The phenomenon opened the doors for more British recording acts. The American public couldn't get enough of them. *Billboard* estimated that three dozen British acts hit the U.S. charts to varying degrees of success. The public then recognized new names—Petula Clark ("Downtown"), the Zombies ("Tell Her No"), the Swinging Blue Jeans ("Tobacco Road"), to name a few. When reasonably possible, American acts tried to

British Invasion

BILL GAVIN: " this is one of the greatest records I've heard all year!"
FENWAY REPORTER: FOUR STAR SPECIAL. " will score just as big in the U.S. as it is doing in England!"
BRITAIN'S NME: UP TO 7TH and climbing!

PETULA CLARK'S SURGING SINGLE

"DOWNTOWN"
5494

A WINNER!

The British Invasion of America in the mid-1960s featured Petula Clark, whose impressive hits in the States included "Downtown," produced and written by Tony Hatch. As a child, Clark began her career singing during World War II. By the 1950s she had become a recording star in England. Unlike most of the younger bands and solo artists of the British Invasion, Clark was in her early thirties when "Downtown" hit big and launched a volley of Hatch-produced hits that included "I Couldn't Live Without Your Love," "Colour My World," and "My Love." His songs, often co-written with wife Jackie Trent, were fresh and upbeat. They contrasted sharply with the Rolling Stones, the Zombies, and other British acts of that era. A half-century later, Hatch's songs and Clark's vocal interpretations stand as some of the best pop music of the 1960s.

fool the public into believing they were British. The Sir Douglas Quintet from Texas, and the Buckinghams from Chicago, became hot on the red coattails of the British. The Invasion continued until the Americans finally regrouped in the late 1960s, but even then, the British were here to stay.

B-Side

"Flip side" of a 45-rpm single. It was not intended for primary airplay, but sometimes the recipient of it. Famous B-sides included "That'll Be the Day" by The Crickets (1957), "Chantilly Lace" by the Big Bopper (1958), and "La Bamba" by Ritchie Valens (1959). Surprisingly, "Ebb Tide" by the Righteous Brothers in 1965, was a B-side. The Bs didn't have to be labeled that way, but it helped radio music directors know right away which side the record companies considered more worthy of airplay. That certainly meant a lot in those days, but some radio guys bucked the system. If they thought the B-side was better, they played it. However, most B-sides were immediately relegated to the dump heap of vinyl. Only a few of them broke out of the B-side ghetto. By the mid-1960s, record companies got smart and placed noticeably inferior songs on their B-sides to discourage DJs from playing them. Even so, a few "Bs" broke through the barrier. Even some children's records had B-sides. In later years, fewer Bs reached the charts as often as they did in the 1950s and 1960s. This stemmed from a gradual loss of local control by disc jockeys and program directors, and the radio chains' reluctance to take a chance on something unfamiliar. On the other hand, some famous B-sides included "The Twist" by Hank Ballard and the Midnighters on King Records in 1960. The A-side, "Teardrops on Your Letter," also received considerable airplay. In addition, the Five Satins' B-side "In the Still of the Night" surpassed its A-side, "The Jones Girl." As music historian Bill Griggs once wrote, "[Jack Scott's] recording of 'Leroy' was zooming up the charts, destined to become a huge hit. Then the song suddenly stopped climbing. Why? Some DJs had flipped it over …." They found "My True Love." Another B-side that turned into a monster instrumental was "Wipeout" by the Surfaris. The A-side, "Surfer Joe," got its share of airplay as well. "Wipeout" was so appreciated that DJs broke the same recording again—as a new release—in 1967. (See **Rock Instrumentals** and **A-Side**.)

Bubblegum Music

A potpourri of catchy, upbeat songs, often with nonsensical meanings. At the time, AM dominated the airwaves by playing singles. If a record executive hoped to receive airplay, he or she *had* to make a commercial record. Because only a few formats existed then, Top 40 stations played mainly commercial rock and soul. But sometimes they slipped in an oddball record from adult contemporary pop, country, and occasionally jazz. At one point radio program directors started veering over to ultracommercial rock to expand their audience with younger listeners. But there was more to it. Radio stations and record producers loved that old commercial hook line. Bubblegum provided it. The sticky craze had begun in 1967 with some experimental records. A year later, bubblegum was luring independent producers—Jerry Kasenetz and Jeff Katz led the way—who were attracted by records with lower budgets and a good-time sound. The two worked with promotion wizard Neil Bogart at Buddah Records in New York to coin the name bubblegum music. Kasenetz and Katz perfected their idea, which opened space in the market for a pre-teen sound. The subgenre of rock occupied a murky place between the familiar Top 40 recordings and the ultracommercial young teen recordings. In fact, bubblegum *was* the epitome of commercial. Kasenetz and Katz's Super K Productions became a mini industry unto itself. Within a couple of years the young producers—in their early twenties—sold six million records. In 1968, their number-four hit "Yummy Yummy Yummy" became the prototypical bubblegum song, and one of the most memorable. Songwriter-vocalist Joey Levine helped create it for Super K. He had fun while also singing in a nasally tone on a number of other Super K's bubblegum hits, including the Express' "Chewy, Chewy." Levine, like most bubblegum studio musicians and songwriters, realized the secret to making the idea work was not taking it too seriously. After all, the music was supposed to be fun. Buddah soon became known as the premier bubblegum label, though the company and its subsidiary labels did release a healthy number of other types of hit records, from Bill Withers' soul to Melanie's pop. Today, the name bubblegum music is used frequently, but its original meaning has evolved with a new generation. These days it is applied to just about anything that sounds remotely like a happy, sing-along recording. For example, the 1967 hits "Apples, Peaches, Pumpkin Pie" and "Keep the Ball Rollin'" by Jay and the Techniques were not bubblegum records. Neither was producer Paul Leka's "Green Tambourine" by the Lemon Pipers—a real work of studio art with a creative arrangement and strings. They were commercial Top 40 hits. So were Tommy James' "I Think We're Alone Now" and "Mirage," although they were written and recorded by a couple of future bubblegum producers. Edison Lighthouse's "Love Grows (Where My Rosemary Goes)" was not a bubblegum record, either. Real bubblegum came with over-the-top lyrics and fanciful band names such as the 1910 Fruitgum Company ("Simon Says," "1, 2, 3 Red Light"), and the Kasenetz-Katz Singing Orchestral Circus ("Quick Joey Small"). Super K, which trademarked band names, hired musicians to go on the road and perform under the name of the hit groups. Studio musicians rarely performed with them. When more labels and producers

Bubblegum Music 29

Crazy Elephant was one of many creations of bubblegum record producers Jeff Katz and Jerry Kasenetz. Their New York–based Super K Productions specialized in radio-friendly records aimed at the pre-teen market. Hits included "Yummy, Yummy, Yummy," by the Ohio Express, "1, 2, 3 Red Light" by the 1910 Fruit Gum Company, and "Gimme Gimme Good Lovin'" by Crazy Elephant. The young producers looked like accountants, not rock 'n' roll titans. Fittingly, by the time they were twenty-three they had sold six million records. Usually, the duo hired studio musicians, writers, and producers to make the records. Then Kasenetz and Katz managed and marketed their "ghost groups," using fanciful names that the younger Top 40 radio audience loved.

jumped into the bubblegum pool in the late 1960s, and competition grew, bubblegum sounds grew crazier. A&R departments and advertising agencies dreamed up even more strange and funny band names. The goal was to combine silliness with music, and a strong hook line. Highly respected writer-producer Jeff Barry, who once worked with Phil Spector, wrote and produced the number-one hit "Sugar, Sugar" by the Archies in 1969. The group was fictional, coming from an animated television show. They hit the top ten again with "Jingle Jangle." Though more bubblegum hits by other producers would follow, "Sugar, Sugar" represented the music's high point. Nonetheless, producers continued to cut bubblegum records into the early to-mid 1970s. The bands' goofy names included the Eye-Full Tower, the Carnaby Street Runners, 1989 Musical Marching Zoo, Patty Flabbies' Coughed Engine, the Charles E. Funk Rebellion, Salt Water Taffy, Crazy Elephant, the Yellow Balloon, Fat Man's Music Festival, Sunny Day and the Comic Strip, Marshmallow Way, The Sugar Canyon, Mellow Brick Rode, The Magic Circle, Silver Caboose, the Two Dollar Question, Professor Morrison's Lollipop, the Care Package, the Waterproof Tinker Toy, the Toy Factory, the Detroit Road Runners, the Fun and Games, and, not to be forgotten, the Bubblegum Machine. Someone had a great job—naming bubblegum acts.

Bubbler

One of the most familiar jukeboxes in history. The humpbacked Wurlitzer Model 1015, made in the mid–1940s, featured colorful neon that bubbled while playing 78-rpm discs.

Bubbling Under the Hot 100

Chart that debuted in *Billboard* on June 1, 1959. Though the number of records listed varied at different times. By 1963, it listed numbers 101 through 135. The gap between 100 and 101 was as wide as the Mississippi. In sales, however, there was little difference. The cellar-dwellers were not all unhappy residents. Some singers and bands made "careers" in the cellar. Not that it was bad. Landing on the Bubbling chart meant the entertainers were hot in at least one big radio market and maybe two or three others. However, for once-popular acts whose records now languished, the Bubbling chart was a death sentence. The freefall from the top ten on to, say, 110 on a follow-up record was an ego-buster, but it happened all too often. Who inhabited the underworld of records? The names read like a who's who in music: John Cougar and Perry Como, Nat King Cole and Natalie Cole, Judy Collins and Tommy Collins, Rosemary Clooney and Patsy Cline, Rita Coolidge and Elvis Costello. The non-hits just kept on coming. From

1960 to 1968, the Everly Brothers managed to do it thirteen times. Warner Bros. Records executives must have second-guessed themselves for signing the duo to a lucrative contract. Interestingly, big-name belter Tom Jones lived temporarily in the basement, singing "Take Me Tonight," and as did Janis Joplin with "Try (Just a Little Bit Harder"). Even Motown star Marvin Gaye, the man of many hits, resided in the Hotel Bubbling—twice. Pity the poor unknown and little-known who peaked at 101, coming oh-so-close to the coveted Hot 100. Actually, hitting the Bubbling Under chart was considered a morale booster for unknown acts and those who put up money to promote them. Sales in that strata ranged from 15,000 to 30,000, and up, depending on the week and how many records the competition was selling in a market or markets. (See **Regional Hits**.)

Budget Lines

Songs recycled from original tracks and released on LPs. The covers were basic, often with no liner notes. The artists were the originals. Record company low-budget lines were continued on compact discs, but they're not as prevalent as they were on vinyl in the 1960s and 1970s. Some companies had specialty budget lines, such as Harmony Records from Columbia. They were from a time when consumers could find many lower-priced LPs featuring light classical, orchestral, and middle-of-the-road albums made specifically for the bargain hunter. Some companies, including London, also marketed low-budget-line audio cassettes. (See **Low-Cost Field**.)

Bull Frog

Singer or disc jockey with a deep voice.

Bullseye

The hit predictor. The *Cash Box* Bullseye of the 1960s listed country singles that the magazine's staff believed would be or could be hits. The listing became a popular feature in the magazine. Listed were new singles with no-doubt possibilities plus others that were graded as B+ (very good), B (good), C+ (fair), and C (mediocre). Nashville producers hoped to land a listing in the Bullseye, for everyone in the business, including radio personnel, would see it.

Butt Splice

Joining two ends of a tape together. When audio tape came into widespread use in the early 1950s, engineers discovered that they could cut it and splice the two ends together to eliminate a bad note or some other unwanted sound. This simple technique was revolutionary, for it saved everyone the trouble of recording another take. How many hit records were created using the "butt splice" method? No one knows. But probably most of them were, especially as musicians and engineers started using it as a safety net. The term spilled over into television, where engineers used the method to splice film. However, butt-splicing was much less reliable with film. As a result, television engineers rarely used it.

C

Capitol Tower

Designed and built in Los Angeles in the 1950s to resemble a stack of 45s. It is still the headquarters of Capitol Records. (See **Full Dimensional Stereo**.)

Car Songs

Music that teens could appreciate because they involved driving. Label operatives called them car songs. In the late 1950s and early '60s, young people identified with the songs because they bought or borrowed them more often than their parents did. Car songs gained speed in the early 1960s. Subject matter was not restricted to car-appreciation songs. They could be anything remotely involving an automobile. Some car songs could also be classified in other subgenres, such as tear-jerkers and novelties. But no matter. A car song was a car song, and the public remembered it that way. Jan & Dean had a gruesome one with "Dead Man's Curve." The Rip Chords sang "Little Cobra," which helped introduce teens to racers, and the Beach Boys came along with "Little Deuce Coupe," a souped-up Ford model eighteen. Then came their "Shut Down," another racing song, and "Car Crazy Cutie." But the Beach Boys were not only the kings of surf. They were the kings of cars. "Fun, Fun, Fun" and "I Get Around" also focused kids' minds on wheels. Two offbeat car songs were not only car songs, but tear-jerker songs as well. In the spring of 1964, as the British Invasion was hitting America, an independent producer named Sonley Roush discovered J. Frank Wilson and the Cavaliers. He took them into a new studio, Accurate Sound, in San Angelo, Texas. Roush and studio owner Ron Newdoll produced "Last Kiss," written by singer Wayne Cochran. It was unlike many of the songs coming from the Zombies, the Beatles, Petula Clark, and other Brits. Wilson's record sounded like it was from 1957. The record, about a young man whose girlfriend is killed in a car crash, went to number two on the *Billboard* chart. Surprisingly, Wilson's only big hit has endured for decades. One of the better car songs of all time came not in the 1960s, but in 1955, and it was rockabilly. Charlie Ryan, known mostly for his car songs, recorded "Hot Rod Lincoln" that year. He had written the song in 1947 and continued to polish it for the next three years while performing in Idaho. Soon he recorded it for his own Souvenir label in Spokane. Then in 1960 he recut it for the 4 Star label of California. On the latter version he was credited as Charlie Ryan and the Timberline Riders. "When I wrote the song," he recalled twenty-five years after the record hit, "we were riding in a '41 Lincoln with a twelve-cylinder engine. I still have that car, too. Real incidents led me to some of the things I talked about in the song, although some had to be exaggerated for the song's sake." Ryan went on to carve a career out of his hit, which reached number fourteen on *Billboard's* country charts and number thirty-three on the Hot 100. It was enough to earn him a spot on one of singer Johnny Horton's national tours. Ryan's record featured the band's steel guitar imitating sirens and speeding cars. Later, his single "Side Car Saddle," another disc that saw national chart action, was covered and remade by other artists, including the country star Johnny Bond, who had also covered "Hot Rod Lincoln." No matter. The song was enough to keep Ryan working into old age. In his seventies, he sent music reporters post cards from the road, proudly proclaiming that he was on tour again. In his twelve-cylinder Lincoln? "Not even close," he said. "I had an old bus by then." Producers and writers turned out many car songs, before radio and record labels turned to more serious subjects in the late 1960s. Car songs seemed trivial next to songs about Vietnam and anti-war protests.

Cartridge

An essential part of a phonograph. It is used to "transform into an electric signal the vibrations picked up by the needle as it travels the record groove," Capitol Records explained to its late–1950s customers. "But the important fact about a stereo cartridge is that with one needle, two sound messages can be kept separate." Cartridges replaced the old acoustic phonograph needle, and many were made of ceramic housings. Today, with the revival of the phonograph, cartridges are back.

Cassette Theory

Idea that audio cassettes would damage the record business. When Philips Phonographic Industries introduced the audio cassette recorder in November 1963, then followed with the prerecorded cassette, the record business began debating the so-called cassette theory. In some quarters the theory had no real name, but the idea was the same: audio cassettes would damage the music industry by enabling consumers to copy vinyl records.

The threat from prerecorded cassettes seemed even more obvious. They would siphon sales from vinyl albums. By the early 1970s, however, fewer industry observers believed in the cassette theory. Cassettes were soon competing against the eight-track tape. The vinyl record survived both of them.

Cassingle

An audio cassette with two cuts. When the 45-rpm single began to fade in the late 1980s, record companies started releasing audio-cassette singles for consumers, complete with attractive artwork and two songs, like a 45. The 45, still needed for jukeboxes and mail-order sources, existed simultaneously with the cassingle for a few years. Though a young audience accepted the cassingles, many jukebox operators and radio stations did not. As the *Country Music Reporter* noted that June, "The possibility that the 45-rpm single could soon become extinct is most troubling to makers and operators of the nation's 225,000 jukeboxes, the largest consumers who BUY records of this type.... Many operators told us they.... WOULD NEVER revert over to cassingles tapes or CDs." Cassingles had a good run in the stores, until the cassette format began giving way to compact discs.

Chart Hyping (or Hyping)

Records were hyped onto the charts—that is, inflated figures were given as a favor to somebody at a record company. It was common knowledge that some records hit the bottom of the chart for a week or two and then died, because their hype did not carry them further. The idea behind hyping was to gain attention, hoping that other radio stations would see the chart entry and start playing the record.

Cherry Pie

Singers, actors, studio engineers, and disc jockeys used the name cherry pie to describe jobs they might pick up on the side to generate unexpected income. The word was used mainly from the 1940s to the '60s.

Children's Records

Children's records became more profitable than they had ever been after World War II and the subsequent baby boom. This coincided with the introduction of the 45. They complemented each another. You don't hear as much about children's records in these days of fewer children and music streaming and digital books, although music for kids is still viable in modern formats. Mostly the older discs for children were the seven-inch variety. Naturally, the basics of these records have changed since the 1960s, when the independent Golden Records operated out of New York. Golden, founded in 1948 by Arthur Shimkin, was a leader in the field. In 1964, Golden sold its singles for twenty-nine cents, EPs for forty-nine cents, and LPs for a dollar and ninety-eight cents. This was below the average prices for adult records. (See **Kidisks**.)

Cincinnati Sound

Lonnie Mack, whose twanging soul-rock guitar influenced two generations of guitarists, led the blues-rock movement known as the Cincinnati Sound. He sang blues, country, and rock, often melding them within one song. He voice was soulful, but it was his guitar that spoke the loudest. His top-ten guitar instrumental hits in 1963 were "Memphis" and "Wham!" Though other good blue-eyed soul singers and bands came out of Cincinnati in the 1960s, none became as famous as Mack. He practically carried Harry Carlson's independent Fraternity Records in the early part of the decade.

Music that mixed a little country with the blues and came out as blue-eyed soul. In 1963, guitarist Lonnie Mack became the city's most well-known example after he hit the top ten with "Memphis" and "Wham!" If Mack wasn't the father of the Cincinnati Sound, he surely was its cherished guardian. His bluesy roadhouse music, laced with a touch of country, was defined by hot guitars and—sometimes—horns. He impressed a young guitarist named Stevie Ray Vaughan, who would later perform with Mack and even record his song "Wham!" Cincinnati's Fraternity Records mined the genre successfully in the 1960s. Other bands fell into this category, including the Dapps, Troy Seals and the Cincinnati Kids, and Beau Dollar and the Coins. Working with James Brown at King Records, Dollar—born William Bowman—helped set the standards for funk drumming. Though Cincinnati's eclectic country, bluegrass, and R&B music is often referred to generically as the Cincinnati

Sound, the Queen City's music had no single, defining musical style. It was too broad to be classified as one entity. In the 1960s and into the early 1970s, local rock musicians and disc jockeys simply referred to the blue-eyed soul as the Cincinnati Sound—the roadhouse blues-rock of Lonnie Mack and his followers. The presence of King Records, the label of James Brown and the Famous Flames, helped Cincinnati become a soul and blues-rock Mecca.

Clapping

Rhythmic clapping as part of the musical track. Some songs depended on clapping to drive home the beat. Others used it more for sonic decoration. In the early 1960s, clapping became the focus of records for R&B singer Shirley Ellis. She hit the top ten with "The Nitty Gritty" and "The Clapping Song."

Classical 45s

Hooked listeners on shorter classical compositions as well as on the new 45-rpm record. In the early 1950s and into the 1960s, some classical music was released on 45-rpm discs, particularly by labels which produced classical albums (RCA Victor, for example). Then demand slowed for the classics on seven-inchers. By 1968, however, the classical 45 had returned on labels such as Deutsche Grammophon, which promoted the new records to rock, progressive, easy listening, and Top Forty stations. Some of the new 45s, on Columbia, Colgems, and other labels, were tie-ins with then-current films, such as *Elvira Madigan*, *Rosemary's Baby*, and *2001: A Space Odyssey*. The classical single had all but died when rock 'n' roll arrived in the mid–1950s. The 1968 comeback didn't last too long. It seems that the 45 just wasn't the vehicle of choice for most classical listeners. The 45 was suited mainly to the promotion of classical pieces that were featured in major films.

Clicking with Flicks

Movies plus teenage music. When rock 'n' roll arrived in the mid-'50s, film companies turned out inexpensive rock movies that featured the new singing stars. In September of 1961, the trade magazine *Music Vendor* picked up on a trend and named it "clicking with flicks." Record executives called it making money. The trend was already becoming obvious: "Record fame is opening the gates to a promising film career for many pop disc artists today. A flood of popular singers are cashing in on the movie sweepstakes with more expected." Some of the pop singers hoped to leap from music to film as a career, while others simply wanted to use film to bolster their vocal careers. *MV* noted that American movie producers were being forced to turn to the teen market because night-time television and foreign films were grabbing much of the older adult market. As *MV* put it, "The movie moguls have discovered that instead of arduously developing their own stars for the teen market they [can] enjoy ready-made box-office attractions in today's pop singers—who are already teen idols." But many were unable to act or carry; they were mere live props to draw kids into the theaters. Elvis Presley's entry into movies taught the movie and record industries a lesson: The RCA Victor star could actually act in meaningful roles. Presley's rise coincided with the drive-in theater's continued success. American International Pictures and director Roger Corman exploited passion-pit viewers to the fullest. Meanwhile, film companies couldn't get enough of teen pop stars. Pat Boone exuded a clean-cut image for the movies. So did Frankie Avalon, a major young recording artist who appeared in some big-time films, including *The Alamo* with John Wayne as well as *Voyage to the Bottom of the Sea* and *Sail a Crooked Ship*. The more hit records he turned out, the bigger his reputation grew as an actor. He also teamed with Disney star Annette Funicello in the lower-budget beach movies. Avalon's Chancellor Records label mate, Fabian, appeared in *The Longest Day*. Bobby Darin appeared in *Hell Is for Heroes* and *State Fair*. Other singing stars who did limited film work during the early 1960s included Bobby Vee, Brenda Lee, Tommy Sands, Ann-Margaret, Jimmy Clanton, and Chubby Checker. After the Beatles turned the recording world upside down with their records and their own films, the trend of turning American pop stars into movie idols slowed. Films, and society, turned more serious. Today, some recording stars still star in the movies, but there is no stampede to Hollywood as there was in the early 1960s. Clicking on flicks has been eclipsed by music videos as well as clicking on downloads and streaming.

Coarse-Groove Records

Older 78s with deep grooves. In their heyday they were about all that was available in disc recordings. They were fine for acoustically recorded music and talking records of the early phonograph era, but not for records made with the new electrically recorded sounds of the late 1920s. Originally, 78-rpm discs had coarse grooves with 83 to 100 grooves per inch. Coarse groove records played at, on occasion, 120 rpm and higher. For obvious reasons, 1950s disc jockeys simply would not touch a coarse-groove record. Sometimes called the big groove, the coarse grooves were manufactured in the late nineteenth century until the mid-twentieth, although few of them were made in the later years. By then they were anachronisms, replaced by discs with smaller or tighter groove patterns, and then by vinyl records.

Coin Man

Any jukebox outlet owner-operator, but also anyone who owned other types of coin-operated machines, including pinball and other entertainment machines. Of course, women also worked in the coin machine business, but they seemed impervious to the term "coin man." The name sounded suspiciously and unfortunately like con man.

Cold

Status of a recording artist's career. Opposite of the hot career or record. No doubt cold was one of most-used words in the record business language. If you were cold, baby, you were not selling. Usually you had not been selling for quite some time. Even worse, you might not have a label deal. As a result, you were knee-deep in history. Record business types used to say that one year off the charts equaled five years in obscurity. It was all about what the artist had done in the last six months. The whole industry considered his or her career dead. Cold was hard to overcome. It was like trying to get warm on a ten-degree day. Who was cold? Just about every act in the business at one time or another. The now-formally famous B.J. Thomas, for one. In 1966, his first big record went top ten. It was "I'm So Lonesome I Could Cry," and it brought him gigs and some modest fame. He must have thought it was easy to have a hit. Not so. Definitely not. Soon his luck got so bad that when he came back with a modest tear-jerking hit, "Billy and Sue," it wasn't even on Scepter Records, then his current label. It was something he had recorded previously for another label. He followed it with a couple of poor-selling, bottom-of-the-charters on Scepter. Then he hit a wall like a NASCAR racer. It's a wonder that Scepter's shrewd A&R guys didn't pull the plug on him. But he was good, very good, so they stuck with him and offered his services to indie producers. A full two years (and two cold winters) later, Thomas returned to hit town again. He was rescued by Chips Moman, the up-and-coming indie producer. In his Memphis studio Moman cut "The Eyes of a New York Woman" for Thomas. Fortunately, the record returned him to the chart's twenties and, better yet, propelled him onto the narrow radar screen of the nation's radio music directors. A few months later Thomas came roaring back to life with a terrific follow-up, the top-ten hit "Hooked on a Feeling." Though he would go on to have his ups and downs over the next ten years, Thomas recorded multiple big hits, sang movie themes, and became a star concert attraction. Finally, he realized he was the opposite of cold. He was hot. As hot as a two-dollar pistol, as DJs used to say.

Cold Stop

A record that ended abruptly but naturally. By necessity records almost always ended that way in the pre-tape days of the early twentieth century. These days, the cold stop is more prevalent and gaining popularity among record producers. Top 40 disc jockeys in the '50s and most of the '60s preferred the slow fade so they could talk while a song was fading out. But a cold stop would not keep a good record off the air. It was easier to use a slow fade when a producer was using tape and the modern console. (See **Fade**.)

Colored Wax

Colored vinyl, usually in the form of the 45-rpm disc. When RCA Victor introduced the 45-rpm single in 1949, the color gimmick was used extensively. The effect was achieved by adding a color to the vinyl instead of a substance used to turn it black. Colored vinyl was more expensive to make because it required special pressing-plant setups; most jobs were pressed in the standard black. The company believed its color made it easier to identify types of records. According to a company sales brochure from the early 1950s, classical music was pressed in ruby red; popular, in midnight blue; country and western, grass green; children's, lemon-drop yellow; blues and rhythm (folk), cerise; and international, sky blue. Of course, the general type of 45 was black. According to RCA, the colors showed "the psychological and esthetic color connotation of the type of music represented." Unlike earlier colored discs, the later ones were translucent. In later years, special-issue discs and some promotional discs used colored vinyl. The most popular colors were red, green, blue, and yellow. Today, colored vinyl discs usually sell for slightly higher prices, if the record itself is worth collecting.

Comical Songs

So-called comical songs, a subgenre of the novelty record of the 1920s and '30s, dates back to the late 1800s, when the phonograph was in its infancy. They were often sung in a humorous voice, or accent. Many were about the foibles between men and women, but some poked fun at ethnic groups and races. A number of them lampooned rural people. Some mainstream singers recorded an occasional comical song, but not exclusively. They included the famous tenor Billy Murray, who in 1923 recorded "Me No Speak'a Good English." He cut a number of these songs in the later part of his long career. Today, many comical songs would be considered anything but funny. They would be considered racist and xenophobic. Interestingly, the comical song hangs on today, but in modern form. You see one every so often. Its topic is contemporary, bordering on the bawdy instead of silliness. Comical songs are sometimes featured in comedy albums and in live performances.

Commemorative Record

Used to commemorate an event or occasion. The commemorative record was often labeled that way on its cover. It could be a single or album. A surprisingly large number of singles were released, including one on which television personality Hugh Downs announced a moon landing.

Commercial

A type of record, usually a single. "The record is *so* commercial," producers used to say, meaning attractive to radio and consumers. When a program director used to say a record was commercial, he or she meant something specific: the record had a catchy melody, a hook line, and a running time of three minutes or less. Commercial records were made for Top 40 AM radio in the late 1950s, the 1960s, and into the early 1970s. By the 1980s, you didn't hear the term used so often, and when it was used it often referred to commercialism in the more general sense. These days, many singles sound no more commercial than what album cuts did thirty years ago.

Commercial Folk

Had its heyday as an impressive Top 40 vehicle from the early 1950s through the early 1970s. Disco all but chased its last stragglers from the airwaves. Unfortunately, the times of Peter, Paul and Mary and "Leaving on a Jet Plane" are gone. But a long history and fervent supporters remain. A forerunner of folk began in the late nineteenth century. When genres of music began to evolve and be identified in the 1920s through the 1940s, record companies adopted the term *folk* most often to describe rural white music. It was relatively simple, with sparse instrumentation. Used interchangeably with hillbilly into the 1940s, the name folk became a marketing term. In the later years of its dual use, it was applicable to guitar-strumming vocalists like Clyde Moody, who recorded for King Records and other labels. One can see how the term eventually became used by the folk singers of the 1960s, the real heyday of the single folk singer. To baby-boomers, folk music generally means one singer or a group accompanied by acoustic guitars, although many observers widen the scope of folk music to include folk-rock bands and electrified instrumentation. The first wave of modern folk music arrived in the late 1940s with Pete Seeger and in the 1950s with more "hip" trios and groups such as the Kingston Trio, which turned out sing-a-long hit records. Many folk acts (and non-folk) recorded the old black spiritual "Michael, Row the Boat Ashore," a song that originated in post–Civil War days. After losing popularity with the mass commercial audience during the early Cold War years, folk music resurged during the turbulent 1960s, when Joan Baez, Buffy Sainte-Marie, Bob Dylan, Ian and Sylvia, and many other acts sang about civil rights, social justice, the war in Vietnam, and other liberal causes. Specific labels popped up to accommodate the burgeoning number of new and different folk artists. The heyday of coffeehouse folk music thrived, especially in urban settings. Folk music never died among its hardcore folk fans, and soon it expanded its base and lived again. It just slipped into the background, continuing to comment on politics and the human condition. (See **Conservative Folk Music**.)

Commercial Label

Record labels owned by a company or an individual and aimed at record sales as a business. No other businesses are involved. In other words, this commercial is the opposite of custom recording.

Compact 33

Trade name for an RCA Victor effort to compete with the LP. The Compact 33 took the size (seven inches) of a 45-rpm single and married it to the speed (33⅓ rpm) of an LP. It usually contained four songs. In the early 1960s, RCA marketed the disc as the Compact 33. The name never caught on. The seven-inch disc with multiple cuts was called the extended-play record or the EP.

Compatibles

Special discs that could be played on both monaural and stereo phonographs without damaging the disc. Interest in them peaked in the mid-1960s, when the phonograph industry was slowly moving into its stereo phase but, due to the sheer numbers produced, monaural records and players continued to have their niche.

Conservative Folk Music

Opposite of liberal folk. To young people of the 1960s, folk music meant acoustic guitars and an intimate performance. And it also meant a left-leaning lyric about social issues and war. Just because a singer was politically conservative didn't mean he or she hated the folk style. This was rare, however, because conservative youths' image of folk music was of liberals such as Joan Baez, Buffy Sainte-Marie, Bob Dylan, Peter, Paul and Mary, and others. There were standouts in conservative folk movement. Janet Greene, an Ohio-born entertainer who began her career at age eight, and later became a children's TV host in Cincinnati and Columbus. Vera Vanderlaan worked on her family's dairy farm in Vermont when she wasn't strumming her guitar. Bunny Kop, a nurse from Massachusetts, often performed with Vanderlaan. Tony Dolan, a student at Yale, must have had a strong will and indomitable courage to sing one note at Yale. Obviously, a conservative folk singer had no chance of getting a major-label deal in New York. That didn't bother Greene, who had the well-groomed good looks of a pop singer. She signed with Chantico Records of California. The label was an offshoot of Dr. Fred Schwarz's Christian Anti-Communist Crusade, a well-known organization on the right. Greene toured with him and his conservative speakers. She sang and recorded original material, including "Termites" and "Comrade's Lament." After a performance one night in Cincinnati in the mid–'60s, she challenged Baez to a duel—with guitars, not guns. Apparently, Baez was too busy performing to care. Vanderlaan and Kop both recorded for another California label called Round Table Music. Dolan cut a small-label album for which the conservative-libertarian intellectual William F. Buckley, Jr., host of *The Firing Line* TV show, wrote the liner notes. (A Yale connection here, no doubt.) Dolan performed at coffeehouses in Connecticut, where liberals found him amusing. How things have changed. Dolan moved on to other political causes in the 1970s, eventually landing a gig as a speech writer for Ronald Reagan. Greene left Chantico in the 1970s and sang a combination of folk songs, show tunes, and pop music at restaurants and small clubs around Long Beach, California. What happened to Vanderlaan and Kop? They were forever lost between the lines of music history.

Contemporary Music

In the 1960s, when the Beatles and their popular songs caught the ears of all ages, music trade writers and record label executives needed a term to describe the new music. They called it contemporary, especially when an older pop artist was recording it. The new music was any written or sung by young performers. When Andy Williams recorded a Beatles song, he was called a standard artist singing contemporary. In 1968, standard performers universally adopted contemporary music. Jukebox operators loved it. Columbia A&R man Jack Gold told *Billboard* in 1969 that standard acts were tripling their sales by recording contemporary music. "The standard artist must deal in repertoire that people have heard recently and want to hear now," Gold said. (See **Standard Artist**.)

Conversion

From mono singles to stereo. Executives from the middle to late 1960s assumed that the conversion to stereo would bring a much-needed price increase for 45-rpm singles. Even debating whether to embrace the stereo format for singles might seem strange to us today, but back then the proposal received strong opposition in some quarters. People were (and still are) reluctant to change, especially when it would cost a little more. The issue was a particularly important one for independent, singles-based labels such as Fraternity in Cincinnati. Though over the years it had released a few albums, Fraternity mainly sold singles. "That's what kept us afloat," owner Harry Carlson once said. While he was earning a small profit on his singles, he had to battle vinyl counterfeiters, who were actually selling their versions of his records to the stores. Yet converting to stereo would add a little to his pressing costs. Nonetheless, proponents of the change marched onward into stereo land. In 1968, the pro-conversion *Record World* published an editorial called "The Stereo Single—Key to a Price Increase." Two weeks later, the magazine followed with another editorial, "You Can't See the Profits for the Squeeze." The magazine pointed out a sad reality: The profit from a hit single was tiny after deducting the costs of production, promotion, pressing, and distribution. Then there was the whopping cost of selling wholesale to distributors and one-stops. This knocked off another 30 to 40 cents per single that sold in stores for a dollar—if the label was lucky. Often the stores wanted to sell them for less than 80 cents. What really troubled the record chiefs was the cost of supporting their "bombs." There were a lot of them, too. *Record World* estimated that of the innumerable singles released each year, ninety-seven percent of them did not make the charts. Supposedly, record companies earned only three cents profit per single. One unidentified "important industry figure" pointed out in the magazine's second editorial, "You want to talk about volume? Sure—go into a department store, a five and dime, and watch them selling the top 10—I mean the *top 10*—singles for *50 cents* a throw. That's volume, all right. With volume like that who needs to file for bankruptcy?" Fortunately, the stereo single did arrive over the next few years, but it was not the savior the industry expected. Yet the single remained alive, sucking up profits. It was too important, and entrenched in the minds of buyers, to eliminate.

Coordinators

They made us see, while the A&R staff made us hear. In the earlier days of rock 'n' roll, artist management and record-label personnel performed the task of coordinating the wardrobes of bands and solo singers from various musical styles. Rock took precedent for the enforcers, probably because they figured the adult contemporary singers had the good sense to "dress up" and the kids did not. However, this was not always the case. Young people of that generation were indoctrinated by their parents with the idea that one should wear clothing appropriate for different events and occasions. So when the garage bands began hitting big and generating significant income for record labels, managers, producers, and booking agents, the pressure was on to present the proper image. Naturally, matching suits were popular with bands. Such clothes projected a team image. A little later in the '60s, matching suits gave way to hip and stylish clothes, including Nehru jackets, paisley shirts and ties, and bell-bottom pants. (For the fashion-challenged, Nehru jackets were hip-length coats with mandarin collars.) Groovy clothes became *the* thing. Bands were proud of them. Clothes and music seemed to blend. Behind the scenes, especially in the earlier years, the personal managers suggested what to wear. Major labels had someone on staff who made sure this "suggestion" was enforced, particularly for album-cover shoots and publicity pictures. Look at photographs of the Beatles from 1963 to 1965, when they wore "mod" matching suits. Other bands, no matter how obscure they were, dressed appropriately for gigs, photos, and even for travel. Smaller labels left the enforcement task to the managers. Hippie bands were more reticent to obey orders. By the end of the decade the hippie fashion style began dominating the scene. Hippies eschewed anything relating to the establishment, so out went the suits and stylish "happening" clothes. In came the love beads and jeans.

Copy Record

Often used interchangeably with cover record. There was a slight difference, however. A copy record, much like the cover record and the sound-alike record, is now just another faded term from the 1950s. The copy peaked then. A 45-rpm single *copied* the original recording, right down to every last little lick in the arrangement, either to ride the coattails of the original and compete with it for radio airplay or to sell in mom-and-pop stores. The original definition can be illustrated by the story of Rusty York, a Cincinnati rockabilly and country performer in the 1950s. His record was both copy record *and* cover record. Immediately after the release of Buddy Holly's "Peggy Sue" in 1957, a King Records A&R man called York and asked, "Can you sing like Buddy Holly?" Though York hadn't heard Holly sing, he answered, "Sure I can!" The King producer told York to come over to the studio right away. There was no time to lose in the copy business. The guy ordered York and the studio musicians to copy—exactly—Holly's record. After the taping, King hurriedly pressed its version and released it in hopes that it would jump onto the chart and compete with

Holly's original. This was the goal of the copy. Ultimately, King sold about 60,000 copies of York's record, which generated a small, but much-needed, profit. Using record trade publications' definition of that era, if the King producer had asked York to record "Peggy Sue" a few weeks or months later, his record would have been called a cover. But King didn't. It jumped on "Peggy Sue" right away. For this reason, label owners despised copy records because they were in the same genre as the originals. This confused radio station music directors and DJs. While the copy sounded exactly like the original version, the cover did not necessarily have to sound this way. Sometimes a cover was done with a different arrangement, and even a different style of singer than the original—for example, a pop cover of a country or R&B record. To further complicate the situation, a second cousin to the copy and cover record was the venerable sound-alike disc, which copied the original and was sold specifically as a less-expensive alternative for buyers on a low budget. The sound-alike made no effort to compete on the charts. It simply provided another sales option. Often it was released by a label that specialized in sound-alikes. Like the copy, the sound-alike featured the vocal style and arrangement of the hit version. The cover was so much like the copy that they could be considered twins. Obviously, they were not identical ones. Covers were more creative and up-front about their status and intentions. They paid royalties to songwriters of the originals. More subversive copies tried to slip onto the radio airwaves by stealth. Even many people in the record business didn't always understand what the trades were talking about when their reporters wrote about covers, copies, and sound-alikes. But label owners knew a copy when they heard one. To their disgust, the copy didn't have to be advertised widely or even promoted much at all. No need. It did its dirty deed by simply existing. Independent labels, more often the victims of copies, went on the offensive. In 1955, Syd Nathan, founder of Cincinnati's King label, became so annoyed at copy records that he started filing lawsuits to stop them. (Never one to miss a trick, once in a while Nathan issued a copy himself, including Rusty York's.) Joining Nathan in the lawsuit counterattack was a competitor, Savoy Records of New Jersey. Radio didn't appreciate the copies, either. Program director Bob Smith of WINS told *Billboard*, "When an original disk is followed by 'copies,' WINS will play only the originals." Interestingly, copies didn't always focus on R&B originals. Many targets were country records. Smith said his station sent warning notices to top disc jockeys, including Alan Freed (who wasn't likely to play a copy anyway), Peter Roberts, Jack Lacey, and others. According to WINS, originals that were copied included LaVern Baker's "Tweedlee Dee" on Atlantic, Billy Vaughn's "Melody of Love" on Dot, the Penguins' "Earth Angel" on Dootone, Chuck Berry's "Maybellene" on Chess, and pianist Roger Williams' "Autumn Leaves" on Kapp Records. Though the more long-shot copies usually didn't generate as much profit, they must have been worth the trouble of making them or else they would not have stuck around for so long.

CORD

A co-op of record distributing companies. In 1966 a group of record distributors, dealers, one-stops, and rack-jobbers met in Chicago with an agenda. They wanted to present themselves as professional. They formed CORD, which *Record World* described as "a countrywide co-operative organization." (Loosely, CORD meant co-op records.) The trade magazine observed that CORD's profit-sharing policies were "bound to get much reaction in the industry." No wonder. Squeezed by declining profits on the sale of singles, CORD members decided to save money by buying in larger quantities for their members. They set up a system by which they could receive record shipments overnight. They sold singles to stores and other customers at cost, plus fifteen per cent. CORD members saved up to thirty-five cents on each LP. The group distributed profits of forty percent to CORD management and supplier members, and twenty percent for purchaser members. Membership cost $1,000 annually, a fairly expensive fee for smaller companies at that time. Unfortunately, in the long run the company didn't catch on with enough dealers.

Cores

Interiors of cylinder records. Some cylinder manufacturers of the late 1800s and early 1900s, particularly the Lambert Co. of Chicago, boasted that their cylinders could withstand "a flurry of activity." Lambert promoted its cylinders as indestructible, using the slogan "Can't Break 'Em." Of course, they were not indestructible. Cylinders depended on their cores for durability. Cores were made of various substances, including cardboard, glass (with a thin paraffin coating), and thread, with cardboard being the most popular.

Counterfeits

Illegally duplicated tapes and records that looked and sounded exactly like the originals. Their covers looked authentic, too. Counterfeits often competed for sales with the originals, thereby robbing songwriters, artists, and labels of revenue. Counterfeiting was and still is a worldwide problem for record companies. (See **Piracy**.)

Country-Soul

Country music with a touch of soul. Conway Twitty, the "It's Only Make Believe" man, defined the better of two genres. In the late 1950s and early '60s he combined country and soul music that drew similar audiences. The difference was that early country was popular among whites, and soul among blacks. Both had soul. Rockabilly couldn't restrain Twitty. Neither could a switch to stone country and duets with Loretta Lynn. No matter what type of music he sang in the 1960s and '70s, Twitty always achieved a soulful sound, whether it was with one word or with an entire line. "Hello Darlin'" comes straight from the heart, and crosses both styles. The term country-soul peaked in the late '60s and '70s. Two Southern soul-rockers who epitomize music are Roy Head, the "Treat Her Right" vocalist who went country, and Billy Joe Royal, the singer with the incredible voice whose "I Knew You When" contradicted the perception that you had to be black to sing with soul. Head had some success in country; Royal revived his career and had more hits as a country act than he did as a rock artist. Interestingly, at the end of his career he returned to rock. No matter what he sang, though, he was belting out soul.

Cover

Perhaps the most well-known older term still in use from the record industry of sixty years ago. It is still used as both a noun, as in "a cover version of a recording," and as a verb, as in "the singer covered the record." But today, the meaning has evolved. Often multiple covers were issued on various labels nearly simultaneously with the original. Their interpretations of the songs could be different, or similar. The idea was to compete with the original. Usually, there was no reason to be surreptitious. Everyone in the business understood the practice. The new definition of the cover—at least in the record business—has expanded over the years to mean any song that is redone, regardless of how many years have passed since the song was originally released. As a result, today the terms *cover* and *remake* are used interchangeably. Sometimes the remakes overshadowed the originals. For example, R&B singer Eddie Bo's unheralded version of "Tell It Like It Is" was released by a label in New Orleans in 1960. Aaron Neville's 1966 remake of the song, also on a Crescent City label, hit the Top 40 as a remake. Billy Joe Royal's 1988 country version was also a remake. In 1967, Brenda Holloway went to number thirty-nine with "You've Made Me So Very Happy" on Tamla Records, a Motown subsidiary. Two years later, Blood, Sweat and Tears remade it and it soared to number three. Earlier, the cover recordings of the 1950s and '60s were even more interesting. When Shelby Singleton produced Tom T. Hall's song "Harper Valley PTA" in 1968, it was immediately covered by pop singer Bobbi Martin on United Artists Records and country vocalist Ricky Page on Spar Records. Spar also promoted its version as pop. Both labels bought full-page advertisements in *Billboard*, but they could not overcome Jeannie C. Riley's version on Singleton's own Plantation Records. Surprisingly, the life of the genuine cover record lasted from

WE HAVE A SMASH
AND THE WHOLE WORLD KNOWS IT!!
<u>THE ORIGINAL!!</u>   <u>THE HIT!!</u>
"HISTORY REPEATS ITSELF"
Buddy Starcher
Boone 1038

Hit cover records are famous, but few people know ones such as "History Repeats Itself" by country performer Buddy Starcher. He co-wrote it with Minnie Pearl and recorded it with "Battle Hymn of the Republic" playing in the background. This one was a recitation country record, and the Boy from Down Home tore it up. Starcher released it on his own small label, then leased it to the independent Boone Records in Kentucky. A television performer, Starcher had had one big country hit in 1949. Then "History Repeats Itself" arrived in 1966. The song pointed out the many uncanny similarities between assassinated presidents Abraham Lincoln and John F. Kennedy. Just as Starcher's single had started to rise, Cab Calloway, the veteran jazz musician and band leader, came out with his version on Boone Records. By then, however, Starcher's version had firmly established itself with the country radio audience, which helped boost it onto the pop charts. It became a huge country hit, landing at number two, and even cracked the Hot 100's top forty records.

the 1940s to the 1970s. But the practice of covering predated radio. Years before radio began playing records in the 1930s, sheet music companies dominated the music business. They often covered popular songs at the urging of song publishers. A popular song's sheet music might feature three or four big artists' photos because they all recorded the same song. When sheet music sales slowly declined, and radio supplanted them as the main exposure for new songs, the act of covering switched more to records. By 1970, however, the radio cover record was fading, although still kicking. "Seldom does a record company pushing a 'cover disk' recoup its investment," Marvin Schlachter, head of Janus Records in New York, told *Billboard* that summer. Nonetheless, some labels still tried, despite obstacles. The label issuing a cover had to pay for extra promotion and advertising, he said at the time, making the effort too costly in the modern market. Schlachter was frustrated because Janus had suffered from covers of its hits and even some of its misses, particularly Pickettywitch's "That Same Old Feeling," an excellent song that was covered by the Fortunes on World Pacific Records. As a result, both the Janus and World Pacific versions competed, and both ended up landing in the sixties on the *Billboard* chart in 1970. In 1955, when covers flourished in pop, *Music Guild* magazine published an editorial titled, "Should You Run for Cover? Or Should You Program a Single Recorded Version of a Hit Tune?" It was aimed at jukebox operators, who apparently faced a dilemma: The original, the competition, or both? Editor D.M. Steinberg wrote, "The situation poses a problem for the operator.... The choice or choices of versions is up to the operator." Also that year *Billboard* proclaimed that the cover record "is an integral part of the disk business" and "regarded as completely ethical by all." But some label owners claimed they worked hard to record and promote a record, especially an R&B record, only to be scooped by a larger label's pop version. One interesting cover story came from Texas, where Slim Willett recorded "Don't Let the Stars Get in Your Eyes" for his Willett Records. It sold 250,000 copies and spawned covers in country and pop, including versions by Ray Price, Red Foley, Skeets McDonald, and Perry Como. Most of them hit the national charts at the same time. Judging by the number of releases, the cover record peaked in the 1950s, when R&B and rock 'n' roll were still developing. Some companies covered their own releases with their subsidiary labels in country, R&B, and pop. Other people in the business did not share *Billboard's* viewpoint. Often cover versions stole sales from the original and kept the original lower on the charts than it could have climbed. Sometimes, however, two versions of the same song became big hits. Then there's the incredible example of "The Ballad of Davey Crockett," which hit big in 1955. Crockett actor Fess Parker's version went top five, as did "Tennessee" Ernie Ford's version. Actor Bill Haynes topped out at number one for five weeks. Imagine the royalties for the writer! This didn't even include several country versions. Then there was "Tonight's the Night" by the Shirelles and the Chiffons. Both records peaked in *Billboard* on September 12, 1960. Had the Chiffons not recorded the song, the Shirelles' version might have crested higher than number thirty-nine. The Chiffons' record ended up in the seventies. By the late 1960s, the cover record had declined in popularity among record executives as rock music firmly took root. Reasons for the cover's decline also included the increasing costs of recording, the ever-increasing postage rates, the overall decline of the single as an individual musical entity, and the decline of the Tin Pan Alley songwriting. Traditionalists live by this explanation: a cover is a cover, and a remake is a remake. And never the twain—or the refrains—shall meet. (See **Cover Hit**.)

Cover-Cover

Original version of a record that covered its cover versions. For example, in an unusual occurrence in 1973, a single called "Soul Makossa," by thirty-nine-year-old African musician Manu Dibango, became a big hit on Fiesta Records in France. He and his band performed all over Europe. (The name Makossa referred to a well-known African musician.) A Brooklyn company, African Market Exports, imported copies of the record and sold them around New York. The company reportedly moved 30,000 units; some retailers charged up to ten dollars a copy. Meanwhile, enterprising producers launched cover versions of the African rock song, complete with chants by guys who were allegedly African chiefs. One cover's U.S. distributor took out ads in the trades, announcing "New York City's Number 1 Smash Blockbuster!" by the Original Nairobi Afro Band. The band's single was issued by the Town Hall One Stop label in Brooklyn. The company introduced sales gimmicks, such as a Soul Makossa Contest that promised "valuable prizes" to fans of its "TRUE MAKOSSA arrangement which builds up to a TRUE MAKOSSA 'FRENZY' ENDING. An exciting dance smash! Also, the only recording that features the 'MYSTERY VOCAL' at the end." The label claimed it was receiving airplay on radio stations in Philadelphia, Washington, D.C., and greater New York. Even more, the lucky contestant who sent in "the best translation and most complete explanation of what the second [African] chief is saying will WIN THE FIRST PRIZE—a Free TV SET." Seeing how this frenzy could lead to big-time sales, Atlantic Records stepped in and took control of what *Cash Box* was by then calling "the 'Soul Makossa' Sweepstakes." Atlantic execs went to Paris to lease Dibango's *original* master from Fiesta. Atlantic president Ahmet Ertegun said, "We are normally reluctant to do covers, but in this case we are covering the covers with the original." In the trades that June of '73, both labels—David and Goliath of the record business—battled in advertisements over "Soul Makossa." The Atlantic Goliath won, claiming it shipped 150,000 copies in only one day. (See **Cover**.)

Cover Hit

A cover record that was a hit. Often it out-dueled the original and possibly other covers to become the dominant chart version.

Crossover Hit

A record that appealed to across-the-board genres. The term, used most often in the heyday of the 45-rpm single, referred to hits that made it in various genres. Because so few radio formats existed then, country hits sometimes made it onto the top pop charts. So did adult contemporary records and an occasional jazz record ("Take Five" by Dave Brubeck). Examples of a successful crossover are Charlie Rich's "Behind Closed Doors" and Glen Campbell's "By the Time I Get to Phoenix." Both were hits in country, pop, and adult contemporary.

CSG Processed

The process of adapting stereo records to play on monaural phonographs. The process, created by Holzer Audio, was applied to the master tapes during the mixdown phase. In that era, quite a few mono phonographs were still in use, particularly older models from the 1950s and early 1960s and some of the smaller, carrying-case phonos aimed at the teen market. Without getting technical here, let's just say that the process did work. But it was criticized for supposedly making the record sound different than its creators intended. The vocals seemed to stand out better in mono. The heyday of the CSG process was short—1968 to 1970, though it continued in use sporadically throughout the '70s. By the time the process really got rolling, the switchover to stereo had come on like a tidal wave. Stereo phonographs were plentiful. CSG was no longer needed. A Vanilla Fudge single on Atco Records was labeled "CSG Processed Mono Master."

Cue

DJs would find the first note of the record, then rotate it back one half to three-quarters of a turn to avoid a "wow" factor. This was done to make sure the music or vocal would begin immediately when the DJ announced it. When DJs played records on the air, they didn't use tape in the early days of rock. They had to first cue them up because the turntables had to get up to speed.

Custom Label

Recording studios and pressing plants owned their own custom labels for which clients could record or release their tapes. Because so many hometown rockabilly and country artists released their music on custom labels, they have become sought-after collectibles today. Some larger record companies used the term custom to refer to the independent labels that they manufactured and distributed. Atlantic Records in New York often used the term this way.

Custom Pressing

A job done for an outside group, label, or individual. One of the larger custom pressing companies was RCA Victor Division, Custom Record Sales. It pressed not only for independent labels and individuals but also for radio stations. In the late 1940s and early 1950s, stations routinely ordered discs for programs and commercials and special events that were to be broadcast. The work kept pressing plants busy. As the number of independent record companies grew in the late '40s and early '50s, they turned to the major-label pressing plants for manufacturing. Only a few indie labels—King Records and its Royal Plastics division in Cincinnati, for example—invested in pressing equipment and engaged in outside custom work. The majors often made a handsome side income by providing custom work; in fact, RCA pressed not only for its own label but also for other majors. Columbia, the largest American label in the late 1950s and 1960s, operated Columbia Record Productions, a custom service. One of CRP's albums, *Remember How Great,* featured hits of the late 1950s and early 1960s by pop and rock performers (from various labels), including "Tequila" by the Champs and "Hawaiian Wedding Song" by Andy Williams. An independent custom label, Dixie Records, made by Starday, released some surprisingly good records.

Custom Recording

Made in studios that rent their facilities to anyone. Independent producers cut some of the biggest hits of the 1960s, including "Wipe Out" by the Surfaris, as custom jobs.

Cut

Making a record. Used as a verb, as in to cut a record, and as a noun, as in a good cut (or track). The term dates back to the early days of the phonograph, when wax cylinders were actually cut. In later years, discs were mastered, or cut. Then an engineer transferred the sound from a mixed-down master tape through a console, which used a lathe and stylus to cut grooves into a lacquer-coated aluminum disc.

Cut-In Record

Snippets of different records put together to make one theme. The cut-in was made possible by the full-scale arrival of commercial tape recorders in the early 1950s. Prior to this time, when records were recorded on acetate discs, such a practice would have been difficult if not impossible. Besides, the timing wasn't right. Only the crazy 1950s could give birth to the cut-in. Producers of cut-ins carefully spliced tiny parts of familiar recordings into the recording artist's narration, thereby creating a whole new record and making the radio audience laugh. (Today this practice would be called sampling.) The first huge cut-in hit, and possibly the first cut-in record, was released in 1956 by Dickie Goodman, a New York music-business operative. "The Flying Saucer" was both a cut-in and a topical record, for flying saucers had become a national craze by the mid-'50s. He followed it with a string of other cut-in flops, near-misses, and hits, most notably "Mr. Jaws" in 1975. By then, only the master could manage to squeeze a cut-in record onto the fast-evolving radio charts. The days of the cut-in were numbered. (See **Break-In Record**.)

Cutoff Groove

Pushes the stylus or needle to the end of the disc.

Cut-Outs

You could find them in record stores and discount stores all the time. Older people remember the days when cutout bins offered LPs for twenty-five cents to fifty cents, and singles from ten to twenty-five cents. (In the late 1960s, you could buy a new single for ninety-eight cents, and cheaper if on sale.) Cut-outs still exist for modern record products. Record labels sell their unwanted product to special firms, which supply cut-outs to stores at bargain prices. In the heyday of the single, the cut-out bin was a repository of failed dreams. You could find dozens of obscure records on major and minor labels and everything in between. And at ten for a dollar, you could take a chance on some records that sounded good but never received enough promotion.

Cutting In

Giving someone a piece of a song. Often this was payment in writer royalties in exchange for something, usually for promoting or producing a record. James Brown was a master of cutting in. He once assigned co-writer credit to his audio engineer for his long-time ability and dependability. In the 1950s, the practice reached a peak when rock-and-roll arrived. Many record label owners and disc jockeys were "cut in" on the deals, only to be cut out when the practice fell out of favor in the 1970s. As an example, it has been said that Duke Records owner Don Robey often "cut in" on songwriter credits by adding his name to some of his hit songs to maximize his profits. It wasn't illegal, and he did own the publishing rights, but such activity is not as common today. It simply is not tolerated by the big-business songwriting world.

Cylinder

Delivery system of recorded music that lasted commercially from the 1880s to 1912, and into the 1920s for office use. Some cylinder recorders continued to be made into the mid–1920s. Everything began on cylinder in the 1870s, when Edison invented the phonograph. By the end of the century it had competition from the disc machine. Cylinders were made of wax in the earliest days of the record business. Sizes of cylinders varied, but the most common ones were a bit larger than the cardboard in a roll of bathroom tissue. They were highly breakable if dropped. Into the twentieth century, the disc won the battle, something on the order of VHS defeating Beta for the preferred videocassette format. The Depression all but wiped out the cylinder trade for recorded music, though the format hung around for some years in other forms.

D

Dance Records

Promoted new dances through Top 40 radio in the 1950s and through the early 1970s. They celebrated dances that often had been conceived and choreographed by hip young kids who loved to rock on the dance floor. Other dances of the period were created by musicians and songwriters who knew what people wanted to hear. Some early teen dances were improvised by kids who attended Dick Clark's *American Bandstand* program in Philadelphia. There was a difference between the teen *dance* record and the *dancing* record. Teen dance records were usually tied to one or more dances and had related lyrics. When the 1950s arrived and spawned rock 'n' roll, shrewd record companies recognized teen dance trends and over the years capitalized on them. The labels released vocal records to promote colorful dances called the Fly, the Twist, the Mashed Potato, the Shimmy, the

Watusi, the Jerk, the Stroll, the Swim, and others. The records inspired kids to create new and more fanciful dances, nationally and internationally. A few of them, including the Twist, became household names. Probably the most famous was Chubby Checker's massive hit "The Twist." He built his popularity on dance records. Checker's number-one record "Limbo Rock"

A hit record with a nonsensical title that came out of Memphis in 1965 prompted dancers to invent their own routines to fit the music. Though "Wooly Bully" by Sam the Sham and the Pharaohs was not a traditional dance, like the Watusi and the Twist, it translated well on the dance floor with a solid, steady beat, just right for line dancing. Domingo "Sam" Samudio, the lead singer and organist, wrote it. It was pure good-time music with seemingly unintelligible lyrics. But everyone on the inside of cool knew what Sam was singing in "Wooly Bully." The song introduced the term L-7 into the public lexicon. L-7 meant unhip, uptight. Sam went on to write and record more hits, but "Wooly" remains his most-remembered hit.

sold 1.3 million copies. "It is another feather in the cap of the young lad who has become the 'Dean of Teen Dance,'" *Cash Box* proclaimed on its cover in 1962. As Checker, who was by then the undisputed king of the dance record, helped push the limbo dance, his label, Cameo Records of Philadelphia, became a leading singles label. The company signed him to a new five-year deal based on his success with the two dance records. Other Checker dance hits included "Let's Twist Again," "The Fly," and "Pony Time." His albums also sold well. Adults and kids alike had fun doing the Twist and singing to the record. Even people with two left feet could do it. The simple dance song was first written and recorded by Hank Ballard on the indie King label, which also placed his version on the charts. Down in Memphis, Sonny Burgess and the Pacers decided to capitalize on the dance craze in the late 1950s by promoting a dance called the Bug. He once said, "The Bug dance is when you're itchin' and scratchin,' and each musician acts like he's throwing a bug on another guy. Then he throws it into the corner, into the crowd. Then the band jumps into the crowd and sings." One time, Burgess jumped and his guitar hit him in the mouth. Even after the Beatles changed the music scene in 1964, teen dance records remained popular. The mid-'60s also brought some other new, and more stylized dances. The Robot Walk, for instance, encouraged dancers to move around like robots. In 1964, the Little Mark label released "The Robot Walk" by Tony (Robot) Alamo. He looked like Fabian in a metal outfit resembled a medieval knight more than a robot. In 1965, James Brown, who sang some dance music on stage, hit with "Papa's Got a Brand New Bag." His record paid tribute to a number of then-current dances. By 1969, however, things began to change with the nation's darkening mood. When the flower-child movement and its hippie rock bands arrived in full force, and the Vietnam conflict preoccupied young people, monster-selling teen dance singles slowly began to disappear. Although dancing music of all kinds continues to be released today, those innocent Top 40 teen dance records like "The Twist" are a relic from the early to mid–1960s and the heyday of the 45.

Dancing Records

Named by phonograph trade magazines of long ago. At the time, there were neither baby boomers nor their dance records, so everything was a dancing record. Many were instrumentals. They have been made since the early part of the twentieth century to accompany specific dances, such as the Waltz, the Fox Trot, and later the Jitterbug. Instrumental dancing records have a long history, almost as long as the phonograph has existed. In 1914, the trade magazine *Talking Machine World* noted how the records brightened the nation's spirits and helped pull the record industry out of an economic slump. Thanks to dancing records, the magazine pointed out, the Victor label earned nearly one-third more profit between 1913 and 1915, up to $21,682,055. Over the next thirty years, dancing records continued to be big moneymakers. They were popular during the big-band days. Although you can dance in some form to about any record, the dancing record was and still is perfect for couples trying the latest dances, or just for dancing in general. Though some old dancing records came with vocals, their lyrics were unrelated to the dances. Early on, a strength of the instrumental dancing record was that anyone, including people who didn't even dance, could appreciate it on another level—for its instrumentation and melody. This has continued. The dancing record outlasted the teen dance record because musically it stood on its own, without being tied lyrically to any particular dances. Dances became dated. Instrumentals lasted longer. They often came with names that suggested a certain dance, but that's as far as it went. The lack of words allowed listeners to imagine whatever they wanted when the record played. Many huge R&B instrumentals, such as "The Horse" by Cliff Nobles and Company in 1968, were named for specific dances. Thanks to disco, instrumental dancing records had another renaissance. As the decades passed and new dances and generations arrived, the physical styles of dancing changed. It became fashionable for people to dance by themselves or without partners actually touching. But one thing remained the same: the music still moved them. Fortunately, dancing records are still popular, especially in clubs that promote dancing.

Dead Wax

The part of a record that lies between the paper label and the grooves—the smooth part that returns the tone arm to its resting place. Dead wax carries at least a record's number and maybe even an interesting message. Sometimes mastering engineers wrote their initials in the dead wax. Don Robey, of the Duke and Peacock labels in Houston, made the practice popular. In 1949, he became upset about bootlegging of his discs, so he started writing Don D. Robey in the dead wax to make bootlegging more difficult. In the early 1960s, "Wall of Sound" producer Phil Spector wrote his first name in the dead wax with that of Ronnie of the Ronettes.

Defectives

Discs, usually 45s, damaged in the factory. By 1972, *Billboard* called the situation a crisis. As one jukebox operator put it in a letter to the magazine's editor, "In our modern world of advanced technology, the recording industry is doing nothing to improve the quality of its product." He was referring to the 45, of course, for jukebox operators used mainly singles. One of the problems was the pressing plants of the era. They were growing older, and some were not updated to handle the new sound of stereo and more sophisticated needles and phonographs. Other defective issues were even worse. Records were often off center or bent, and labels were torn.

Deluxe Packaging

Fancy record album covers. By the early '70s, eight of ten new albums featured artistic, colorful covers and/or double-fold jackets. Only a year earlier, only sixty-five percent of LPs came in deluxe. Some label executives said the new approach allowed their companies to feature more photos and longer liner notes, although many of their artists didn't care about the notes. Buyers came to expect deluxe albums—and notes. The term was not new to the record business. In the late '50s, the trade magazines were using the name to describe expanded LPs. One particular kind was called the folder, which contained longer liner notes and photographs inside the jacket. This type was used mainly for some classical albums and for musicals. In 1958, Columbia released its "super deluxer" package for two albums—*The Confederacy* and *The Union*, which featured a box containing expanded notes, photos, and text. And the Civil War centennial wasn't coming until 1961.

Demo

Recorded to showcase a song to a producer or record label. Some were basic guitar-and-vocal efforts. Others, such as Carole King's "It Might as Well Rain Until September," were so good that they could—and did—become records. In the 1950s through the early 1970s, many demos consisted of a songwriter singing his song with a piano or guitar or with minimal backup. Some were more elaborate, especially ones done in New York. If you find an acetate disc put out by a publishing firm from those days, you might hear a popular songwriter doing his or her thing in the rough. These days, demos are usually complete, closer to masters. The reason? Publishers don't want prospective A&R reps with weak musical imaginations to work too hard. Other than that, a demo is a suggestion. When a songwriter writes a song, he or she records a demo in hopes of enticing a producer or artist to record a song. Producers also have used demos as blueprints, building their records on the demo's basic ideas in phrasing, licks, and tempo. "It Was I" by Skip and Flip, a top ten hit in 1959, was cut as a demo. Bobby Shadd heard it and released it on his Brent label in New York. Routinely labels received demos recorded by their artists. Often record companies slapped the better demos on singers' albums to fill them out and save money. Now, in this high-tech era, homemade demos often end up molded into a final digital recording. (See **Acetate**.)

Democratization of Music

Opened a new era for the rise of independent labels, R&B, and rock 'n' roll, and thousands of new song publishers who want their music played on the radio. Before radio, sheet music was king. For decades, the big sheet publishers held what amounted to a monopoly on popular songs and Broadway performances. They were the barons of sheet music who introduced their songs through performances and theater musicals. Some people in the record business and in politics believed the 1950s brought the "democratization of music," as it was called. Not coincidentally, it paralleled the rise of radio's interest in playing records. This was a more lucrative venue for the new country and R&B labels and exposed new songs to millions of people through radio airplay. In 1958, the president of BMI, Robert Burton, maintained that new technology changed the old ways of promoting music through well-known singers and popular bands. He claimed this was in effect "a tightly held monopoly" operated by Tin Pan Alley in New York and songwriting and recording centers in Hollywood. In the new era, he told a U.S. Senate panel, BMI could compete with ASCAP and smaller record companies could compete with the major labels. It was done, he said, through accessibility—the introduction of tape recording and the pressing of new hi-fidelity, unbreakable records.

Demonstration Record (Promotional)

Often featured a well-known performer or performers to promote a product, cause, or company. On one such disc in the late 1950s, Columbia Records sold an album to promote its pop line. Majors and independents also released discs—both singles and albums—to promote everything from phonographs to washing machines. *Bonanza* star Lorne Greene made at least one demonstration record.

Demonstration Record (Sales Tool)

Known in the trades as a demo. It was truly a *demonstration* record. Record companies distributed demonstration discs to audio stores to give customers some idea of how phonographs would sound at home. In the early 1960s, vinyl LP demos came with a limited number of songs. This irked some audio dealers, who wanted a variety of songs and styles that would appeal to people of all ages and tastes. One dealer complained that a demo record should feature cuts ranging from classical to jazz to show tunes. Another complained that the pressings themselves were often poor and scratched. If a customer was considering shelling out up to $5,000 for a state-of-art hi-fi system, audio store owners argued, then he or she deserved something better than a shoddy record with too few music samples.

Descriptive Record

Descriptive records sold in record company catalogs and in stores of the 1890s. For example, "Morning on the Farm" was an audio recreation of a realistic barnyard experience. The label bragged that the sounds were "so real and exact that it requires but a slight stretch of the imagination to place one's self in that delightful position, the result of which is the drinking in of copious drafts of fresh air and numerous other pleasures attainable only on the farm." Descriptive discs faded as the phonograph and the listener became more sophisticated.

Detroit

Regional music center that was so overshadowed by one record label that the city's contributions to rock and other types of music went underappreciated by the average teenage radio listener of the era. In the early 1960s, Motown Records—it combined a smooth pop sound with black soul—caught fire and didn't stop. Berry Gordy, Jr., did a good job synching his business and his dream to his *place*. The city was a major regional entertainment and recording center throughout Motown's years in Detroit. Songwriters, arrangers, producers, and other behind-the-scenes operatives worked for the label. But there were other labels, including Hot Wax Records, and other non–Motown hits. Everything in the Detroit's music business was by some degree overshadowed by the goliath Motown. In this way, Detroit was typecast. Motown racked up so many big hits for so long that people thought of the Motor City as the smooth soul capital of America. Rock music bubbled under the surface in area clubs, and spawned the Bob Seger System, MC5, and other bands. In 1958, the rockin' Royaltones from Detroit cut their instrumental hit "Poor Boy," charging in with two saxophones blasting, and backed by a hot guitar and solid rhythm section. The band featured top players as guitarist Dennis Coffey, sax player George Katsakis, and bassist Bob Babbitt. Over six years, the group recorded for Jubilee, Warwick, Mala, Twirl, and other labels. Detroit rocked as hard as it crooned. Singer Herman Griffin, one of Motown's earliest recording artists, said the city's radio stations were also an overlooked asset. They made sure Detroit stayed well-rounded—at least to the region's people. Though today the best days of Motown are in a museum, things keep rocking in Detroit.

Dialect Stories

Comedic records done with imitations of America's regional dialects as well as those of immigrants, blacks, and rural people. Voices included East Europeans, the Irish, and Germans. The records were popular in the early 1900s, but slowly faded after the electric recording era arrived in the mid–1920s.

Diamond Disc

Quarter-inch thick record that featured vertical grooves. Because it used a diamond-tipped stylus instead of a steel needle, the Edison Diamond Disc phonograph became a forerunner of modern phonographs. It was also Mr. Edison's answer to the growing threat of Victor's disc machines. His cylinders, while technically sound, had been losing in the battle with the disc. Columbia, which had manufactured both cylinders and discs, finally gave up on cylinders as their popularity declined in the early years of the twentieth century, but Edison stubbornly continued to make them. Finally, the Edison company realized that the future was in discs, so in 1910 it introduced the Diamond Disc and a special phonograph to play them. The new phonograph featured a diamond stylus on a floating head that operated much like the modern phonograph's tone arm and reproducer. The rigid, heavy tone arms on other machines used the steel needle. Diamond Disc cases were as attractive as a Victrola or any other machine, but the Diamond Disc did have a difference: its records could not be played on other machines. Their steel needles would damage the Edison discs, which used the hill-and-dale groove system. The phonograph was also different because its turntable revolved at about eighty revolutions per minute. To adjust the volume, the operator simply turned a special volume control, which connected to a ball of felt that plugged the internal acoustic horn speaker. The Diamond Disc record and its accompanying phonograph peaked during the years immediately after World War I, but continued to be sold until the Depression hit in 1929. (See **Re-Creation**.)

Diaphragms

A forerunner of the modern microphone. Mica diaphragms of varying thickness used in the acoustic recording era, 1878–1924. Horns gathered the sound. The thin diaphragms were used to record softer sounds; thicker ones to record the louder sounds on recorder-player machines. Often the sounds were captured on wax cylinders.

Dime Store Records

Sold for about twenty-five cents each in the late 1920s. Their peak years were the 1920s and '30s. They were forerunners of later budget lines sold by various labels and some stores. Dime store labels featured little-known performers singing and playing well-known songs. People then were more interested in hearing a certain song than they were hearing any particular recording artist. The Banner Records label was made by Plaza Music Company in New York for sale in the S.S. Kresge Company's five-and-dime stores in the 1920s and '30s. Banner's titles reflected a number of genres to appeal to a wide range of Kresge customers' musical tastes. Another dime store label, Oriole Records, was sold by the McCrory stores. A McCrory competitor, Woolworth, sold records on its Crown label, while W.T. Grant stores sold records on its Bell label. The larger stores, including Sears & Roebuck, sold their own records as well. Sears' labels included Challenge and Silvertone. Dime store labels died out for two main reasons: The Depression and a trend toward customers wanting records by well-known artists.

Direct-to-Disc

Recording a live performance directly to disc, instead of on multitrack tape—was started for jazz performers in the 1980s. Actually, the work is much older. Some of the earlier recordings were made directly onto disc and cylinder. In New Orleans in the '40s, audio engineer Cosimo Matassa recorded black blues and R&B singers with a Presto recorder, three electrical outlets, and a prayer. This type of recording process has a long history.

Dirty Blues

Radio and record-business nickname for risqué rhythm and blues records in the late 1940s and early 1950s. They often employed a double entendre in their titles and sold well. King Records, an independent in Cincinnati, released many of these records, but so did other labels. The King releases included "Sixty-Minute Man" by Billy Ward and the Dominoes, "I Want a Bowlegged Woman" by Bull Moose Jackson, and "Slow, Smooth and Easy" by the Drivers. The dirty blues records faded in the mid–1950s when the public finally caught on to them and the labels decided the records made more trouble than they were worth. A King Records executive felt forced to apologize for ever releasing them. Except for "Sixty-Minute Man," which sold well through the music underground and received some play on black radio, and was covered and remade, most of the dirty records didn't attract as much airplay as the "clean" hits.

Disc changer

A devise used to change records and speeds. Popular in the 1950s, when the single and the LP were competing. One such unit, Webcor's Magic Wand Disc Changer, could handle seven-, ten-, and twelve-inch records. Its advertising slogan read, "Now you can sit back and enjoy Microgroove records for hours!"

Disc-Charger

A small silver cylinder that contained radioactive material that ionized the air, drawing static electricity generated by vinyl discs. In the mid–1950s, the Mercury Scientific Products Corp., Los Angeles, sold the Mercury Disc-Charger. The static electricity caused records to hold dust, so the device helped eliminate a common problem by allowing the stylus to clean the record in a few plays. The device clipped to the record player's pickup arm. It cost $4.50.

Disc-O-Mat

Attempted to sell the top hits in unlikely places. In early 1969, the Dot, Capitol, and Columbia labels expressed interest in the new Disc-O-Mat vending machine, developed by entrepreneurs Don Orsattis and David T. Gorwitz of Los Angeles. They sought to sell the top 100 hits as the discs were being promoted to record distributors, rack-jobbers, and radio stations. Plans called for 100,000 machines to be placed in supermarkets, teen retail stores, schools, fast-food restaurants, and recreation sites. To help boost interest, the Disc-O-Mat owners planned to give away copies of *Go* magazine at each machine. Unfortunately, after a promising start, the Disc-O-Mat just didn't go.

Disco Mix

Recording mixed for dancing. Some were originally recorded for that purpose. Others were singles that ran as long as a disco mix could. As the disco craze hit in New York clubs, the term disco mix began to germinate in the Big Apple. By 1976, it was firmly inserted into the moves of the disco beat. The term means a longer, more resonant cut with a focus on the beat and rhythm. The beat made the disco mix, and certain recording engineers specialized in it. The so-called Father of the Disco Mix was Tom Moulton, the guru of the disco continuous-mix sound. He even wrote a column in *Billboard* named, appropriately, Disco Mix. In it he discussed the latest releases and commented briefly on them. As for the mix itself, it enabled record companies to release a shorter seven-inch single version of a song as well as a longer, one-song twelve-inch version. The twelve-inch records often had long stretches of instrumentation, which allowed the dancers to go longer. Radio airplay was not necessary, because the clubs took the place of radio exposure. Moulton started his career in the record business as a sales and promotion man for several labels. Later, he started mixing, then got into disco. He mixed Gloria Gaynor's important disco album *Never Can Say Goodbye*.

Discotheque

Dance club of the early to mid–1960s. A decade before disco music began percolating in New York clubs, the discotheque ruled the dance floor. Like disco, the discotheque fad resonated with record companies. The name had a familiar French ring to it. Most discotheques featured live music. As these clubs became the "in" places to be seen and unwind in the mid-'60s, record labels started using them to sell records. Albums were issued with the word discotheque emblazoned on their covers. Singles tried to use that angle, too, although with far less success and effort than in the coming disco days. In March of 1964, the trade magazine *Music Business* described discotheque as "dancing to recordings with shill dancers displaying the latest monkey, frug, Watusi or what have you." Art D'Lugoff, owner of the Village Gate in Greenwich Village, told *Music Business*, "One thing is definite. Dancing is back and is in. Live dance bands (not the big bands of yesteryear) are definitely on the scene combining blues, jazz and folk material to meet the current tastes of youth." To take advantage of the trend, he installed a new dance floor at the Village Gate. He used both live and recorded music. He also formed a record label, opened a restaurant, an art gallery, and a café called Top of the Gate. The discotheque concept burned like a rocket for a few years, then died down in the turmoil and social changes of the late '60s. But dance clubs did not die. They just waited to be reborn as disco clubs.

Disk Men

Trade magazine name for record producers and record label owners.

Diskery

Another popular slang term for a record company. It originated in the late 1940s and 1950s. It was used by trade magazines, and rarely by the people who worked at record companies.

Discotheque Vol. 2 was issued by the Command label in New York. It represented the height of the discotheque era, the mid-1960s, a decade before disco clubs became popular. At age sixty, Enoch Light was a little old to be a hip discotheque guy, but the bandleader, recording engineer, and classically trained violinist knew a commercial opening when he heard it, and it was America's fascination with big-city discotheque clubs populated by dancing girls in white go-go boots. This album represented the discotheque sound: horns, a bright organ, and guitar. The songs, including "Love Potion Number Nine" and "Sha La La," sound like pieces from a 1960s soundtrack.

Diskin' Data

Popular column in *Music Vendor* magazine in the late 1950s. It featured news about artists' bookings, their new records, and brief commentaries. The column was credited to Dave. Probably he was staff writer David Steinberg. He mixed Diskin' Data, one of the *Vendor's* regular features, with new pop and rock records. At the end of the March 31, 1958, column, Steinberg wrote: "Education Note: Our teenagers are interested in the two r's—rock and roll." Few of them read *Music Vendor*, but their jukebox-operator parents and grandparents did.

Distribbers

Record distributors. A late-1940s trade magazine slang term.

Distribution Deal

Record companies selling other labels' records. In the early 1960s, the majors and larger independents decided they could make more money by distributing independent labels. The larger ones charged pressing fees to the new client and received a royalty on each record sold. Sometimes, such deals made sense, especially if the smaller label could not break into the rich land of the better distributors and marketers. Larger labels took the small labels on, usually sensing that their time had come for a big hit. King Records agreed to distribute Beltone Records in New York, and Four Store Records in Los Angeles. Immediately, the deals paid off, with "Hot Rod Lincoln" by Charlie Ryan in 1960 and Beltone with "Tossin' and Turnin'" and "One Track Mind" by Bobby Lewis in 1961. Though Ryan's record was successful, despite reaching only the low thirties on the *Billboard* chart, Lewis' "Tossin' and Turnin'" hit number one and "One Track Mind" number nine on the magazine's pop chart. On the downside, the profits were substantially less for the smaller labels because the distributing label had to press the records, promote them, advertise them, and store them.

DJ Convention

Radio personnel gathered to discuss the trade and propose improvements to radio. Sometimes record company A&R men stopped to play their latest offerings and seek support among the DJs. Record promoters used the conventions to break new records. They had a captive audience. DJ conventions also featured various kinds of night-time entertainment.

DJ Platter

Promotion copies—records, or "platters"—for radio stations. Term used by RCA Victor, then picked up by most labels and until the end of commercial vinyl in the early 1990s.

Dog

Jukebox operator's name for a record that occupied vital space in a jukebox, but received few "spins," or plays. Also known as a stiff—a dog. Every dog would have its day—in the cut-out bin.

Double A (AA)

A "Double A" was a record with two A sides—both with the same song or cut. In modern times, it was mainly used for promotional copies, but not exclusively. The reasoning behind the double A-side was to prevent DJs from playing the flip side. Also, double A-sides saved a little money because the flip side needed neither recording nor mastering. Occasionally, record companies had to use the double A side because no B-side was available.

Double Cover

A strange practice that had a record company competing against itself, or at least milking its songs to the maximum. A so-called double cover was a record that covered another—on the same label. Quite a few companies released double covers in two musical genres, such as pop and country or soul and country. The pop-rock doubles combination was not as prevalent. King Records did it in the 1940s and '50s, occasionally releasing a triple cover in pop, country, and soul. But by the early '60s the triple was as rare. Examples of double covers include "Tonight," a pop version by former big-band leader Ralph Marterie, and a Top 40 version by Jay and the Americans. Both records were released by United Artists in 1961, and both failed to chart on the national top 100. When *Music Vendor* heard about the simultaneous double releases on UA, it noted: "The company has the jump on the only renditions of the song being timed for release with the opening of the movie *West Side Story*, in which the tune is featured. Columbia clicked on Johnny Mathis' treatment of the song when the show was popular on Broadway." (Mathis' version did not reach the Hot 100. It did not count as a cover because it was released well before the Marterie-Americans releases.) UA had issued double covers before. They included "Never on Sunday" by arranger Don Costa and its double cover by the actress Melina Mercuri. "We were quite successful with both," a company spokesman said at the time. Costa's version was the most successful, reaching number nineteen on

Billboard's Hot 100 in 1960. Another double cover was "Let's Get Together" by Annette Funicello and Tommy Sands on Buena Vista Records, the Disney label. It did not chart. The song was used in the company's film *The Parent Trap*. At the same time, Disney also released a "Let's Get Together" double-cover version by the popular young English actress Haley Mills, who co-starred in the film. She hit big with the song, landing it in the top ten in September of 1960. By the mid–1970s, double covers had faded. (See **Cover**.)

Double-Face Records

Two recorded sides on a 78-rpm shellac disc. They officially began in 1908, when Columbia introduced them, but forerunners had appeared as early as 1900. When Columbia's new double-sided records arrived, many competing record firms advertised that single-faced records—ones with only one recorded side—were better because the customer did not have to pay for two songs. People already were accustomed to buying cylinder recordings, which had only one song or offering. But the future clearly was in double-face records. The standard continues to this day. The single-face disc did stick around until the 1980s, when acetates were distributed as test pressings and rush-release singles. But these discs were not for sale for public consumption. (See **Single-Face Record**.)

Double One

Single that hit number one on the national charts from *both* sides. It made the two-sided hit look cheap. Having a double one was more than rare. It was nearly impossible to achieve, for the ferocity of competition among hot singles varied each week. In the rock 'n' roll era, Elvis Presley did it with "Hound Dog" hit number one and "Don't Be Cruel" in the summer and fall of 1956. This occurred when Presley was hotter than a meteorite. The manner in which "Hound Dog" hit one is confusing, however, for the magazine's revered Hot 100 pop chart debuted about the time the record was hitting. Nonetheless, "Hound Dog" did hit number one on two other *Billboard* genre charts at the time. "Don't Be Cruel" arrived in time to reach number one on the Hot 100. Meanwhile, competitor *Cash Box* reported the two sides as separate number-one hits on its pop singles chart. Between the two sides, Elvis held the number one slot for ten weeks on the *Cash Box* chart and eleven on *Billboard's* charts. (See **Two-Sided Hit**.)

Double Play Disks

Weekly *Billboard* listing called Double Play Disks, which referred to records with "two-sided action." This listing was aimed at jukebox operators, who needed such information for "maximum programming effectiveness." The term was the jukebox operators' version of the two-sided hit. The listing's ten most popular 45-rpm singles had to be currently or recently on the Hot 100. On March 23, 1963, for example, double hit disks included "Let's Limbo Some More" and "Twenty Miles" by Chubby Checker on Cameo Records, "I Wanna Be Around" and "I Will Live My Life for You" by Tony Bennett on Columbia, and "Laughing Boy" and "Two Wrongs Don't Make a Right" by Mary Wells on Motown. One of the more memorable Double Play Disks that week was "Can't Get Used to Losing You" and "The Days of Wine and Roses" by Andy Williams on Columbia. (See **Two-Sided Hit**.)

Drive-Hole Marks

Tiny depressions visible around the center hole of 45-rpm discs. They were made in the pressing process by the master lacquer.

Dual Distribution

One record label using two distributors in one territory. Usually, labels set up a network of individual distribution companies across the country, with each distributor working its area (Cincinnati, Houston, Memphis, etc.). With dual distribution, labels would work with two distributors in some cities. Neither of them liked the idea, but the labels got saturation coverage in 1963, when the mini-trend began. Nonetheless, most labels continued to do business the traditional way, with one distributor.

Dual Forty-Five

One of the first compatible singles, from early 1968. Compatible for both stereo and monaural phonographs, the new single was a breakthrough for 45s because finally they could be played on the more expensive stereo phonographs of the day. It cost record companies about one cent more per record to press the Dual 45. Its purpose was to interest adults in buying singles, improve the sagging singles market, and bolster sales to jukebox outlets. People behind the new system included Cal Roberts of Columbia and Paul Leka, producer of the Lemon Pipers for Buddah Records, a proponent of the early stereo single. The dual single was a good idea, but it didn't last too long. When stereo finally took hold, it came on quickly. Record buyers started acquiring stereo phonographs, making the compatible 45 about as obsolete as the mono single.

Dual Programming

Extended play albums and singles offered on a jukebox. By 1958, Seeburg Corporation, the Chicago-based jukebox manufacturer, had expanded its options for customers, jukebox operators, and record companies. Seeburg's new system allowed both EP albums and 45-rpm singles to be played on several of the company's models. The jukeboxes add "Dual Programming to Dual Pricing to present operators the opportunity to profitably merchandise both kinds of records," according to a company advertisement. "With new Seeburg Dual Programming, EP album records (two tunes per side) are programmed in the brilliantly illuminated, self-advertising upper display panel." Single releases were displayed on the lower display panel.

Duophonic

Term synonymous with simulated stereo. Record companies came up with a number of early methods in the 1950s and early 1960s. One of them was Capitol's Duophonic Sound, which was remixed for "stereo." The method, which used mono with added echo, first appeared in 1961. That year Capitol re-released fourteen all-time hit mono albums with the Duophonic method. Audio buffs complained that the method—also known as electronically rechanneled stereo and more colloquially as fake stereo—sounded different than the original mono versions. This was due in part to echo. In the early '60s, record companies had more mono than stereo albums in their catalogs, so they wanted to use "fake stereo" that might appeal to the stereo-only buyers as well as the mono buyers. By 1968 everyone conceded that the public wanted real stereo, particularly in the album field. By then even the kids were asking for stereo singles. Unfortunately, the older rechanneled stereo records sounded bad when buyers compared them to the pure stereo albums.

Dupes

Illegally duplicated tapes and records. Their makers were also known in some quarters of the business as dupes. By the early 1970s, they received fifty cents of every dollar earned by the American tape industry, according to Jerry Geller, who led the tape division of Scepter Records. Legitimate tape duplicators could do little to thwart the practice because illegal duplicating was a misdemeanor at the time.

As the 1950s were turning into the 1960s, the Seeburg Corporation of Chicago introduced one of the jukebox industry's last attempts to regain the power it once held over the music industry. The 200 Model was a gorgeous piece of Americana, glowing with red, blue, and yellow lights. By offering both EPs and 45-rpm singles, the jukebox company hoped to attract teens as well as adults who might be more interested in big-name pop and country acts with EP records.

Dying Singles

A hit or charted record that had begun falling from its peak position on the chart. Once the decline began, some records dropped hard and fast, while others hung on, gradually falling off the charts after several weeks. Either way, they were seen as dead weight. Even the few that remained static on the charts were finished. On record charts, the artist is either on the way up or on down. One is always moving in one direction or the other. No one is in between. In the record business of the 1950s and '60s, Charlie Lamb, publisher and editor of the Nashville-based *Music Reporter*, believed that the dying single had no place on the national charts. "Eliminating the deadwood from the Big 100 Singles Chart [the MR version of *Billboard's* Hot 100] has another very desirable objective," he wrote in a story published in 1963, the year he axed the deadwood from his charts. "It makes room for more newcomers and live products which on the basis of exposure and under the prodding of advertising and good promotion could reach the very top." As Lamb said, the records on his chart were there because of their "ascendancy." He added, "As they climb gloryward [sic] there must be no 'hangers on' to clutter up the way."

Dynagroove

A name trademarked by the Radio Corporation of America (RCA) prior to 1963. Dynagroove was the marketing term for RCA's recording and pressing technology. Dynagroove was printed on most RCA LPs and 45s through the 1970s. The company even issued an LP with a red cover called *New Thresholds in Sound.... Dynagroove: The Magnificent New Sound Developed by RCA Victor.* Inside, the sleeve featured a lengthy story by audio writer Hans H. Fantel, detailing the achievements of Dynagroove: clarity of musical texture, fidelity of musical tone, presence, and absence of stylus noise. He wrote that RCA engineers developed an electronic computer to modify the audio signal fed into the recording stylus. A result, he said, was some fine listening. Dynagroove was a great name that sounded futuristic and powerful, like dynamite. Producer Bob Crewe once had a label called DynaVoice.

E

Echo Chambers

Gave recordings a fat, ethereal sound, the ghost that lingered after the original faded. The old-style, acoustic echo chamber was in a building, a hallway, or any room that echoed sweetly enough to be used in recording. Original echo chambers were intriguing because each one had its own personality, its own sound. They were all different. The echo chamber was a big part of the hits of the 1950s and 1960s. It provided clear, smooth, and lengthy reverberation that gave tracks a dynamic sound. Echo was the rage of the era. Gold Star Studios in Los Angeles, where Phil Spector produced many of his "Wall of Sound" hits in the early 1960s, had one of the world's more interesting and effective echo chambers. Spector effectively applied the chamber's big sound on four tracks. Also in Los Angeles, another first-class echo chamber operated at Western Recording. (Listen to the echo on "Like to Get to Know You" by Spanky and Our Gang and "This Diamond Ring" by Gary Lewis and the Playboys.) Echo chambers varied in size and sound from studio to studio. Some audio engineers had a knack for setting them up; others got lucky and found a room where sound echoed beautifully. Producer Lee Hazelwood resurrected a metal grain bin for use as a chamber, and it worked well. Some of the greatest records ever made were recorded with live echo from a chamber, especially at the Columbia Records studio in New York. Its echo chamber was underground. Tony Bennett's voice bounced off the chambers' walls and into the hearts of pop fans. Echo itself is a recording signal's regular repetition and the ingredient that helped make early rock records distinctively recognizable. Capitol Records' echo chambers in Los Angeles still operate, as they have been for decades. They have been used on some of the "most memorable recordings in modern history," as Capitol explains on its Web site. The trapezoidal chambers, which reportedly all have different "personalities," lie thirty feet beneath the building. But those chambers are an anomaly in the studio business; most studios use digital methods of achieving the echo effect. At Cinderella Sound in Madison, Tennessee, owner-engineer Wayne Moss built a small concrete-block building as his echo chamber. When singer-songwriter Mickey Newberry came in to cut an album, he wanted to overdub cricket sounds. So he placed a can filled with crickets inside the dark and dank echo chamber. Unfortunately, the can tipped over, spilling the crickets throughout building. Moss had a hard time getting them out. Months later, he could still hear the crickets when he turned up the echo. So he switched to electronic echo that by the late 1970s was replacing the old chambers. (See **Slapback** and **Reverb**.)

Eight-Track Tapes

Paralleled the cultural development of the 1970s. Some industry experts predicted in the late 1960s that the cumbersome eight-track prerecorded tape would kill the audio cassette, but that never happened. In fact, after a good run into the 1970s, the eight-track died and joined the four-track on the garbage heap of sonic history. Still, the eight-track has its collector fans, who dig anything from that era. But the old eight-track had three major drawbacks. When one side of the tape ended, the tape paused with a loud thud before resuming. It was larger and more difficult to store and take to the beach. And, of course, you couldn't buy blanks and record on them. (See **Four-Track Tapes**.)

Eighty-rpm

Ran a little too fast for most people. In the 1920s, Sears recommended that its Silvertone records be played at 80-rpm to give the listener an enjoyable experience. The company claimed its engineers had designed their records that way, instead of using the more conventional 78-rpm version. Of course, the 80-rpm disc soon faded. By the 1930s it posed no real threat to the grand old 78-rpm record. In the heyday of the 80, Sears recommended the use of four grades of steel needles: soft tone, medium tone, loud tone, and extra-loud tone. Soft tone was not mentioned further, so it must not have been considered a truly dependable alternative. Medium was described as "most satisfactory" for home use, and loud and extra loud for dancing, outdoor use, and band pieces. The company warned buyers that at no time should the new diamond, sapphire, or any other jewel-point needles be used on a Sears disc—or any other phonograph designed for the steel needle. The Edison Diamond Disc phonograph and its records used the diamond-tip type. (See **Diamond Disc**.)

Electrically Recorded

In 1925, microphones were first being used in recording, replacing the old acoustic recording horns. Musical sounds were converted to electric currents, which were amplified to drive a cutting stylus. Many discs from the late 1920s carried the words "electrically recorded" to let buyers know that the selections were made with the new electric microphones—and higher quality recording devices. The designation was important, for the new system was much superior to the old method of capturing sound. For once, record buyers could actually hear a close approximation of the concert hall.

Electronic Ear

In the late 1950s, a two-track stereo from Ampex. Nicknamed the Electronic Ear, it caught on for a few years, then grew into three tracks.

EP

Extended-play record. Like the 45-rpm disc, the EP is seven inches in diameter. In the 1950s and '60s it came with a hard cover, like an LP, and ran an average of twelve minutes, enough for four to six brief songs. If necessary, it could hold sixteen minutes total. RCA called theirs the 45 EP. Company advertising writers bragged, "We don't know of an EP that's ever worn out!" Perhaps this is because they didn't sell well to the general record buyer. By the late '50s, RCA had built up a catalog of at least 1,000 EP titles. In May of 1958, *Music Vendor* noted that the Sterling Title Strip Company was printing more song strips for jukeboxes than ever before. This probably was the high point of the EP. As the magazine's story concluded, "EPs definitely have become part of intelligent programming." However, EPs sold far fewer copies than singles or LPs because they were made mainly for jukeboxes. Eliot Tiegel, a *Billboard* staff writer, observed in 1964 that the EP "generally has not been that successful for the industry." They nearly died out in the 1990s. These days, the EP is making a small comeback.

Error-Proof Single

In the spring of 1972, Allied Record Company, the custom pressing firm based in Los Angeles, announced that it had invented the impossible. The error-proof single that would end manufacturing problems associated with making 45s. The new technology used three different systems, including a new compound created for making discs and new offset printing equipment.

Etching

Etching was another 1950s trade slang term for a record. It had nothing to do with an artist's etching or the era's hipster pickup line, "Hey, baby, why don't you come up to my pad and see my etchings."

Event Records

Peaked in the mid–1960s, when the genre became old-fashioned. What was an event record? It was any recording connected to an event, usually something in the news but not necessarily. One example was the Vietnam conflict. Between January and early June of 1966, more than one hundred Vietnam-related records were released, according to a *Billboard* story at the time. Five of them hit the magazine's Hot 100 singles chart, while a dozen landed on the country singles chart. As *Billboard* reporter Aaron Sternfeld reported in the magazine's June 4, 1966, issue, "Event songs are as old as the history of songwriting." The War of 1812 spawned "The Star-Spangled Banner," and the Civil War prompted "When Johnny Comes Marching Home" and other songs. In the nineteenth century, event songs were published by sheet-music companies. When records came along in the twentieth, event songs were released on records. As the reporter put it, "Event songs tied in with wars have been an integral part of the U.S. musical heritage."

Evergreens

Older records that continue to sell steadily to jukebox outlets. As *Music Vendor* put it: "One-stops, through intelligent programming, have been servicing operators with standards for years. However, these have never been reflected on the charts, because a good evergreen may outsell a rock 'n' roll record number over a period of three years, the latter cannot make the splash which the former can in one month, which will make it a chart contender."

Exclusive Artists

Recorded for one label and were paid per side. In the early days, most recording acts were freelancers. Then came exclusive artists, who recorded for only one label. For that privilege modern performers can thank a shrewd old recording star named Cal Stewart. Being tied exclusively to one company sounds odd to us today because we live in a time when practically all conventional recording artists make music for one label. Can you imagine Elvis and the Beatles recording for any label that paid them per session? It would have been audio pandemonium. But in the early days of the phonograph, performers did record cylinders and 78-rpm discs for multiple companies. They came into the studio, recorded their songs, and left with a few dollars in their pockets. It was actually good money for that time. Royalties? Forget it. Then in the early 1900s, Cal "Uncle Josh" Stewart, a popular actor, comedian, and recording star, demanded and received royalties. He was one of the first talking machine stars to sell a million records, but he did it by recording for at least a dozen labels, including Edison, Victor, and Columbia—the Big Three at that time. He also was among the first to receive a contract from one label, Columbia, in 1903. It was to his advantage because Columbia could promote him heavily, and as a result he could sell more records. The less successful acts could make a little more spending money by recording for multiple labels. Columbia was so elated with the one-label idea that it started displaying "Exclusive Artist" on its discs. By the time Vernon Dalhart became the first million-selling ("Wreck of the Old 97") rural act in 1924, vocalists had found a way around the exclusivity requirement: They used pseudonyms, or aliases, on records they made for smaller companies. In Dalhart's case, his one hundred fake (at least) names were all built on a primary alias. His real name was Marion T. Slaughter. Today, it would look silly to see "Exclusive Artist" on a record.

Exclusives

An advance copy of a new record sent directly to important personality disc jockeys in the 1950s. Security was the key. It was nearly as tight as the government's atom-bomb security. When record company owners feared that a competing label might suddenly intercept their new record and cut its own cover version, they would order acetate copies to be sent directly from the recording studios to the DJs via a secure delivery service. In case the new record had already been pressed and was ready for release, copies were hand-delivered to the DJs by local record company promotion men. By offering exclusives, record labels believed they could sell more records because the most popular disc jockeys had reputations for "breaking" the hits. "I'd put an exclusive on the air," former WSRS personality Jack Gale said, "and sometimes play it seven, eight times in a row. I'd bring the artists into the studio for interviews. Exclusives were important to the record labels and to radio. They made the DJs powerful record-breakers." As Top 40 radio began to dominate in the early 1960s, however, the exclusive faded with the personality disc jockey. Labels might send out an acetate to rush a record onto the radio, but by then record promoters were more concerned about receiving airplay on as many stations as possible.

Executive Producer

The designation was listed more often on the fine print of album sleeves, and sometimes on 45s. Executive producers were often the main investors or label executives who oversaw the financing and picked a producer to do the work. The term was less prevalent in the record business in the 1960s but has been used more since the 1990s brought big-money record deals, branding, and other modern practices of the international record business.

Exploitation Records

Capitalized on movies or an event. In the less litigious years of the 1950s and 1960s, exploitation records were singles named after soon-to-be released movies or other identifiable situations and events that would give the records instant name recognition. Sometimes, the recognition would go to new movies. Studios would ask songwriters to compose songs with the names of upcoming films. "Wives and Lovers," written by Burt Bacharach and Hal David and recorded by Jack Jones on Kapp Records, was intended to exploit the film by the same name. The same thing occurred with Bacharach and David's "The Man Who Shot Liberty Valance," recorded by Gene Pitney on Musicor Records. People assumed the songs were from the films.

They weren't. If a producer tried to make one today, he'd probably be sued for $200 million. But the hype worked in those days when film companies, songwriters, and record labels all helped each other make money on a single project.

F

Face

One side of a record. The term was used in early years, and continued in Europe, particularly in France, into the 1960s and later. Face 1 was Side A; Face 2, Side B. (See **Single-Face Records**.)

Fade

The DJ's friend in the heyday of Top 40. The fade, (also known as the fade-out), is itself fading with the times. Though the fade is not extinct by any means, today more recording artists and producers prefer definitive endings to their songs, hanging onto a vocal note or strumming a final strong chord. Once, recording engineers routinely faded the recording. Over the years the fade became the ending of choice for many producers and engineers. DJs liked it because they could talk over the slow fade. It became second nature to many producers; they rarely thought of doing it any other way. This also was radio's preference during the years when vinyl records were played on the air, before the era of tape and digital recording of entire shows. A fade gave DJs a warning that the record was ending. Though many recordings still fade, the technique is not nearly as prevalent and popular as it was from the 1950s to the '70s. (See **Cold Stop**.)

Falsetto

Reached its peak in rock 'n' roll in the 1960s and 1970s. Falsetto, or high-register singing mainly by male singers, was a carryover from the 1950s and even earlier. But it seemed to have prospered in early rock and soul, particularly on uptempo numbers. Frankie Valli and the Four Seasons depended on the falsetto, and they are known for it even today. Valli could do it with the best of the "falsies," as some record-biz personnel nicknamed the style. Another terrific falsetto singer, Lou Christie, could quickly go into and out of falsetto. Hear him wail on "Two Faces Have I." The Bee Gees did their version of the falsetto for years. In 1969 the smooth R&B man Eddie Holman used the top of his vocal range to take "Hey There Lonely Girl" to the top of the pop charts in all the trades. As the years have passed and public tastes have altered the falsetto has become a self-conscious technique.

Fan Clubs

Promoted rock bands, disc jockeys, and vocalists in the days before the Internet. Fan clubs had been around for years before rock 'n' roll arrived in the 1950s. Personal managers courted particularly passionate fans to form clubs and solicit members. This wasn't hard to do. Fan club presidents already knew many of the young admirers. The fan club became particularly significant to early rock bands because it kept the faithful connected through a monthly or seasonal newsletter, usually edited by the gushing club president. Newsletters featured artists' itineraries, and noted the performers' favorite foods and clothes, and other personal observations. Nearly every nationally known rock band of the mid–1960s, including the Left Banke and the Walker Brothers, had a fan club. Even New York disc jockey Murray the "K" had his own club, called Murray the "K" International Fan Club. Its slogan: "Be What's Happening, Baby." For only two dollars, the fan received an album, newsletter, and personalized ephemera from the famous jock. The club concept continued in the 1970s and later, until interest in fan clubs waned in the 1980s. Today, the official fan club seems quaint. Anyone interested in a singer or band can obtain gig information on social media and Web sites, and public relations managers can send emails to lists of hundreds of potential fans and post news of the artists on social media.

Film-Theme Singles

Big money from movies. *Billboard* reporter June Bundy called 1960 the year of "the film-theme single." That's when record executives discovered that movie themes could sell as 45s, if the performers stayed true to the original. In this respect it differed from the blatantly obvious exploitation record, which shared nothing in common with a movie or play except the title. One of the biggest film-theme singles—a number-one record in February of 1960—was "The Theme from *A Summer Place*," by Percy Faith and His Orchestra on Columbia Records. He remade the original theme music about the time the movie was released in late 1959. Actually, it was the film's love theme, not its main title theme, but who's quibbling over something that sold over a million copies and broke a record by remaining at number one for nine consecutive weeks. Kids enjoyed the record's lush sound and pleasing melody, but probably most of them didn't see the accompanying "adult movie," *A Summer Place*. Today's Top 40 listeners might think it strange to hear Percy Faith on the same radio station that played records by Jan & Dean. It was not. Radio used an eclectic mix of music then. Many film-theme singles were remake interpretations by artists not connected to the pictures, but the artists' versions stayed true to the original song. Other

Flip Side

Film-theme kings Ferrante and Teicher, the tuxedo-clad piano duo that hit the pop charts with regularity in the 1960s, seemed unlikely occupants of what fast became a teen-dominated realm. Arthur Ferrante and Louis Teicher began performing in 1947, coming from the Juilliard School of Music. They were all about easy listening music, yet their records competed with the Beatles and the Rolling Stones for coveted chart positions. They succeeded by recording film themes, including "Theme from the Apartment," "Exodus," and "Theme from Lawrence of Arabia."

singles were used in the original film soundtracks. The preferred choice among record people was the film-theme remake. It could be promoted as something new by an already big act, and not just a one-shot movie theme. A pioneer in mining these kinds of discs, United Artists Records, delivered Ferrante and Teicher's "Theme from the Apartment" and "Exodus" Both hit the top ten that year on the trades' top 100 charts. Over the coming decade, Ferrante and Teicher gave UA two more top-ten film singles, "Tonight" (*West Side Story*) and "Midnight Cowboy." The dual pianists also provided their label with several other nationally charted records during that decade. Another smaller but nonetheless recognizable UA single was composer John Barry's "Goldfinger" in 1965. But for UA management, "Exodus" was the most satisfying of the film music 45s. They told Bundy that it was the fastest-breaking single in the label's history. (See **Instrumentals**.)

Flip Side

Term mainly reserved for a 45's B-side, or for the side not slated for attention by radio stations. Thankfully, the flip is back in style. Novelty and break-in king Dickie Goodman even recorded a track call "B Side," which was the flip side of "Ben Crazy" on Diamond Records in New York. (See **B-Side**.)

Flipping

Radio programmers turning over a record to play the B-side. Many "flipped" sides became big hits, including "Wipe Out" by the Surfaris in 1964.

Flip-Side Play

A patron could hear both sides of a 45 in succession, if selected that way in advance. The feature became available in 1971, when Wurlitzer manufactured the Zodiac, which came with the trademarked name Flip-Side Play.

Folk Music

Songs and singers appreciated by the common man and woman. Once used almost interchangeably with hillbilly, rural, and western music, the genre name was known in the early 1900s and perhaps earlier. It meant the music of the people. Pioneers in the field included Cal "Uncle Josh" Stewart, whose humorous recorded monologues about life in the fictional Punkin Center included original songs such as "I'm Old but I'm Awfully Tough." The Virginia native recorded for Columbia, Victor, Edison, and other labels until his death in 1919. Into the 1920s and '30s, the record business stamped the name folk music onto anything rural in origin, including mountain music, cowboy songs, and old-time music. Performers included Walter "The Kentucky Wonder Bean" Peterson, a vocalist who played guitar and harmonica. Other folk recording acts included Carson Robison and Vernon Dalhart. An interesting aspect of folk music was its sincerity and simplicity. As fans in that era pointed out, pop music lacked the intimacy of folk. But even more interesting: Folk acts tended to write their own material in a time when most of them were uneducated or undereducated. Yet they crafted heartfelt songs that are still played. The term folk as it related to rural music faded by the early 1950s, when country-and-western came along to embrace the older western, folk, and hillbilly music. Suddenly, guys like Cowboy Copas and Jimmie Osborne were called country. The name folk began to take on a different style of music. (See **Folk Music Hits**.)

Folk Music Hits

Came into vogue after the name had evolved to include protest songs. Folk singers will exist as long as there are stories to tell and causes to champion or protest. Sadly, the era of the mega hit folk single is blowin' in the wind. Times have changed. Music has changed. But pure folk remains pretty much about same. In the 1950s and '60s, folk stars brought us songs, acts, and messages that appealed to wide audiences. The genre's more commercial songs were catchy and well-performed. Some became genuine Top 40 hits. They included "Green Green" by the New Christy Minstrels, "Walk Right In" by the Rooftop Singers, and "Don't Let the Rain Come Down" by the Serendipity Singers. This popular music with a decidedly folk sound was hot in the early 1960s, the early years of Top 40 radio. Other well-known artists who embraced the music's more commercial side included the Kingston Trio, Chad Mitchell Trio, Theodore Bikel, the Highwaymen, and the Four Preps. Commercial folk-pop still lives, but not as robustly as it did on the charts in those times, when Joni Mitchell, Joan Baez, Peter, Paul and Mary charted with topical, socially-conscious classics. In 1963, this new style of folk even had a magazine—*Folk World*—devoted to the music and the style. A story titled "Newcomers Hit Spotlight Overnight as Folk Invades 'Pop' Territory." explained how television had introduced the more commercial folk acts to "millions of receptive viewers." Acts featured through the growing medium included Odetta, the Smothers Brothers (they had their own TV show), and the Brothers Four. As the magazine noted, "The tide has turned for folk acts. The climb to stardom that used to take years can be done with a first album these days—as Peter, Paul and Mary proved last year." That tide on radio continued for well over fifteen years.

Follow-Up Records

The follow-up record—also known in the business as a "follow"—is another industry term that has changed over the last fifty years. It now means a performer's next record. In the early days of R&B, however, the follow-up was something very different. Music historian Bill Griggs explained it best in a 1992 story: "A follow-up record is usually done by the same artist using the same subject matter as the original hit. It could be an answer or it could be a continuation of the song." He cited an example: the Jewels' "Hearts of Stone" was followed by "Hearts Can Be Broken." He noted that most follow-ups were poorly received. But a few did make noise. As Griggs pointed out, Danny and the Juniors' hit with "At the Hop" in 1958. Three years later they "followed up" with "Back to the Hop," which climbed to only number eighty on the Hot 100. In the days of Top 40 in the mid- to late '60s, follows often used similar titles, arrangements, and themes. The theory was, if people enjoyed the first version, they would like more of it in the follow-up record. Often this theory did not work, simply because the follow song was inferior to the original one. Fortunately for listeners, most follow-up singles did not try to copy the first one. This approach seemed more natural. Sometimes the strategy backfired. "Neon Rainbow," the offbeat follow to "The Letter" by the Box Tops in 1967, sold far fewer copies. But then, "The Letter" was hard to match.

Foreign Hits

Records that occasionally broke loose in the pop field in the United States. The old foreign hit's unlikely success in Top 40 radio was due to the support of welcoming radio stations, even though their young audiences had no idea what the singer was singing. Even in the early '60s, picking—and playing—a record like that in a competitive Top 40 market took courage and confidence. Or at least a super-persuasive record company promotion man. How many kids understood the words to the Singing Nun's "Dominique," a cheery, folk-style record in 1963? They called her Soeur Sourire, or Sister Smile, and she sang in rapid-fire Belgian French while strumming an acoustic guitar. The A&R staff at the Philips label, a part of an international record company, was probably as shocked as anyone else when the record shot to the top of the American charts. Equally intriguing is "Sukiyaki" by Kyu Sakamoto. The Japanese singer and actor also hit in 1963, on the Capitol label. Both "Dominque" and "Sukiyaki" were number-one records on *Billboard's* Hot 100. "Dominique" was a sensation, lodging itself at the top for four weeks. The Singing Nun, in habit, appeared on the covers of magazines and was the subject of TV interviews. Her record stayed on the American *Billboard* Top 100 chart for a total of thirteen weeks. The slower paced "Sukiyaki" sounded like a love song, even though the name sounded more like some Asian nation. Most teenagers didn't know that sukiyaki is a Japanese meal of meat and vegetables cooked fast, with soy sauce, sake, and sugar on it.

Formats

The most popular radio formats were country, Top 40, R&B, and MOR (middle of the road, pop). Top 40 stations would often play a few records from the other formats. This gave listeners exposure to musical styles they might not otherwise hear or want to hear. For example, a teenager might recognize the country music of Buck Owens, the pop music of Andy Williams, and the soul of James Brown. All this changed with the arrival of FM and later more radio formats.

Forty-Five

Slang for the 45-rpm disc, introduced by RCA Victor in late March of 1949 to compete with Columbia's long-playing album, which was introduced the previous year. In a 1998 interview with *Classic Records*, former RCA record development executive George Avakian said the company selected the 45-rpm speed and name by subtracting 33 from 78, although this sounds like corporate myth. The speed had to be calculated precisely, and the 45 had been in the planning and development stages for many years. Once it was on the market, the 45 started the War of the Speeds. The first 45 to hit the *Billboard* pop-music chart was Perry Como's "You're Adorable," on May 7, 1949. RCA advertised the new disc heavily. "The new RCA Victor record and changer constitute the sensible, modern, inexpensive way to enjoy recorded music. The product is ready … the public is ready.… Its advantages will eventually make it the only way to play music in the home." On this point, the company's prediction partly came true. Arrival of the 45 brought about the swifter demise of the old 78-rpm disc. Some six years later, the 45 helped develop the rock-music market by giving it a more portable and "unbreakable" medium primarily for teenagers. On February 26, 1955, 45s surpassed sales of 78s in the United States. Soon they were buying small record cases and other accessories related to the less expensive 45. Today, the 45 is the symbol of an era in which rock and pop music became a major force. The little seven-incher is, to use a woeful cliché, a true cultural icon of the second half of the twentieth century. And it's back. (See **Vinyl**.)

Forty-Five/Forty-Five System (45/45)

In stereo, sounds are recorded from two points of view and, ultimately, engraved on each side of the groove. Because the two sounds are engraved at 45-degree angles from the record surface, record cutting was often called the 45/45 System, according to Capitol engineers of the late 1950s.

Forty-Five Players

RCA Victor needed something on which to play its new singles. In 1949, the company announced a new line of phonographs for the 45s. The players were small compared with the other phonographs of the period. Early on, the new machines carried various stock numbers, but by 1950 they had their own, starting with the number 45. For example, customers could choose from the deluxe table model (45E44), a regular table model (45EY3), and another machine that could be plugged into larger phonographs to use their speaker systems. For kids, there was the Disney decorated 45EY15 model. Some adult models came equipped with maroon cases with gold-colored trim, RCA's Silent Sapphire pickup, the Golden Throat tone system, and a stylus that exerted only five grams of weight on the 45's surface. Magazine advertisements boasted that the machines could hold fourteen discs. One special sale in 1950 offered the 45EY2, plus a forty-two-page book called "Listener's Digest," and ten RCA Victor "45 EPs" for only $39.95.

Four-By

Introduced by Capitol Records in the late summer of 1964. The "4-By," a seven-incher, featured four songs like the EP, but Capitol's marketing department went to great lengths to identify their new product as anything and everything but an EP. *Billboard* called it a "space age, super single concept." It came with four songs and a paper sleeve with a photo. The paper sleeve identified the thing as a single, Capitol noted, whereas the EP came with a hard cover like an LP. Another difference was the purpose: The EP was a mini album, and the 4-By was a large single. The first one was called "4-By the Beach Boys." Its four songs came from the group's album *All Summer Long*. Capitol promoted "Little Honda" as the plug song because it had never been released as a single. Perhaps the label chose the Beach Boys to launch the line because they believe that if the hit group couldn't succeed with the 4-By, than no one could. Despite the label's best efforts, the concept didn't catch on with the public. Buyers couldn't understand anything more than the two-sided single 45-rpm and the LP. The 4-By became just one more challenger to the 45 that ended up in the cut-out bin.

Four-Track Tapes

Before eight-track tapes became popular, four-track tapes were adopted by teenagers and adults alike. They were a big innovation that was supposed to supplant bulky reel-to-reel tapes. But four didn't last long. They sold from about 1962 to 1972, although in their later years they were nearly finished. Like the eight-track, the four-track came in a plastic cartridge. Both looked similar. "In short," *Billboard* noted in 1970, "two situations caught up with four-track as an attractive configuration: Bootleggers [tape pirates] and time." Four-track tapes were most popular in California, Texas, and Florida. Consumers preferred the new eight-track tapes and cassettes. Goodbye, four-track tapes.

Free Singles Survey

A label's nefarious practice of giving free 45-rpm singles to some surveying—or reporting—record stores to "hype radio station playlists," as *Billboard* staff writer Earl Paige put it. To determine which discs were selling well locally, stations obtained information from their designated reporting stores. Stations reported the latest hot records to trade magazines, which in turn used the information to compile national and regional charts. Though stores didn't pay for the singles in question, they did sell them to their young customers. Sometimes, the freebie records jump-started regional hits because stations unwittingly added them to their playlists. The bogus practice first occurred in larger markets, but soon spread to the medium-size ones. The guilty labels had obvious motives. They sought to boost chart positions and obtain reviews for new artists and those who were trying to make a comeback. This happened in the 1960s, long before the music magazines used computers to track record sales. In some markets, record stores knowingly faked sales figures to the trades. Paige checked on the problem in Peoria, Illinois. WIRL program director Robin Walker told Paige: "When we call a store here and are told about singles that are not being played on WLS in Chicago or in St. Louis, we know something is wrong." To counteract the hype, WIRL started making fifty random calls to consumers three times a week and checked the popularity of various records being played by local jukebox owners. Soon the National Association of Record Merchandisers (NARM) got involved, and the practice of giving away free singles ended.

Frozen Shellac

Restriction of the distribution of shellac during World War II. The materials were known as frozen commodities. Shellac, used to coat 78-rpm discs, became known as frozen shellac. On February 6, 1943, a *Billboard* columnist noted that there had been talk lately that the government would ease up on its restriction of shellac. "If shellac becomes available, the lists [of new records] should grow quickly," one insider told the magazine. "The demand is there for new ones—a frantic demand, in some cases." (See **Shellac**.)

Full-Dimension Stereo

Capitol Records' term meaning "a dynamic fidelity in the recording of music—fidelity that returns the music's full range, balance, and depth." It was also a company marketing gimmick used to promote stereo discs in the early 1960s, when record labels were scrambling to find a way to interest the public stereo albums. The company even released an album called *Full Dimensional Sound from the Capitol Tower*. The process of creating the sound remains nebulous. The cover features a night photograph of the fully lighted Capitol building, designed in the 1950s to resemble a stack of 45s. The name Capitol Records is displayed on top in lights, and today the building is as important as ever.

Full-Track Mono

Music and vocals on one track. Quarter inch tape had one full track. Engineers had to mix the volume coming from each microphone on the spot. They couldn't remix later; everything was on one track.

Furniture Store Records

Discs sold in furniture stores in the days before record stores were widespread. Around 1900, when discs were in their earliest days, phonographs, cylinders, and discs were sold in furniture stores along with sofas and chairs. Phonographs in those days were made of wood with fancy external horns. They could easily sit atop a table or other furniture. No one could earn a living from the sale of records. So furniture stores became a natural sales outlet. Record companies soon ditched their old morning glory horns for oak and maple furniture with acoustic horns inside. As the years passed, and record shops became the norm, fewer furniture stores bothered to sell records. But they continued to be sold in department stores and other businesses that could make a little money selling discs. They took over the job of selling most of the records. Still, furniture stores continued to sell records, along with phonographs and furniture-style cabinets, at a few isolated outposts until the 1960s.

G

Gabel Automatic Entertainer

An early music machine, a prehistoric jukebox. It entered the market in 1906, using discs instead of the usual wax cylinders that had been popular in music machines in those days. The Automatic Entertainer offered the customer a choice of records, and this feature helped the machine capture a large market share for twenty years. It was displaced only when the Automated Music Instrument Company (AMI) brought out its electrically amplified machine in 1927, thus bringing in the modern jukebox period.

Garage Bands

Bands that practiced in garages during the British Invasion of the mid–1960s. The nation had fallen under the juggernaut of the Beatles and other UK bands, so garage bands started popping up everywhere, hoping to be the next international superstars. Kids as young as twelve years old were trying to organize bands. The teen band fad became a phenomenon. No matter where they practiced—basement, living room, Aunt Fanny's back porch—they were all dubbed garage bands and they always will be. Locations didn't matter—big city, small city, rural villages, and medium-size towns. From 1964 to 1974, garage bands flourished beyond comprehension. Many of them went straight from the garage to live venues and big-time record deals. Some landed on *American Bandstand*. Though the garage band will always exist, it won't have the mystique that once swirled around it when the Beatles were huge and teenage girls swooned over any high-school guy with a guitar. The garage-band movement was successful, for it turned out many excellent groups for large and small record labels. Their names were often colorful, sometimes as colorful as their music: Question Mark and the Mysterians (the leader was also known as ?), the Knickerbockers, the McCoys, and the Exiles. As the years passed, bands continued to practice in garages across the country, but the culture had changed. Expanded sports opportunities, computers, and other distractions reduced the interest in forming local bands. The 1960s will remain a high point for them. It was a time when independent labels with clout flourished, and seemingly every label chief was looking for the next Beatles. The most incredible part is, these teen musicians often came up with some of the more intriguing and creative songs of the era.

Ghost Band

Studio musicians paid to create a record for a producer, usually an independent, who had only a concept and no real band. The nonexistent group was given a name and musicians were hired to take the band on the road. Voila! The ghost band was now a real group with either a hit or a miss. The premier ghost-band creators were Jeff Katz and Jerry Kasenetz, producers of the Ohio Express, Crazy Elephant, and other bubblegum groups. Many, but not all, of their bands were created with a concept first, and musicians second. Many bubblegum producers also followed this route.

Girl Singers

Young or older woman singer of the 1950s and '60s. Women were not as well-represented as their male counterparts in the 1950s and early '60s. They had far less presence in the ranks of producers and songwriters. By the late 1960s, however, all types of women singers, including pop vocalist Barbra Streisand, pop/R&B singer Barbara Lewis, and R&B vocalist Barbara Harris, were breaking out. *Record World* made a point: Increasing numbers of women were fronting vocal groups. They included Elaine "Spanky" McFarland of Spanky and Our Gang, Grace Slick of the Jefferson Airplane, Janis Joplin of Big Brother and the Holding Company, Linda Ronstadt of the Stone Poneys, and Gladys Knight and the Pips. The future was coming. It had taken a long time for women to step through the door. In the 1960s, female vocalists were called girl singers and female vocal groups as girl groups. Judging by today's standards, record men were downright paternalistic. But the guys didn't think much about it. Keep in mind that this happened at least a half century ago. Even then, however, no one described a male vocalist as a boy singer or a group as a boy band. (That would take a couple of decades.) Before introducing Jackie DeShannon and her new single "Oh Boy" on his popular *American Bandstand*, Dick Clark asked a teenage girl in the bleachers if she liked girl singers. Yes, she replied. Clark told her in all sincerity that she must be in the minority, for most girls don't like girl singers. He must have known that the girl-singer term was used by record men, radio men, record-collector men—oh well, let's be honest: Just about every man and even some women of that era used the girl-singer name. Though female vocalists were prevalent throughout the last half of the twentieth century, by then the name girl singer was solidly in place because women were living and working in a man's, man's, man's world. A 1968 story in *Record World* noted, "If the old saw is true that it's difficult for girl singers to break onto the singles charts, it is becoming equally true that much of the news behind new groups is the presence of a lead femme singer." Old trade magazines are stocked—and stacked—with advertisements promoting records by women vocalists. In the 1950s, Patti Page, Rosemary Clooney, and other women ruled. Also, the big bands of the '40s often featured female vocalists. But they commanded nowhere near the influence and numbers of the "boy" singers.

Glue Job

Slang for splicing audio tape. In the pre-digital era, splicing was an indispensable method of editing recorded performances. If a producer had, say, four takes of a song, and he liked parts of each one, he could pick the best lines from each and splice them all together. The reference to glue comes from the adhesive backing on the splicing tape used to hold the edited portions together. At least this is one theory. The term is old and no one really knows exactly how it originated. An interesting story about splicing comes from England. Cubby Broccoli, a partner in the James Bond movie franchise, knew Frank Sinatra well, and was the godfather of Sinatra's daughter, Nancy. She was a singing star in the States then, in 1967, so Broccoli decided to hire her to sing "You Only Live Twice," the title song from his next James Bond movie. Recording the song was a challenge. Soundtrack composer John Barry once said she was chosen against his wishes. Barry, an expert in matching songs with singers to achieve their best performances, brought her to London to record. Immediately, she was intimidated by the presence of the London Philharmonic, and by Barry himself, a rising soundtrack star and about as close to a musical genius as is possible. Barry asked her to do take after take; she had problems with the song. Finally giving up, Barry decided to do "a glue job," as he put it in his autobiography. He and an engineer took all twenty-four takes, cut and spliced the tapes, and came up with one whole song that consisted of her best efforts. "There was just no way that we'd ever have got it in one take," he told author Eddi Fiegel years later. Another good story about splicing comes from Cincinnati, where in 1965 King Records engineer Ron Lenhoff was ordered to edit James Brown's "Papa's Got a Brand New Bag" tape. Brown and his band had recorded the song in Charlotte, North Carolina. They just let it rip—one long blast. Then Brown sent the tape—with a seven-minute song—to his label. There was no way that radio stations would have accepted a seven-minute single in 1965. Thanks to Lenhoff's skill and determination, however, the first funk hit in history went to the pressing plant as a master that lasted under three minutes. It was a masterful glue job. Now, in the age of computers, splicing is even more prevalent. It's simply done digitally.

Gold Record

Award started by the Record Industry Association of America (RIAA) in 1958 to certify million-selling singles, and albums that earned one million dollars in sales at the wholesale price. Prior to this time, record companies awarded their own gold records, mostly unauthenticated ones. After the RIAA decided to use accountants to keep track of record companies' sales on records submitted for gold status, some indie label owners fumed. They did not wish to be scrutinized by what they considered prying, eagle-eyed pencil pushers. Those record guys didn't bother to enter the contest. That's why some "million-sellers" prior to '58 are not *officially* gold. In fact, some of them are suspect. Of course, many of those big records were no-doubters, but the ones that straddled the line were iffy. For some late bloomers, gold-record certification came years after the records were released. Companies did not have to sell a million copies in the first few months. This was sort of like the Baseball Hall of Fame inducting the old-timers who didn't make it on the first go-round. This was a good thing. The first official gold single, issued in 1958, was Perry Como's "Catch a Falling Star," and the first album was from the soundtrack *Oklahoma!* In January 1989, amid declining singles sales, the RIAA changed the criterion for gold singles—500,000 copies sold. The new gold standard for the album also became 500,000. Imagine: the million-sellers—the real gold ones, mind you—of the 1960s would be genuine whoppers today. Nuclear-cloud-size gold. The industry would have to have a new category called double gold. If the more recent rule had existed in the '60s, gold would still be paving just about everything, including suburban streets across the country where the producers live.

Gold Standard Series

After RCA Victor introduced the new 45-rpm single, the company brought out a line of its all-time hits on in the new single format. The discs sold for eighty-nine cents each.

Golden Age of Records

Began in 1912, the year that saw the emergence of many new labels and important artists. According to *Billboard*, 1912 also signaled the end of the cylinder record. Finally, the disc record had no significant competition. The first golden age ended in a mighty thud when the Great Depression nearly killed the record industry. Record sales dropped from $75 million in 1929 to $18 million in 1931, and $11 million in 1932, and $6 million in 1933. At $7 million in 1934, things looked just as grim. Unfortunately, sales wouldn't surpass 1921 levels until World War II ended in 1945. As shellac restrictions lessened and the GIs returned home, sales shot up to $218 million in 1946. The second Golden Age of Records is debatable because of timing and format. If it is in vinyl, and judged by sales, then the 1960s and early '70s would be the second Golden Age of Records. Buoyed by the rise of stereo, better technology, and increased creativity, record sales hit $1,051 million in 1967 and $1,124 in 1968. Like the first Golden Age of 1912, many new acts—in rock 'n' roll, adult contemporary, and country music—emerged. The independent record label also blossomed in the 1960s.

Golden Throat

Term dreamed up by advertising people to describe RCA Victor's latest phonographs, particularly the new smaller ones that played 45s. The company used the term to reassure the public that its latest record players hadn't lost the dependable old sounds of the Victor.

Gramophone

Trade name chosen by Emile Berliner for his hand-cranked acoustic flat-disc player in the early days of the talking machine. We celebrated its centennial in 1987. Today, people often mistakenly call the cylinder talking machines Gramophones, but technically they were not. The American Graphophone Company made cylinder players, which early on were known generically as phonographs. The real confusion set in after 1902, when the talking machine companies added and dropped specific terminologies. A century after the Gramophone's invention, its name was still often mistakenly applied to phonographs of all kinds.

Gramophony

Art and craft of designing and manufacturing gramophone records. Of course, the work was a closely guarded secret understood only by pioneer Emile Berliner and other high-level executives.

Graphophone

Talking machine used wax cylinders was a competitor of the early disc phonograph. If the cylinders had won the war, you might be firing up the digital cylinder right now. The Graphophone was synonymous with the cylinder, not discs.

Groove Jumping

Problem found on less expensive transcription players and the early phonographs that played vinyl discs. The sapphire stylus jumped out of the groove at times, causing a disruption in play.

Groove Selector

Columbia Records product used to prevent the stylus from scratching the disc while the user was selecting a specific band of music. The device was sold in the 1950s.

Grooved

Slang term used by record trade magazines to explain the comings and goings of 78-rpm discs. "The platter seems grooved for hitdom," a *Billboard* writer observed in 1943.

Groovy

Happy, nice, and good. It did not originate with the hippies. Nor did it originate in the twentieth century. It came into common usage in the late-1960s, but it occasionally popped up in magazine stories as early as the 1890s as "groovy" and "groovey." It meant the same thing as it would mean later, but less enthusiastically and much less varied. So what does "groovy" have to do with the old record and music industries? Plenty. The hipster's word slipped into common usage in the days of flower power, and from there mushroomed into an all-purpose word to fill dead air space. Instead of a guy replying, "OK, sure," he would simply say "Groovy." Record label s and A&R, public relations, and advertising departments went berserk with the word. Soon groovy drifted into the consciousness of everyday people (usually under the age of forty but, sadly, even some guys over fifty), started saying it, too. Using attractive design elements, record labels incorporated the word into fancy album covers and ad designs with paisley borders. Once the word started being overused by hippies and some elites on television, groovy became fair game for professional songwriters. They mentioned it in otherwise good songs—and, for heaven's sakes, even in song titles. There was "Groovy Situation" by Gene Chandler, "Groovin'" by the Rascals, "Groovy Kind of Love" by the Mindbenders, and "Treat Her Groovy" by the New Colony Six. By today's standards, many excellent songs are dated by just one reference to groovy. The word is hardly ever spoken these days, let alone used in songs.

Gruve Gard

Late-1950s trademarked name by RCA Victor. It referred to the center and outer edge of an LP that was designed to protect the playing surface. This was duly noted on the back of album jackets. RCA even commissioned a little Gruve Gard logo that featured Nipper the dog, to display on the backs of albums.

Guitar Instrumental

Picking as only a red-hot rocker could do. As soon as rock 'n' roll arrived in 1955, guitar instrumentals began to surface. Actually, records that emphasized guitars had been around for years, especially during the pre-rock days of hillbilly boogie and R&B. But the era of the teenager—the baby-boomer—embraced the guitar. The instrument became the clear favorite of the kids. In 1963, the guitar instrumental seemed to hit with fury. The Surfaris of California arrived with "Wipe Out," "influential" guitarist Lonnie Mack blew out of Cincinnati with the blues-rock sounds of "Memphis" and "Wham!" on Harry Carlson's Fraternity Records. Some of the more interesting and influential flat-out rock guitar numbers included Duane Eddy's "Rebel Rouser" and "Because They're Young." The Virtues did "Guitar Boogie Shuffle," and Link Wray, an amped-up picker, gave us "Raw Hide" and "Rumble," which he co-wrote. Reportedly he was inspired to compose "Rumble" after he saw the rumble scenes in *West Side Story*. He came up with the rocking guitar instrumental that eventually climbed to number sixteen in 1958. The record was banned in several cities for allegedly promoting juvenile delinquency. To get the raucous sound he wanted, Wray punched pencil holes into his amplifier's speakers, creating a fuzz-tone effect. Music writer and musician Cub Koda once said that Ray kept his vibrato control higher and faster, "leaving the tune's fade-out rippling with an electric intensity that's hard to beat for sheer menace." (See **Instrumental**.)

H

Hammond B-3

The organ that built R&B and rock 'n' roll. James Brown played one. So did Booker T. Jones of Booker T. and the MGs, the studio band at Stax Records and a hit-making group on its own. At one time, nearly every soul-oriented and good-time rock group band used the B-3. Horns complemented it. A sax blended well with the throaty B-3's sound. But there was a major problem. The thing weighed too much. "You're talking close to three hundred pounds," said Wayne Bullock, organist for Beau Dollar and the Coins and other blues-rock bands out of Cincinnati. "I had to lug that thing from gig to gig. One time, the band arrived in a city—in Wisconsin, I believe. The dance hall was on the third floor. The organ wouldn't fit in the elevator." He and two other guys in the band had to shove and drag the thing up the metal fire escape. At the top, the metal let loose and Bullock pushed the organ inside the door at the last minute. These days, Bullock uses an electronic keyboard that simulates the B-3. So do many other organists. Unfortunately, the B-3 sound is not as popular as it once was. Not that it has vanished from the music scene. It's simply not as popular because the kinds of music it worked best with—R&B and rock—are not as prominent these days. The original, heavy, wooden B-3 still has its fans, though, and it always will.

Hemispheric Sound

Columbia Records marketing term in the early 1960s. It identified stereo albums. Called the "360" Hemispheric Sound because it is "enlarging the horizons of listening pleasure."

Hi-Fi

Term that started in the early 1940s, when audiophiles put together custom-built equipment to play their records. The sound was so good, they said, that it gave a high-fidelity response. Altec, the speaker manufacturer, issued an explanation to customers that defined hi-fi's "rules of thumb." They were: separate speaker cabinet; three record crossover selections; separate bass and treble controls; a genuine two-way speaker; and a speaker enclosure that measured at least two cubic feet. Through the 1950s, when hi-fi began its rise, audio fans looked down on mass-produced equipment, as inferior. Real hi-fi equipment was high-priced and custom-built. When the LP arrived in 1948, high-fidelity sound finally had a worthy partner. Vinyl provided a smoother ride for the tone arm and a better sound. No doubt the average record-player buyer of the early 1950s had a much different definition of hi-fi than did the fanatic audiophiles. To the buyer of a little 45-rpm phonograph, hi-fi meant little more than a clear sound and the capability of turning up the volume as loudly as possible. To audio buffs, however, the term meant crystal-clear (for that time) sound—and more. "There is a theory," wrote Christopher Faye in *High Fidelity* magazine in 1955, "that high fidelity is simply technology's latest and more picturesque attempt to achieve mankind's subjugation." In a story in the November 1950 issue of *Radio and Television News*, writer James F. Becker, a consulting engineer for Concord Radio Corporation, said hi-fi has three characteristics: the ability to reproduce sound from the lowest to the highest tones; reproduce that sound uniformly; and do it free of all extraneous noises. In the same issue, L.M. Dezettel, of Allied Radio Corp., said hi-fi developed because many people had become dissatisfied with regular store-bought equipment. He said the making of the modern phonograph cartridge gave rise to the true hi-fi sound.

Highway Hi-Fi

When the new 1956 Chrysler cars arrived in September 1955, a few came equipped with something special. It was the Highway Hi-Fi, a record player encased in rubber and mounted under the dashboard. The system played 7-inch discs with a 78-rpm-style hole in the center. They could play 45 minutes of music. Chrysler explained: "The pickup arm, though conventional in appearance, moves only in a horizontal plane. Hence, there is no problem of the arm itself bouncing when the car travels a rough road. Only the stylus can move vertically, and this is spring-loaded to hold the point against the record with a pressure of two grams. The pickup arm is also counter-weighted, so that its center-of-mass is at the pivot point.... [It] has proved extremely difficult to jar the arm off the record or even make the stylus jump a groove." The system was used until a modified automobile phonograph system replaced it in 1959.

Hill-and-Dale

Grooves made so the stylus will vibrate in an up-and-down motion on the disc. Used in the Edison and Pathe companies' recordings. The term is synonymous with vertical cut. (See **Vertical Cut** and **Lateral Cut**.)

Hillbilly Music

Forerunner of country or country-and-western. The genre hillybilly music became popular in the late 1940s and early 1950s. Use of the term gained popularity with records labels in the 1930s, as rural white music began to flourish and sell well. Companies needed a marketing tool, or a name for the folk music they were selling… The derogatory hillbilly name stuck. It was probably first applied by record company employees in New York. Independent labels that sold primarily hillbilly records in the '40s, including Syd Nathan at King Records, campaigned to change the name, saying it was insulting. A few years later, radio stations started calling it country-and-western. Then country.

Hip Pocket Records

Small records. Philco, owned by Ford Motor Company, developed what it believed to be an innovative concept in recording. The company called it Hip Pocket Records. In the 1960s, ads touted "the LP, the EP, the HP." For sixty-nine cents, kids—the market was thirteen to seventeen-year-olds—got two "big hits" on "a disc so small [three and three-fourths inches] that kids can carry a couple of dozen in their pockets." The company's ads claimed that HP discs can be dropped, sat on, stepped on, and so forth, within reason, of course. The Hip Pocket was going strong by 1968 with full-page ads in the trades. Unfortunately for Philco, its new threat to the EP, LP, and 45 fizzled.

Hip Sounds

The so-called hippie music of the late-1960s, but also the cost of recording it. Record executives described it as the "hip sounds," but they had little to do with cutting-edge music. Actually, the term referred to pretentious rockers taking too long to record albums. Composed of self-indulgent baby boomers, the new bands began taking excessive time in the studio, creating what they wanted for as long as they wanted. Middle-aged label executives resented the bands for wasting time smoking marijuana and drinking in the studio while creating their hip sounds. An independent producer told *Billboard* reporter Eliot Tiegel, "The Beatles really spoiled it for everyone by spending so much time in the studio." An album by the American band the Association cost Warner Bros. $80,000—big money in the late '60s. Known for its haunting singles "Never My Love" and "Windy," the Association could hardly be mistaken for a Haight-Ashbury band, but they ran up the tab like one. Meanwhile, emboldened recording studios began adding accommodations, being part hotel room and part studio. The Jefferson

Airplane returned to the studio to add more music to an album that already had been completed. By then, the create-it-in-the-studio idea had sunk into the heads of many unlikely bands, many of them with little or no track records. As costs shot out of control, independent label owners felt threatened because they knew they couldn't compete with the majors. "These kids want to go into the studio and rehearse at $60 an hour," the unidentified producer told Tiegel. Once other young bands heard about the long sessions, they wanted to try it, too. As flower-power sounds finally lost steam in the mid–1970s, the majors came back to reality and further restricted the amount of time bands could stay in the studio. Costs were contained.

Hit Bound

Up-and-coming new singles and albums in the 1960s. The term was used extensively in advertisements, in stories, and just about anywhere. The name was hit bound. Stations used it on their free local charts that were distributed to record shops. Hit bound became a popular trade-advertising and DJ term into the 1970s. It is rarely used anymore.

Hole

A drop-off in sound created when two speakers are placed too far apart.

When early stereo phonographs came into more widespread use in the 1950s, engineers warned buyers against creating "a hole," meaning the drop-off.

Hook First

Opening singles with the catchiest part of the song, the chorus, often known as the hook line. Producers and arrangers believed the record was more commercial and sounded better with the hook-first approach, but often the producer wanted listeners to hear a song's catchy chorus as many times as possible during a less-than-three-minute radio record. The hook-first approach gained popularity in the 1960s. It is still used somewhat today, but hooks are not considered so vital to receiving radio airplay. The repetitive approach was nothing new. Some hymns, including "Lift High the Cross," began with what would now be considered the song's hook. One important factor was the melodies of the verses. If they weren't as strong as their chorus melodies, then the song was a good candidate for a chorus-first opening. Some songs, like "She's a Lady" by Tom Jones, could go either way—chorus first or verse first. Others, like "Ain't Nothin' Like the Real Thing" by Marvin Gaye and Tammi Terrell, simply felt better melodically by going with the chorus first. Other examples included two 1963 hits, "Midnight Mary" by Joey Powers and "Denise" by Randy and the Rainbows. Both were one-hit acts.

Hook Line (aka Hook)

A song's chorus or refrain, intended to "hook" the listener with a repetitive line. Though hook lines are still an important component of songs, they aren't as influential as they were in the 1960s. Then, songwriters and publishers, DJs and radio program directors, and everyone else seemed obsessed with hooks. The first comment a producer would make is, "I like the hook." Or, "Where is the hook?" The hook often featured the song title, so it was important to emphasize the record title to listeners, who would then request it at the store. The thinking at the time was that consumers wouldn't remember the song's title if it didn't have a hook. Nevertheless, many records without hooks became long-lasting hits.

Hopefuls

Singles that producers and reviewers believed had an excellent chance of hitting big. As with baseball teams in spring training, all records were "hopefuls" to a degree. But in reality, all singles were not created equal. Radio was the judge. The public was the jury.

Horn

Metal horns used to project sounds from phonographs that played cylinder and disc master recordings. Two important terms in the early 1900s were horn and hornless. Horns were the forerunners of modern phonograph speakers. In the late 1800s, phonograph companies started making talking machines with metal horns—often made of tin—mounted on wooden boxes, or phonograph cases. From these horns emerged recorded sound in the acoustic era. As phonograph exteriors became more sophisticated and attractive, record companies—many made their own phonographs then—started creating new phonographs that were touted as being "hornless." Actually, the new machines had horns, but they were built inside phonograph cabinets or smaller wooden phonograph bodies. A famous hornless, the Victrola, became a hit for Victor Records in the early part of the twentieth century. By the 1950s, the name was used extensively on new 45-rpm record players. In the acoustic cylinder-record days of the turn of the twentieth century, horns were also used to record sound directly onto wax cylinders that were used as masters. Singers and bands sang and played loudly in front the recording horns, which inscribed the sounds onto wax cylinders.

Horn Bands

Rock groups that featured traditional instruments as well as multiple horns. The horns were significant to such a band's sound. Arrangements were woven tightly into the performances. A typical horn band usually had from two to four horns, although some groups had up to six horn players. Chicago is the most well-known horn band in rock history. Blood, Sweat and Tears is also well known. There was a marked difference between a rock band with one horn, usually a sax, and a horn band. Horns dominated the sound of those groups. The bands thrived on both the national and the local scenes from the mid–1960s to the late 1970s. Oddly, horn bands gained followers during the peak of the British Invasion and its guitar combos. Even the Beatles couldn't knock out the horn groups. Depending on the region, horn bands played different kinds of music. Many played straight rock. Others, including many in the South, played blue-eyed soul and blues-rock music. White soul was popular in clubs around southern Ohio in the 1960s. They battled long-haired garage bands for gigs. "We hated the Beatles," pianist Dumpy Rice said. He played in guitarist Lonnie Mack's band when the Fab Four hit big in America. Another horn band, Wayne Cochran's C.C. Riders, blasted away as its vocalist shimmied and slinked across the stage. Other nationally known horn groups included the Ides of March, which charted four records from 1966 to 1971. Their big hit was "Vehicle"; a moderate one was "Superman." In 1974, a Scottish soul band with horns, the Average White Band, hit big with "Pick Up the Pieces" and

In the 1960s and '70s, hot masters shot across the country like flying saucers. This hot master came from Bullet Records in Hollywood, with Clydie King singing "Loneliness." She was Brown Sugar as well as an in-demand background vocalist. Bullet placed the Brown Sugar master with Wes Farrell's Chelsea Records, distributed by RCA. Chelsea changed the title to "Loneliness (Will Bring Us Together Again)" to give radio listeners a better shot at remembering the name of the song. It was a moderate R&B hit in 1973.

"Cut the Cake." What happened to the horn bands? At least two things: public tastes changed, and the cost of operating a larger band with horns ruined their chances of getting local gigs. Disco, which club DJs loved, hit the horn bands—and all bands—hard in the mid-'70s. Today, rock 'n' roll horn bands still perform in clubs, especially in their hometowns.

Hot Master

A master tape that was wanted badly by nearly everyone in the business. Typically, it was a hot regional hit, or sometimes an unreleased master that labels desired because of the song, the artist, or both. "Hot master" was an important record-biz term from the 1960s and 1970s.

I

Identifiable Licks

Catchy, brief, and repeated instrumentation designed to enhance a recording's commercial appeal on the radio. (In jazz, a melodic phrase played repeatedly is called a riff, and that word spilled over into other kinds of music, being used interchangeably with identifiable lick.) Identifiable licks hit their high point in the 1960s, when they gave a special stamp of individuality to rock 'n' roll recordings. Occasionally, an electric bass was used to create such a memorable lick, as it was on the Animals' "We Gotta Get Out of This Place." That lick came from composer Barry Mann's original version. Not all records had good licks peppered through their tracks. But plenty of them did. A perfect example is "Oh, Pretty Woman" by Roy Orbison. The record is the combination of a good song, a great vocalist, top-grade musicians and production, a good studio sound, and that unmistakable guitar lick that kicks off the record and continues throughout it. It is as much a part of the whole recording as Orbison's sweet vocals. Wayne Moss's unforgettable guitar sound was another reason the record became a classic. These great licks still linger in listeners' minds.

Independent Cooperatives

Smaller independent labels that joined together to promote themselves. In the mid–1970s, the smaller labels that focused on singles faced a major problem. Radio was not welcoming them as it had a few years earlier. Country indie labels had long been a tradition in Nashville, and country radio was open-minded about playing their records. But when an increasing number of important radio stations said no thanks, some indie operators had an idea. Why not form a co-op of indie labels that could help one another with vital matters such as national distribution and promotion? They could hit the secondary radio market, which was all but ignored by the major labels. The idea seemed sound, and it came just in time. This would be the indie's last stand in country music. These low-budget labels were being shut out of airplay with each passing year. In 1974, two new cooperatives opened in Nashville: Nationwide Sound Distributors (NSD) and the International Record Distributing Associates (IRDA). Joe Gibson, founder of Nationwide Sound, signed with twenty-five distributors nationally. So did IRDA. Eighty percent of their clients were country labels. Within a year the cooperatives had accepted a total of sixty labels. Gibson served as his cooperative's A&R man. "I decide which companies can join," he said. "We are not in the business of releasing bad records." His cooperative yielded good results. Soon he had indie label owners calling from all over the country. Both groups pressed client labels' records, bearing the NSD and IRDA logos. NSD returned some veteran artists, who couldn't get a major-label deal, to the charts. Nationwide also promoted and distributed records by talented newcomers. Meanwhile in Nashville, Hank Levine, a veteran session arranger, and Mike Shepherd, who had worked with Monument Records and Warner Bros., founded IRDA. They realized that small indies still managed to crack the lower portions of the national charts, but that window was slowly closing. IRDA distributed a number of established indie country labels, including Fraternity Records in Cincinnati, which released some country product then. Country star Marty Robbins and his son arranged for their label to be distributed by IRDA. One of IRDA's artists was Penny DeHaven, who had been receiving strong airplay on indie labels at the time. Probably some IRDA-affiliated labels were no more than a guy with telephone and a wink. But many were upfront, established small labels that had been on the charts in the past when radio was more welcoming. Because of this, the concept of a distribution union of country labels seemed solid. Both NSD and IRDA began receiving a significant increase in airplay and trade picks. In 1975, Stella Parton, Dolly's sister, ranked number four in *Record World's* Country Single Awards. Parton ranked just under Jessi Colter on Capitol, Emmylou Harris on Warner Bros., and Margo Smith on 20th Century. Also that year, Stella Parton's "I Want to Hold You (in My Dreams)" on Country Soul Records became the only independent artist and label to crack the *Cashbox* Top 100 country singles list of hits for the year. The labels ranged from the unknown to the obscure: Aerie, Boyd, Alexander Street, Hummingbird, Wheat, Ronnee, Maverick, Onyx, and Door Knob. The latter had been around a while, making it marginally on the charts. Owner-producer Gene Kennedy came back with Linda Cassidy's "Tell It to Someone (Who'll Believe It)." On the Antique label, Zoot Fenster went top fifteen in *Record World* with "The Man on Page 602." Unfortunately, by the early 1980s the record business had become too entrenched with corporate radio, major labels, and expensive promotion operatives. Airplay tightened. The economy, struck with inflation, didn't help. Knowing NSD and IRDA could no longer compete, their owners closed up shop. The dollar had been crowned the king of country music.

Independent Distributors

Played an important role in the development of the post-war record business. They have been underappreciated in the written history of the music industry because the job was not glamorous. Nor was it considered creative. It was grunt work: Lugging around boxes of records, calling accounts, and, in some cases, promoting the records made by client labels. The indie companies distributed multiple record labels. The concept peaked about 1957, as the one-stops had begun to slowly take business from the independent distributors. The distributors continued to battle for their share of the market through the 1960s and even into the 1970s. "They [one stops] made it so you [record stores] could buy all the records in one place," said Jerry Blaine, president of Jubilee Records. *Billboard* in the late 1950s ran a column called Distributor News. It featured various distributors across the nation reporting some of their hot sellers. The column featured both major-label-owned distributors as well as the indies, which included Midwest Distributing Company in St. Louis, Melody of Buffalo, Remley of Pittsburgh, and Sherco of Milwaukee. In 1969, Jim Shipley, of Mainline Distributors in Cleveland, predicted the future of his niche and of the record industry when he said, "The pure independent distributor is obsolete.... Nobody needs two middlemen." But no one could deny the impact that indie distributors had on the record business. They were the early champions of the 45. Also a major player in the development of rock and R&B, the indie distributor offered direct routes into record stores and other retail establishments. This type of distribution hit its peak from 1945 to 1970, when indie distributors erred by taking on many new labels that had no previous national track record. At one time, an indie distributor would carry many major labels as well as the top independents, but the majors pulled out in the 1960s in favor of using their own distribution. The biggest complaint about indie distributors was that they often refused to pay the labels that were not generating hit after hit, a policy that put the weaker labels out of business. The old joke used to go, "Getting paid by a distributor is as hard as a bank getting paid by Dillinger." Pay often came a year, or at least many months, late. By then, the cash-starved independent-labels could be out of business. Many independent distributors folded in the 1960s and

1970s. Those that survived were larger companies who had already diversified into other areas of the distribution business. For example, Houston's H.W. Daily Company, which described itself as "wholesale distributors of phonograph records," had been in business since the mid-1940s. When a product changed, Daily changed with it. The company distributed whatever the record business needed. It still does. Founder H.W. "Bud" Daily said in 1976, "We ... have seen a lot of hits come and go. We also have seen a lot of distributors come and go.... We don't push buttons to get sales, but we do kick butts sometimes." As late as 1976, Daily employed thirteen salespeople total in his Houston office and in his Big State Distributing Corporation in Dallas. (Today, Daily's in Houston continues, but Big State does not.) Only the most nimble distributors survived into the late 1970s. Traditionally they covered wide geographic areas and often employed their own promotion men to push records to DJs, stores, and jukebox operators. The larger distributors included Henry Stone's Tone Distributors, Miami; Stan Lewis Distributing, Shreveport; Big State Distributing Corp., Dallas; Fenway Distributors, Pittsburgh; Heilicher Bros., Minneapolis; Gold Distributors, Buffalo; Main Line, Cleveland; A-1 Distributing, Cincinnati; Roberts Distributing, St. Louis; Allstate Distributors, Chicago; and John O'Brien Distributors, Milwaukee. Modern indie distributors have shifted their focus to albums and have aligned themselves more closely with smaller, niche independent labels. (See **One-Stop**.)

Independent Labels

Flourished after World War II, when interest arose in black and hillbilly music and, during in the mid-1950s, rock 'n' roll. They did things their way. From the time the phonograph was invented in 1877 until about 1922, the number of independent labels was limited because the large companies—Edison, Columbia, Victor—tied up the technology used to manufacture discs and cylinders. In 1921, the independent Gennett Records of Richmond, Indiana, and its parent, Starr Piano Co., challenged the patents in court and won a remarkable victory. Prior to that time, fewer independents operated, and they did so only with cooperation of the three majors. (Another memorable indie included the Wisconsin Chair Company's Paramount Records, which was known for its blues.) After Gennett's court victory, more independents arrived, but the Great Depression, which began in 1929, flattened their numbers. More independents opened for business as the late 1930s came along, only to be sidetracked by the war and its shellac rationing. In the late '40s, their return coincided with the rise of R&B and then rock radio. Typically, the independents of the late 1950s were owned by one or individuals who used independent record distributors. In the '50s and '60s, such labels included Specialty, of Los Angeles; Ace, of Jackson, Mississippi; Sun, of Memphis; King, of Cincinnati; and Laurie, of New York. Independents discovered much of the talent in R&B, country, and rock, including Elvis Presley, Carl Perkins, Johnny Cash, and Jerry Lee Lewis (all on Sun); and the hillbilly singers Cowboy Copas, Hawkshaw Hawkins, and Grandpa Jones (on King). Defining an indie label seemed easier then, although by the 1960s there were important nuances. For example, Monument Records, although initially distributed by the large London label in the late 1950s and early 1960s, and later by indie distributors, switched to major-label (CBS) distribution out of necessity in the 1970s and enjoyed the greatest sales of the firm's life. Monument owner Fred Foster maintained that Monument and other labels of the era had no choice but to ally themselves with the majors because of the unreliable payments from independent distributors. (Eventually, Foster returned Monument to the indie distributors.) The golden years of the indie label ran from 1945 to 1970, when large corporations began buying the more successful indies and turning them into divisions. John Broven, the esteemed record-business historian, described the indie record scene best in 2009 when he wrote his seminal *Record Makers and Breakers: Voices of the Independent Rock 'n' Roll Pioneers*. He said, "Dreams and schemes notwithstanding, it was a cutthroat business full of roller-coaster excitement and epoch-making history."

Independent Producers

Brought many fine artists to the record business and operated as de facto A&R operatives. While the name independent record producer is old, its definition keeps changing. In the early 1970s, independent producers peaked in numbers, clout, and productions, turning out some of pop music's most influential and memorable songs. *Cash Box* proclaimed 1960 "the year which saw the indie producer become a major factor in the record business." On a regional basis, some indies often owned their own studios, published hit songs, and scouted talent. Some producers, especially in R&B, had to work with whatever equipment they could find. Early on, they did not even receive credit on the record. The job was often frustrating and grueling. As DJ John Richbourg once wrote, "The R&B producer who had been cutting a lot of his records in back rooms, garages, etc., frequently using equipment he hauled around in his car, had to move into the studio." The modern version of the independent producer started in the mid-1960s, when they began seeing their names listed on the records they made. Major-label staff producers such as Jerry Fuller were ready to leave their day jobs to cut records for the highest bidders. As a staff producer at

Columbia Records, Fuller wrote and produced "Woman, Woman," "Over You," and other hits for Gary Puckett and the Union Gap. As a new independent, Fuller wrote and produced "Show and Tell" by Al Wilson. A few other major independent producers of the era included Richard Perry ("Stoney End," Barbra Steisand), Chips Moman ("Angel of the Morning," Merillee Rush), and Snuff Garrett ("The Night Has a Thousand Eyes," Bobby Vee). Locally, independent producers thrived. Many local ones operated production companies at night and on weekends. By day they were mechanics, barbers, office workers—you name it. They scoured their region for talent. Their operating bases were one city or regions, such as the Dallas-Fort Worth and the Cincinnati-Dayton-Columbus markets. There, a regional hit single that sold 5,000 to 15,000-plus copies could catch the attention of a major label or a larger national independent. Regional hits were often made by producers with strong local labels—Major Bill Smith (Le Cam Records) in Dallas, Huey Meaux (Crazy Cajun Records) in Houston, and many others across the country. Meaux, a former DJ and barber, was one of the most successful over two decades, although he once said some of his records sounded like they were cut in a big tin can. Examples of regional-to-national hits by independents in Texas alone included (regional labels listed first) "Before the Next Teardrop Falls" by Freddy Fender (Crazy Cajun Records; ABC-Dot); "Room Full of Roses," Mickey Gilley (Astro Records; Playboy Records); "Hey, Baby," Bruce Chanel (LeCam Records; Smash Records); "I'm So Lonesome I Could Cry," B.J. Thomas (Pacemaker Records; Scepter Records); "Last Kiss," J. Frank Wilson and the Cavaliers (Newdoll Records; Josie-Jubliee Records); "Chantilly Lace," the Big Bopper (D Records; Mercury Records); and, a later one, "Love in the Hot Afternoon," Gene Watson (Resco Records; Capitol Records). Sadly, the regional singles producer is an anachronism today, although on rare occasions you will hear about one of them breaking loose on radio. It's difficult to have a regional hit in the era of downloading. Consolidation of labels and changing times and technologies have helped put the indie singles producer practically out of business. In the heyday of the independent, producers operated on nearly every corner in small towns and big cities. Now, only an elite class earn a living from it.

Independent Studios

Contributed heavily to the rise of rock music all across America. Although independent recording studios existed well before the coming of rock 'n' roll in 1955, they didn't grow in sufficient enough numbers or cut a significant number of hits, until the 1960s. *Billboard* noted their arrival in 1968 with the story, "'Backyard' Studios—New-Sound Frontier." Reporter

Mike Gross cited studios such as Stax in Memphis, Robin Hood Brians' studio in Tyler, Texas; Norman Petty's studio in Clovis, New Mexico, where Buddy Holly recorded; Huey P. Meaux's Gold Star Studios in Houston, and Rick Hall's Fame Recording in the now-famous area of Muscle Shoals, Alabama. Musician Norman Petty owned and operated a seminal self-named studio in Clovis, New Mexico. That's where he recorded Buddy Holly and the Crickets and another rockabilly band, the Rhythm Orchids, featuring Jimmy Bowen and Buddy Knox. According to Knox, the Rhythm Orchids couldn't record before midnight because of traffic noise on the highway in front of the studio. "You could hear the sound of trucks on the tape, so Norman had to be careful," Knox said in 1989. "We recorded on only one track, so if somebody messed up his part, we had to start over again. To make things more complicated, Norman was a recording engineer who preferred perfection, so our sessions often went all night. The only reason he stopped them was because by morning the trucks were rolling by again." Facing high-tech recording innovations, the smaller indie studios are having a tough time staying in business.

Indies

Name used by reporters for newspapers and trade publications to identify independent record companies in the 1950s and '60s. It was also used to describe anyone in the general record industry who operated independently—that is, free of the majors. They included distributors, jukebox operators, labels, and producers.

Inscription

Mastering engineer's term for what is written in dead wax. It can be seen on a record's spiral—the inch or so of plastic next to the microgrooves—where the stylus travels until it stops. The process, called inscribing, means that a mastering engineer inscribes by hand a record number, matrix number, possibly his or her initials, and occasionally a brief comment. The inscription makes no noise on the disc. You might see a word or initials intended for friendly record label chiefs who were close to pressing plant employees.

Instrumentals

Songs without lyrics that brought a sense of immediacy and diversity to Top 40 radio. The overall influence of Top 40 instrumentals peaked in the 1960s, when 45s dominated the teenage market. Coming from an era when instrumentals of all kinds were popular, the new rock 'n' roll and

In early 1960, former Sun Records artist Bill Justis broke out regionally with the instrumental "Boogie Woogie Rock" for the Play Me label in Memphis. Impressed with his 1957 hit single "Raunchy," NRC Records in Atlanta picked up the master to "Boogie." Some music historians credit "Raunchy" with being the first rock instrumental hit (excluding early R&B instrumentals). Though "Boogie Woogie Rock" did not hit big nationally, it helped Justis enhance his reputation in preparation for a move to Nashville in 1961. There he would become a sought-after arranger.

R&B instrumentals naturally took root. Do not discount the influence that instrumentals—even middle-of-the-road and jazz instrumentals—had on rock radio stations. They included "Take Five" by Dave Brubeck. They were beautiful, no matter what type or genre, though teens were more likely to enjoy the rock versions then. In the late 1950s and throughout the 1960s, instrumentals were as accepted commercially as any vocal record. In Top 40 radio, instrumentals flourished, including everything from orchestral numbers to simple rock-group pieces. Few records are as moody and soothing as Santo and Johnny's "Sleepwalk," a steel guitar instrumental which has been remade many times since it hit number one on Canadian-American Records in June of 1959. But all manner of guitars, though popular in instrumentals, weren't the only lead on instrumental records. Saxophones instrumentals were prominent, as were piano records. In 1968, French band leader Paul Mauriat struck with "Love Is Blue." It was remade many times. When disco music arrived around 1973, the genre discovered a well-heeled benefactor in dancing music. Many instrumentals began in discos, then went on to become radio hits. In 1973, *Cash Box* ran an editorial that saluted the resurging Top 40 instrumental. In April and May of that year, editorial writers pointed out that four top-ten instrumental singles, including "Frankenstein" and "Funky Worm," were in the national top ten. The magazine noted that the record-buying public "seems to want, now more than ever, to get up and dance. The instrumental allows the participant merely to dance and concentrate on the music alone." As the '70s gave way to the '80s, however, Top 40 instrumental hits began to decline. The public didn't abandon them. Radio programmers did. As their playlists tightened even more, and fewer acts played instrumentals exclusively, the genre restricted itself to clubs and specialty fields. Gradually, music overall became more formatted, and tastes changed. Although instrumental hits still linger, their better times have come and gone. (See **Guitar Instrumental**.)

IPS

Inches per second. This is how recording tape passes through a magnetic tape recorder. Usually recordings were made at fifteen IPS, but others were done at thirty IPS. The faster the tape winds through the machine, the less extraneous noise the recorder picks up.

Iron Mothers

Stampers used to press 78-rpm discs in the 1940s and earlier. No connection to heavy-metal bands.

It's Rolling

Audio engineers shouted "it's rolling" to alert the musicians when the tape began to record. Some of them might shout it these days, but usually no tape is actually rolling. It is mostly digital now.

J

Jesus Rock

Arrived in the late 1960s when some counterculture performers from California began embracing Christianity. They helped bring religious rock to Top 40 radio. Despite their spiritual theme, the records often leaped onto the national charts, and teenagers accepted the records as though they were secular. They were not considered traditional gospel, nor were they contemporary Christian music of the period. The records were individual statements from rock 'n' roll performers, who regularly sang secular music. In 1969, "Jesus Is a Soul Man," one of the earlier nationally charted Christian-themed singles, came from a soulful country-sounding singer named Lawrence Reynolds. It was cut in Nashville. By the early '70s, more Christian rock hits came to the charts, including Ocean's "Put Your Hand in the Hand," Brewer and Shipley's "One Toke Over the Line," and, the biggest of them all, Norman Greenbaum's "Spirit in the Sky." The Orthodox Jew enjoyed the feel of gospel music, so he wrote his simple song and recorded it in San Francisco. The record's captivating guitar riff—like a fuzz tone—makes "Spirit in the Sky" the most memorable hit of its period. Capped by some rock operas with religious songs, including "Day by Day," the Jesus Rock period remained on the charts for a few years.

Jukebox

Heavily influenced the record industry and American culture from the 1930s to the 1960s. Early on, cylinder records were installed in prototypical jukeboxes made by record companies such as Columbia and Edison. By the 1890s, the boxes had appeared in a number of urban businesses, including phonograph parlors and drug stores. Possibly the first jukebox—then called a coin-operated phonograph, or a "nickel-in-the-slot"—was installed in the Palais Royal in San Francisco on November 23, 1889, by the entrepreneur Louis Glass. By 1891, a coin-operated box in New Orleans was generating $500 a month, making it the most profitable box in the nation. At first listeners had to use hearing tubes. "All you have to do," instructed an advertisement of the era, "is to drop the coin, wind the crank, put the tubes to your ears—and it does the rest." And what did they hear? Orchestras playing classical pieces, brass bands playing rousing marches (John Philip Sousa was a big star then), sappy ballads, political speeches, and novelty songs and monologues. The coin-operated machines did not hit a major boom in use until they were electrified in the late 1920s and placed in African American juke joints in the Deep South and in Harlem. Prohibition didn't hinder their use. And when the Depression ended, the boxes did even more business. From 1937 to 1949, the jukebox ruled the public music kingdom in what is now known as the Golden Age of the Jukebox. The years were chosen based on the artistic box designs of the period and the popularity of the "automatic phonograph," as the box was called into the early 1930s. At this time the word jukebox began to be accepted throughout the nation. Some historians believe the name juke came from the old Southern word *jook*, a term for dancing that had its roots in Africa. There are other theories on the origins of the name, but jook seems to be the one most widely accepted. At its zenith, the jukebox industry created hits, entertained lovers and families, and helped support untold numbers of mom-and-pop soda shops, restaurants, and diners. In a colorful 1970s *Billboard* supplement called "Jukebox: Extinct but Not Forgotten," Marion Muller noted that the beauty of the jukebox coincided with America's palatial movie houses and upbeat songs of the Great Depression. "Our gathering place was the jukebox," Muller wrote. "It had a bountiful supply of tunes; it lit up our spirits and the price was right." The jukebox, he said, brightened an otherwise dark time with hope, escape, and visions of better days to come. When World War II followed the Depression, people again turned to the jukebox. Operators had a hard time finding enough records, but they managed by replacing harder-to-get pop discs with folk records. The response was positive. People wanted to hear any music. The jukebox industry grew steadily until the 1940s, when it peaked. The boxes were hurt by rising prices and changing entertainment patterns. Television had taken hold. Rock 'n' roll's arrival in the mid–1950s helped bolster the industry for a good decade, and despite the slide, also helped the music machines influence the record business, society, and music in general. As the number of jukebox plays increased, many independent record labels created records especially for that good-time market. This brought the record and jukebox industries together in a common cause. Labels recorded some records especially for jukeboxes. The jukebox industry was once so strong that it rivaled radio for creating hits. Some jukebox hits received little radio play yet sold thousands of records. Today, the greatest jukeboxes are remembered as works of art *and* sound. Some of the most colorful boxes were designed by Paul Fuller for Wurlitzer. His final creation came in 1948—"a last, fantastic effort," Muller called it, filled with technological innovations such as a plastic tone arm, ceramic cartridge, a preamplifier, and a bomber nose window borrowed from airplane designs. In the 1960s, the jukebox industry began a serious, slow decline, which continued to worsen. By the 1990s, the business was continuing to contract. When the 45-rpm single practically vanished from stores in the late 1980s, jukebox operators—who still had plenty of boxes that played singles—continued to order 45s. This kept the vinyl single from becoming extinct. The orders also kept some record-pressing plants in business when they were desperate for business. Finally, the 45-playing boxes were replaced by CD-playing ones. But by then the popular age of the jukebox had come and gone. Though they can still be found in places like older pizza parlors with dine-in tables, it is rare to find jukeboxes in many of their traditional locations, including family restaurants and bars. The jukebox industry continues to operate with the modern version of boxes that feature compact discs. They are made to look "retro."

Jukebox Blues

Originated as a song title in country music. "Jukebox Blues" was written by Maybelle and Helen Carter and published by Acuff-Rose Publications in 1953. Soon people in the trade picked up on the term and used it to describe the emotional state of people who were playing some sad country and pop songs repetitively. Probably jukebox-service employees considered it their theme song. It became a major theme in many country records of the late 1950s and 1960s.

Jukebox Charts

The "boxes" became so popular that trade magazines created special charts on which the most popular jukebox records were listed in the 1940s and 1950s. By establishing exclusive the charts, the magazines paid respects to the jukeboxes in local bars and corner soda shops. The charts often featured between fifteen to twenty-five top-selling records reported by major jukebox outlets from around the country. The fact that the trades ran juke charts is evidence of the sales power of jukebox manufacturers and local operators.

Jukebox Hits

Received so many plays that the records became local, and, occasionally, national sensations. Jukebox hits were more significant than they might seem from a modern perspective. Some national hit records sold hundreds of thousands of copies through direct sales to jukebox outlets, and, as a result of that exposure, to individuals. In rock's early days, jukebox operators were taken seriously because their selections influenced record sales. Before Television and other entertainment media arrived, jukeboxes commanded attention in nightclubs and other gathering places. Record company promoters catered to jukebox outlets, hoping to land new records in the boxes. In 1966, jukebox operators bought $53 million in singles from one-stops, representing forty-three percent of one-stop owners' business, according to a *Billboard* survey published in 1968. Sometimes labels didn't sell these records anywhere else, but often the juke records sold simultaneously as radio hits. Examples were the 1958 novelties "Witch Doctor," a million-seller by David Seville (real name: Ross Bagdasarian), and "The Purple People Eater" by Sheb Wooley, which sold 1.5 million records in just nine weeks. Seville and Wooley could say thanks in part to the jukebox.

Jukebox Labels

Formed by jukebox operators to generate more income. In the mid-1950s, some jukebox trade groups and manufacturers decided to enter the record industry from the other end of the spectrum—as record label owners. They pressed a limited number of records—usually 45-rpm singles and a few EPs—by hometown acts. Familiarity enticed customers to play the records. In November 1955, the Music Operators of America (MOA) followed the lead of other jukebox groups by starting its own National Juke Box Record Corporation, which began signing songwriters and finding material that was in the public domain. Their idea: Sell records to their own established "box" outlets as well as to the general public through traditional radio airplay. The new MOA-owned label, which pressed its records at major-label pressing plants, offered new records to the group's 11,000 members. Meanwhile, Chicago's Bally Manufacturing Company also founded its own label, Bally Records, which officially began operating on January 1, 1956. By this time, other juke companies had entered the record-releasing scene as well. *Billboard* noted that the juke companies decided to start their own labels "with eyes carefully peeled on the profit being raked in by the [record] indie firms." Over the coming years, however, the juke-owned indie labels learned that it was difficult to compete with established independent labels. As a result, most of the juke labels eventually closed. Bally Records ("The Home of Living Performance") closed after less than two years. One problem was the scope of the operations. The companies had set up a system that was too expensive to maintain. The idea was more effective on a local or regional level. Often locals did well enough to pay back inexpensive pressing and recording costs, and eventually turn a profit. Most of these records never went any further than hometown bars and restaurants. Many had a sparse and utilitarian appearance, often using only the artist's name and a basic label name with no logo. Sax player Tommy Wills of Indiana became a pioneer in this field, establishing his Juke Records in the early 1960s. In a few years he was releasing fifteen records a month, an impressive number that surpassed most traditional smaller- and medium-sized independent labels. "People liked it so we expanded," he said. "We had a jukebox of our own in our club, so I thought, 'Hey why don't I make some records for us and other jukebox owners?'" He developed the idea into possibly the largest "small-time" jukebox label in the Midwest, expanding distribution through the Midwest and even into Canada. Wills, operating in a defined, less populated area, continued his label for years. He released singles that featured his own band as well as Denzil "Dumpy" Rice, a Cincinnati-area pianist, vocalist, and songwriter, and other locally popular acts.

Jukebox Mini LP

A marketing term that arrived in the late 1960s. It describes the EP (extended play, 33⅓-rpm) with a hard jacket and usually a blank back. Most of them contained six sides (songs) in the years when songs ran under three minutes.

Jukebox Ops

Nickname for jukebox operators. Through the mid–1960s they were mostly mom-and-pop and small-company operations. A perfect example was Dixie Music, near Cincinnati. Named after its female founder, Dixie serviced jukeboxes for bars and restaurants in an area that its owner staked out through hard work and determination. Such businesses operated across the country. By 1967, however, they were being purchased by vending machine operators who wanted to increase the size and depth of their businesses. Jukebox outlets continue to operate, but not on the scale of the 1960s.

Jukebox Top 25

Already an anachronism by the 1970s. Into the mid–1960s, *Record World* was still providing a jukebox-hit chart called Jukebox Top 25. Its records reflected the top pop chart, for the most part. Jukebox charts, once so reliable and necessary to gauge the success of hit records, were not to be around much longer.

Jukebox Wars

Infighting among various jukebox operators. When a city's larger jukebox operators became embroiled in sticky territorial disputes, things could get tough. Newspapers often described the tussles as "jukebox wars." This occurred in the heyday of the jukebox's popularity, in the 1940s and 1950s, when independent owners wielded considerable clout in the record industry. Juke owners bickered about territorial issues and clashed with local politicians over everything from tax increases to bars' licensing fees. Often the news landed on page one. One way to deal with uncooperative politicians was to unplug the boxes for a short period, creating public protest. The Jukers knew that people in general often blamed politicians for everything, so the public would surely blame city hall for a jukebox strike. This meant little Wally couldn't play Joe Ward's "Nothin' for Christmas" five times while the family ate at Mama Jo's Diner. More serious jukebox wars erupted in violence, particularly in Miami and other large urban areas into the 1960s, when jukebox operators still serviced and installed their boxes in restaurants, coffee shops, diners, bars, and nightclubs. Then there was the Mob's involvement in the jukebox industry in larger cities, particularly in the east. Independent-minded jukebox operators often battled competing jukebox outlets who were also owned by the mob, or were paying "insurance" to organized crime.

Jukes

Slang for jukebox. It was used in the 1930s and later, but now, like the jukebox itself, the word is not widely known. Because the boxes were so popular in lower-class places, they developed a nickname—jukes. According to music historian Tim Brooks, an authoritative writer and researcher of old music, the word jukes "derived from a Negro term for sex, and later applied to a whorehouse or roadhouse, it gained widespread use as the result of a famous nineteenth-century sociological study of a lower-class family." Despite the word's origins, its usage continued.

Jump a Groove

When the stylus or needle popped out of a record groove, disc manufacturers called it groove jumping. Soon the jargon became "jump a groove." When this happened, usually only the disc was damaged.

K

Keyboard

Once, the acoustic piano's place in music was unchallenged—in the recording studio and in concert. Then came the high-tech revolution, and the acoustic piano, that venerable instrument of then and now, was left behind. Its proponents became known as keyboardists. Though certainly not finished, the acoustic piano is struggling to remain relevant in an age of convenience, especially in rock and R&B. As a story in the *Economist* pointed out in 2018, New York used to be the home of one hundred piano makers. Now, most of them are gone. Why? Electronic keyboards, those portable, multifaceted instruments, rule the world of music. They can do almost anything. Musicians can take them anywhere, and not worry about finding a piano at a studio gig or a live performance. Every good studio had an acoustic piano as an indispensable musical instrument. It was used both as the centerpiece of performances as well as in a supporting role in most recordings of the times. Its eighty-eight keys remain the classic configuration that make up the keyboard. All debates over acoustic and electronic aside, the acoustic keyboard changed western music forever when it was invented in the early 1700s. Soon they became the instrument most used by the great classical composers—Beethoven, Mozart, and Hayden. In the heyday of Motown, studio musicians used a harpsicord and a clavichord on some of their pop-rock hits. In live performances from classical to the soul of James Brown, a real, classic piano was a part of the orchestra. Great pianists appeared at their pianos front and center, from Jerry Lee Lewis and Liberace in the '50s and '60s to Elton John and Billy Joel in the '70s. They were honest to goodness acoustic "Piano Men." For those of us who still enjoy the sounds of the acoustic as well as the electronic, there is hope. Some popular songwriters still compose their music on an actual piano keyboard. Today, it's hard to imagine any great piano player being introduced as a keyboardist.

Kidisks

Nickname for the children's record. They called it the kidisk. In 1950 Mercury released thirty-two different songs on ten-inch, non-breakable 78s—kidisks. (See **Children's Records**.)

L

Label

Circular paper that is applied to a vinyl disc, for identifying the artist and song. It also means a record company, as in Ace Records, an independent label.

Label Advertising

A major difference between the record industry of the 1960s and that of the present. In the golden age of the single, three top trade magazines existed. This helped make advertising rates competitive for independent labels. Still, ad space wasn't cheap, but it was more affordable than it is today. Independent labels, which in those days could have huge pop-chart hits, benefited in particular from the more reasonable advertising rates. Companies could afford to take a chance on an unknown act's unknown single by buying a full-page or half-page ad in *Billboard*, *Cash Box*, or *Record World*. As a result, all three magazines—and even smaller ones—carried indie-label advertising from Abnak Records of Houston, King Records of Cincinnati, Red Bud of New York, World Artists of Pittsburgh, Duke-Peacock of Houston, and many others. Today, many indies have turned to niche music to carve out a meager living. They can't afford to consistently run ads in *Billboard* or in any other major publications. Fortunately, they no longer have to, for indie labels aren't expected to turn out top-ten pop single hits to stay in business.

Label Deal

A recording contract. They were the two most important words in any producer's lexicon, for the label deal meant that his recording might be released and he might make some money.

Lacquer

A blank metal disc covered with acetate. A sound engineer used a lathe to cut grooves into the lacquer. A separate lacquer was used to cut each side of a disc.

Lateral Cut

The so-called lateral-cut records were made by Victor and Columbia and other labels. They were the common 78-rpm discs. They had modulating grooves, pushing the stylus side to side instead of up and down. (See **Vertical Cut**.)

Laughing Record

Sub-genre of the novelty record. Obviously, they were records on which the recording "artist" laughed. The early ones had no musical accompaniment. People laughed at hearing a man's recorded laughter. Although the format seems silly today, these recordings fascinated early phonograph audiences, who weren't used to hearing recorded sound. In fact, one of the earliest popular records in the 1890s was George W. Johnson's "Laughing Song" on Emile Berliner's Gramophone label. Surprisingly, laughing records remained popular into the twentieth century. The Mercedes of laughing records came in 1922, when the Okeh label imported from Germany a record on which a man and woman laugh hysterically, backed by a cornet player. Other Okeh laughing records were advertised as "a riot of fun! Laughs, gurgles, chuckles, at every turn of the disc." As record-buyers' tastes became more sophisticated, the laughing discs were doomed.

Lemons

Unscrupulous people—scammers who stole the dreams and the money of amateur songwriters and poets. Throughout the first half of the twentieth century, legitimate music people referred to the crooks as lemons. Hopeful poets who wanted a melody would send a check and never receive a reply from the lemon "publisher." Another kind of lemon actually came through by composing a melody, but did not fulfill the promise of auditioning the song in front of singers and music business people. As musician Fred Mierisch recalled in a 1923 magazine story, "I was a 'lemon' song composer just long enough to find out what my wry-faced boss was doing." Dream-busting lemons still operate today, but not as prolifically. And no one calls them lemons anymore. You know what they're called.

Length

How long a record runs. This simple statement was on the lips and minds of every radio program director, jukebox operator, and record label executive in the 1950s and 1960s. Radio wanted all singles to run under three minutes so DJs could cram as many hits onto the playlists as possible. Juke ops wanted the same thing, so they could make more money from more plays. Of course, record men complied. Some took things to the extreme, cutting records that ran just under two minutes long. But in those days most singles lasted from two minutes and thirty seconds to two minutes and fifty seconds. In 1960, 45s in the top ten averaged two minutes and thirty-six seconds, according to a *Billboard* report in 1970. Surprisingly, in the mid-1960s, the early era of the Beatles, those short records got even a bit shorter. Everything went along smoothly until the spring of 1968 when Dunhill Records released Richard Harris' mammoth production of "MacArthur Park," a Jimmy Webb song with a running time of seven minutes and twenty-one seconds. Reluctantly, radio played it, and things slowly began to change. It broke the hallowed five-minute barrier. But jukebox outlet operators complained. They continued to complain a few months later when the Beatles arrived with "Hey Jude"—a whopping seven minutes and eleven seconds. But even the road-weary juke men finally gave in. They knew the longer single was here to stay. By the early 1970s, station managers and the public had become accustomed to longer singles. Young people preferred them, too. A Vanilla Fudge single came with two long plays—"Some Velvet Morning," the A-side, ran seven minutes and thirty-four seconds, while the flip side, "People," came in at five minutes and twenty seconds. Ultimately, long-plays were welcomed by DJs, who could now run to the rest room without being an Olympic sprinter. (See **Long 45**.)

Listening Booths

Listening booths or rooms where customers tried out recordings that they might want to buy. In the very early days, the 1890s, customers hooked up rubber tubes to cylinder phonographs. They used something akin to today's ear buds. Through the years listening booths evolved and adapted to the times, installing disc phonographs for customers. Store owners added a series of turntables right up front. Customers slapped on 78-rpm discs to decide if they wanted to buy them. Listening booths continued as vinyl records arrived in force in the 1950s. Interestingly, this old-fashioned method of trying out a record continued in some record stores into the mid–1960s. By the 1970s, however, the booths had decreased in number. Booths did survive in some rural towns, just like drugstore soda fountains continued. These days, the listening booth is an anachronism. Today's rough equivalent is a tryout of about thirty seconds on Amazon.com and other on-line digital music sellers.

Listening Fatigue

Term used by phonograph and recording-equipment makers in the early 1950s to describe a problem that habitual listeners developed, marked by tracking distortion caused by record and stylus wear. The solution: a new record. The old one was worn out.

Little LPs

An extended-play single with multiple cuts. The nickname developed in the early 1960s. Never very popular with the general public, the Little LP was used mainly by radio stations and jukebox operators, who liked the four to six sides per disc and, later, the stereo capability of the records. About 1971, Mercury Records became so worried about increasingly long singles and album cuts that it pressed Little LPs mainly for radio stations to provide edited versions of songs on seven-inch discs that played at $33\frac{1}{3}$ rpm. The company hoped that the discs would encourage radio stations with tight time restrictions to play shorter versions of songs that they might not ordinarily consider. Other companies, including Kapp and King, also promoted the Little LPs. (See **EP**.)

Live Sessions

Live performances released on record. After James Brown broke ground by recording an LP of his live performance at the Apollo Theater in New York in the 1960s, live performances for other artists became more popular with the public and the record companies. Albums were one thing; singles another. They had to face a youthful top forty audience. Some label owners worried that the live sound released on singles would not sound like the usual studio-recorded songs. "Little" Stevie Wonder did one of the earlier live-performance singles in 1963 when his "Fingertips—Pt. 2" hit number one on the Hot 100. The live sound, including the audience's reaction, gave the record an electric feel. The difference between a live session and a session done in the day of one-track recorders and disc machines is simple: The live session was a performance recorded before an audience in a club or some other venue outside the studio. Although musicians and singers performed live in studios in the days of one-track recording, they were in a controlled environment with excellent acoustics, echo, and varied electronic machines to enhance their performances. Also, they could record their tracks as many times as they wanted to get the proper feeling and fix any foul-ups. In live sessions, there was no going back. That resulted in a spontaneity an immediacy that listeners preferred.

Live vs. Tape

Sound difference between recorded and live vocals. In the 1950s, people marveled at the clarity of tape recordings over the old acetate disc sounds. Their fascination lasted into the '60s. Audio engineers from Acoustic Research Inc., of Cambridge, Massachusetts, conducted a tape sound test at the Chicago World's Fair from August 31 to September 9, 1962. Their goal was to determine how many people could differentiate between live sound and taped sound. The Fine Arts Quartet played some selections. Unbeknownst to the audience, at times the group acted as though it was playing. The audience had to tell the difference. (Unfortunately, the results of the test were not published in trade magazines.) Fifty dignitaries, including Illinois Governor Otto Kerner, attended. A few years later, Memorex advertised, "Is it real or is it Memorex?"

Lock Jaw

Uninspiring and motionless singers. Known as "lock jaws" to audio engineers and producers of the 1950s, the name was apt. Today, there are few lock-jawed vocalists because audio engineers speed up the tracks and tinker further with Auto Tune and other digital tricks to enhance studio performances. Unfortunately, today's potentially lock-jawed singers sound passable, and individuality is lost.

Lo-Fi

Generally, recording with old-fashioned equipment, particularly tape recorders with only one or two tracks. Also on audio cassette. Low-Fi proponents are dedicated. Some simply enjoy hearing music recorded at its most basic, sonic level. Noise-reduction equipment? Forget it. Lo-Fi is nearly the opposite of Hi-Fi. Low-Fi is to recording what old-time Jeeps are to driving.

Long 45

More about running time than the number of grooves. Known in the business as the long-play single, the "Long 45" became a disdainful term used by jukebox operators in the 1960s to describe singles that ran longer than the preferred two to three minutes. Few longer 45s were made for years because radio and jukebox people opposed them. Short records (to use the vernacular of the era) allowed DJs to cram more records into each radio hour, one already burdened by advertising and tight playlists. Naturally, jukebox operators also liked the short records because customers could play at least two of them for every one long 45. By the late 1960s, a number of affected jukebox owners claimed they had to increase their price to "two plays for twenty-five cents" to offset the increasing number of long-running singles on the market. Imagine: Some companies were releasing five-minute singles. (See **Length**.)

Long Version, Short Version

When mono was battling stereo for dominance in the singles market in the second half of the 1960s, record companies faced a problem. Most AM radio stations still preferred to play shorter, mono records. So some companies, including Atlantic, pressed their DJ copies with the plug side on both sides. One version said "long version," the other said "short version." Thus, both radio camps were satisfied. Soon the short version became obsolete.

Love-Your-Brother Songs

The mid–'60s through the early '70s were the peak years of all sorts of singles. This one is for love-your-brother hits. They did not express romantic love; this was love for fellow human beings. No doubt this type of song gained popularity when the so-called love culture blossomed. Songwriters knew there was a market for it. Keep in mind that radio stations were playing songs about brotherly love while society was in upheaval over the war in Vietnam, the struggle for civil rights, campus protests, and race riots. Singles using this theme, and variations on it, hit big. They included "Get Together" by the Youngbloods, "Put a Little Love in Your Heart" and "What the World Needs Now Is Love" by Jackie DeShannon, "Lay Down (Candles in the Rain)" by Melanie, and "San Francisco (Be Sure to Wear Flowers in Your Hair)" by Scott McKenzie. Today, love-your-brother songs are not so popular. We're too busy yelling at one another.

Low-Priced Field

Segment of the record business that thrived on "lower-end disc product," as *Record World* described it. The so-called low-priced field had been around in different forms for years. But the modern budget lines thrived after the LP hit the stands. The niche started rolling in the '60s. By 1965, Pickwick Records had established itself as the dominant company in the field. Pickwick and other labels stuck leasing deals with the majors and a few larger independents, so the companies obtained the rights to recordings by Jack Jones, Sammy Davis, Jr., Nelson Riddle, and other big names. Pickwick repackaged the original albums and issued them on the Pickwick/33 line. In the early '60s, Pickwick sold many titles at 99 cents each in department-store record departments and other outlets where adults shopped. In a few years, the low cost—as cheap as 45-rpm singles—could have brought Pickwick to its knees. Cy Lewis, president of Pickwick International, gave the magazine one of the classic record-industry quotations of all time: "At that level [99 cents] you really have to sharpen your pencil with your costs figured down to a fraction of a cent with any margin at all. It's really profitless prosperity." Pickwick solved the problem by increasing the cost of its albums to $1.98. Fortunately, that didn't kill the "impulse" buy. Pickwick started a new country label named Hilltop Records, which offered quality covers, good vinyl, color, and liner notes. By 1966, Pickwick was pulling in impressive profits. With Hilltop's success, Pickwick raked in one million dollars in sales. Pickwick alone saw seven million dollars in sales in fiscal year 1964. The good times had just begun. From 1964 to 1967, labels comprising the American budget field generated forty million dollars. The low-priced business continued throughout the remaining years of vinyl, then jumped into the budget compact disc line.

LP

Trademarked long-playing record—dubbed the LP. So-called long-playing records have been around for many years, dating back to the early

1900s. Columbia Records' discs were made in various sizes to achieve longer running times. Somebody was always trying to come up with a record that played longer than the conventional ones. Today, the term LP refers to the vinyl era's long-playing record. (See **Microgroove**.)

M

Madam X

It took her a decade to emerge into the public, but when she finally showed up everyone knew she was worth the wait. Before that, no one knew what she looked like or the purpose of her mission. A sketch of her depicted a slender woman dressed in a black off-the-shoulder evening gown and wearing a little black mask that hid her eyes. A secret file of her origins simply read, "The remarkable background of Madam X." She was that confidential until her arrival in the early years of the Cold War. Code-named Madam X, the lady of mystery and suspense came with her groove on. Deep inside the RCA laboratories in New Jersey through World War II, she was a hush-hush company project that had started in 1939. Her mission? Find a replacement for the old shellac 78-rpm disc. To the company's top engineers and technicians, Madam X became a familiar name. They sought to perfect a record that limited distortion. As a result, RCA engineers created a vinyl disc measuring six and seven-eighths inches in diameter. It turned at forty-five revolutions per minute. The first 45s appeared in the stores in late March of 1949, after being introduced to the public that January. Her 45 still lives, despite its age, spinning its way into history. Madam X is forever unmasked.

Magnetic Tape

Changed the way recording was done. It arrived with much notice in the late 1940s. Its timing was perfect, for R&B was bubbling and soon rock 'n' roll would arrive. Suddenly, audio engineers could cut and splice. Gone were the days when performers had to record multiple takes if they fouled up. By the mid-1990s, tape faded in favor of digital recording. But taped didn't die. Some producers liked its sound, maintaining that tape provided a warmth that digital recording did not. This has given tape-recording a mystique that goes hand in hand with vinyl records. The trouble is, the ranks of recorder "repair persons" keep dwindling, too. There is a shortage of tape doctors. (See **Wax**.)

Majors

For decades the name sent cries of fear and loathing from independent record company owners. The monoliths of the record industry have ruled the music business with their empires of sound ever since the early days of the record industry in the late nineteenth century. Back then, American majors consisted of Edison, Victor, and Columbia. At that time, Edison made only cylinder recordings. Victor made only disc recordings. Columbia made both. The big boys owned the patents that tied up a lot of techniques, so any competitors had to deal with the patent holders. When Gennett Records of Richmond, Indiana, challenged this practice in court, Gennett won, and opened the business to other independents. The story of the majors is complicated and lengthy. Let us distill it. In the days before radio, television, and the Internet, many indies didn't bother to record their own records. They leased them to the majors. Some indies cut a few original recordings, but it was easier to tap the catalog of the established labels. Their rosters were diverse. Take the popular vaudeville actor Cal Stewart, who portrayed a rural character called Uncle Josh Weathersby. He began recording with the United States phonograph company in 1893, then started recording for Edison around 1900. He also recorded for other companies. They all paid him per session, until Stewart—one of the most popular recording acts of the period—demanded royalties. In 1903, he signed an exclusive contract with Columbia. On stage, Stewart performed across the country with a troupe that included his wife, sister, and brother. When his three-year deal expired, he freelanced for various labels again, before signing with Victor around 1907. Stewart is a good example of how the majors courted big stars, and how the stars began to demand exclusivity and royalties. When the Great Depression devastated the recording industry, new majors emerged. Edison Records was gone. CBS had purchased Columbia. Victor was now RCA Victor. Columbia, RCA Victor, and Decca were now the major players, with up-and-coming Mercury and Capitol ready to enter the game. By the 1940s, independent labels such as King, Specialty, Savoy, and others began releasing records, primarily in neglected fields of hillbilly and sepia (or black) music. By the early 1950s, the majors discovered that they could make money in these fields, and they began dipping into the indies' pool of talent and genres. The majors remained at around five for some years, until new mergers created more labels. The gap widened between major and independent once the majors again tapped the independents' specialties, the emerging country and soul. They granted multi-million-dollar deals to all manner of big-name acts and those who had the talent to become big stars. The independents redrew their battle lines and focused almost exclusively on country, soul, jazz, and other fields. By 1990, the indies had retreated even further by specializing in smaller-market fields, such as reissues, blues, and subgenres of hip country.

Master Acquisition

Larger labels obtained the rights to local and regional hit singles. Industry insiders reported the transactions as master acquisitions. It was a fancy term for a simple process that peaked in the 1960s. Many local garage bands zoomed onto the charts thanks to master acquisitions. They worked this way: National labels kept close watch on sales figures from local and regional distributors across the country. If a local label happened to be working a hot single somewhere, usually in a larger market or at least in a medium-size one, the national label's A&R director or owner obtained a copy. If he liked it, he descended onto that town with pen, ink, and contract in hand, to lease the master from the smaller label. Sometimes this resulted in a bidding slugfest among the biggies because they were all watching the hot locals, too. Strictly speaking, the umbrella term master acquisition could be applied whenever a company leased *any* master, period. But big-city indies of that period acquired the majority of their independently produced master tapes *before* they were released onto vinyl discs. Tapes went straight from the producer to the label's A&R department. There was no test marketing by local labels. The deal was made on a hope and a prayer. This type of transaction was more often known in the business as master leasing, as in, "The record company leased the master." Another term, master acquisition, more often meant that a national company had bought the rights to a single that was already proving itself in the regional marketplace. For a straight lease-job or a master acquisition, advance payment for a single generally ranged from as low as $500 to as high as $10,000 for something red hot. This was an unusually high-priced transaction reserved for big-name producers with something worthwhile. Producers called the payments up-front or front money, which ultimately was deducted from any royalties owed to the producers. If the record bombed, the producer kept his advance. Two examples of master acquisitions occurred in Michigan in 1966, when the Philadelphia-based Cameo-Parkway label leased "96 Tears" by Question Mark & the Mysterians from the Pa-Go-Go label based in San Antonio, Texas. Also that year, Roulette Records in New York acquired Tommy James' "Hanky Panky" after a Pittsburgh DJ discovered the song on the little Snap label out of Niles, Michigan. In both cases, the songs were cut in small, local studios and released on small labels. Similarly, DJs from the recording artists' hometowns picked up their records and played them until they became regional hits. Most master acquisitions were made with local labels that launched their records in the towns in which the labels operated. Such smaller labels were usually grassroots organizations owned by disc jockeys, managers, and other people who kept their ears to the local music landscape. These small-time label owners released local records with one goal in mind—leasing their masters to national companies. These days, that hope is gone. With the conglomerate super labels owning the commercial recording industry, you don't hear so much about master acquisitions of local records because the smaller indie labels rarely have big regional radio hits. Today's indies are more likely to focus on specialty sales, and if they receive radio airplay it is usually not concentrated in one of the larger Top 40 singles' markets. Albums are still being acquired, but the day of the regional single's master acquisition has dimmed.

Master Tips

Concept devised by the innovative Fred Foster, founder of Nashville's Monument Records. He thought of his master tip while in pursuit of the latest hot local record. The program began in 1963 as Monument's Mighty Master Contest, which paid a bounty of up to $1,000 to anyone who led Foster to a local record that Monument ultimately acquired—and subsequently promoted to the top ten in any trade publication's charts. Obviously, this contest was about as easy to win as a carnival shooting-gallery game. The idea was used for a brief time without a whole lot of success. Foster insisted that a tipster had to send him a copy of the local record as well as full information. If the record hit the top twenty, the tipster received $500. If a record hit the top 100, the tipster got $100. A Monument A&R man of that era couldn't recall any record hitting the top ten.

Master Wax

This term comes from the often-used terms "wax" and "hot wax" during the 1950s. At times they are still used to describe so-called oldies. What was master wax? It was a substance used to coat cylinder recordings at the turn of the last century. After cylinders faded at the dawn of the Great Depression, Edison Records, one of the cylinder's biggest proponents, continued making Ediphone School Records. During World War II, they were made with a wax that could be recorded properly and "at the same time ... withstand a plating solution for at least sixty hours without deterioration," according to company documents published by historian Ron Dethlefson in 1980. The original wax formula, No. 932, was used for years to make master wax for plating. It consisted of a mixture of stearic acid, Montan wax, lead oxide, caustic soda, and then a final coating of more Montan wax. The six-inch Ediphone School Records could be played on Ediphone dictation machines or the Amberola phonographs and others. Four-inchers could be played on any cylinder phonograph. The dictation cylinders were made until 1960.

Mechanical Reproduction

In early days of radio, primarily in the late 1920s and early 1930s, mechanical reproduction meant that radio stations were legally allowed to play recorded music on the air.

Medley

The medley seamlessly combined two or more songs into one recorded performance. Medleys depended on solid, well-written arrangements to smoothly connect two (or occasionally even three or four) songs. The hardest part of arranging a medley was choosing the right songs. They had to mesh perfectly, sounding enough alike in lyric, tempo, and melody that they could almost pass for one song. They had to sound as though they were meant to be together. The medley trend peaked in the 1960s and early 1970s before losing its appeal. Two examples of well-received medleys were "I Say a Little Prayer"/"By the Time I Get to Phoenix" by Glen Campbell and Anne Murray and "Traces"/"Memories" by the Lettermen.

Memphis Sound

The most famous city of the regional recording era. If you were in the record business anywhere in the world, and you didn't know about the famous Memphis Sound, then you were operating at the earth's core. Atlantic's Jerry Wexler knew about it, for sure. So did a long list of producers and executives and artists. Everyone wanted to rub the genie's belly and receive their only wish—a smash done in Memphis. Of course, it is known for its blues and soul, the sounds of Willie Mitchell, Al Green, Booker T. and the M.G.s ("Green Onions"), and so many others who sang and played in this Mississippi River city where the blues flourished in the early 1900s. But there is much more to the Memphis Sound than meets the ear. Everyone knows that it was that good old Southern soul recorded in the Royal Theater, an old movie house-turned-studio, and the Stax Records studio. But often the city's name attracted players from across the country. Memphis became a magnet that pulled in musicians and producers from across the world. Soon Memphis morphed into soul, blues, rock, pop, and country. It could do it all. If anything, pop was bigger than everything else combined. Petula Clark, of "Downtown" fame, came to town to record pop with producer Chips Moman, as did Brenda Lee, Neil Diamond ("Holly Holy"), and Dionne Warwick. Dusty Springfield cut her masterpiece "Son of a Preacher Man" at Moman's American Sound Studios, with a white band of pop-music house musicians who played on hundreds of national and regional chart records, including "Angel of the Morning" by Merilee Rush, and "Single Girl" by Sandy Posey. Because of this cooking musical stew, the Memphis Sound was really the Memphis *Sounds*. Over at American, Dan Penn produced one of the biggest pop hits of 1967, "The Letter" by the Box

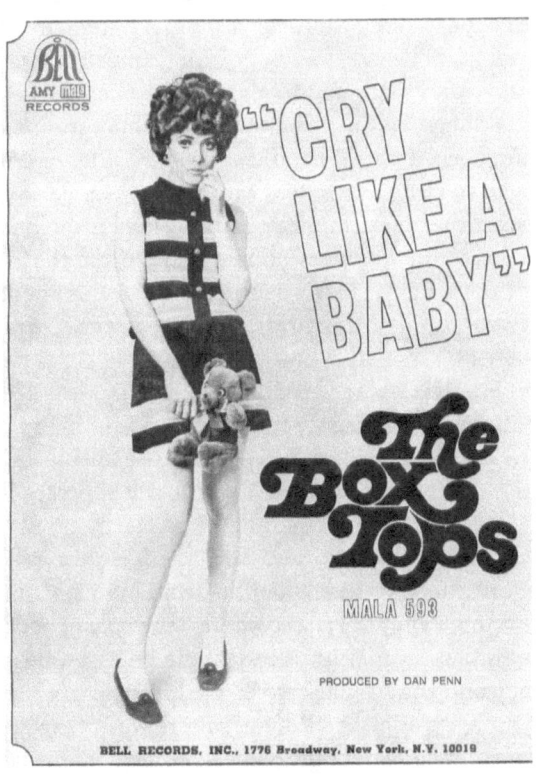

Memphis launched yet another hit in the spring of 1968, when the Box Tops' "Cry Like a Baby" captivated America's young radio audience. The single featured a sitar, a stringed instrument from India. Independent producer Dan Penn, who wrote the song with pianist Spooner Oldham, had already cut "The Letter," a hit for the band, and now Bell Records expected Penn to produce another big hit. He recorded it at Chips Moman's American Sound Studios, where Elvis Presley would later record "Suspicious Minds" and "Kentucky Rain." Under pressure, Penn and Oldham couldn't write what sounded to them like a hit song. Finally, on the morning of the recording session, they sat in a little coffee shop near the studio. Oldham lamented, "I could cry like a baby." Penn jolted to reality. He had his title, and he started to write the song. As they arrived at the studio, he finished it. The record went to number two on *Billboard*'s Hot 100.

Tops, but its follow-up hit, "Neon Rainbow," didn't sell nearly so well. Management at Bell Records threatened to replace him. The equally frustrating thing was, he didn't write either of those songs. He knew his next record was his last if he didn't produce a hit. So he decided to write it with his friend and writing partner, Spooner Oldham, a studio piano player. Neither one of them could think of a song good enough for the Box Tops. They had session time booked at American, and Bell's president knew it. To say there were high expectations would be an understatement. Penn and Oldham stayed up all night before the session, but came up with nothing. Early the next morning, they retreated to a restaurant near the studio, preparing to give up. Oldham laid his head on his arm and groaned, "I could cry like a baby." Penn perked up. "What did you say?" Oldham repeated is comment. Penn began to write lyrics right away. They headed to the studio and took their places at the piano. Fifteen minutes later, as the Box Tops arrived to record, Dan Penn and Spooner Oldham had written the group's next big rock hit, "Cry Like a Baby." Flash back to the 1950s. When Sam Phillips was cutting Sun rockabilly hits by Jerry Lee Lewis and Carl Perkins out of Memphis, a country bass player and truck driver became enthralled with the music business. His name was Slim Wallace. Today, he is an obscure name on the national music scene, and even in Memphis he is not remembered too often. But in 1959, Slim jumped into the business. He was one of the nicest guys in the record business, the mirror opposite of the blustery Syd Nathan at King Records in Cincinnati and Herman Lubinsky at Savoy in New Jersey. Slim was low-key and laid-back. He was living in a brick Cape Cod on Fernwood Avenue when he decided to start his own record label, which he named after the street where he lived. He had watched Phillips do it with Sun, and other guys too, so he believed he could succeed with little money and a lot of hard work. He hired Scotty Moore, formerly Elvis Presley's guitarist, as his A&R man. Moore wasn't exactly rich. He was sleeping in Slim's one-car garage and office. Slim called his label Fernwood Records. It released a number of local hits, but only one became a monster—"Tragedy" by Thomas Wayne and the DeLons. It hit the top five on the pop chart, and the two twenty on the R&B. Its story is indicative of the local record business of that era. Two local songwriters pitched the song to Moore as he was walking on a Memphis street. He liked it, and recorded it on a little studio with a one-track tape recorder. The studio didn't even have an echo chamber. The record broke big nationally and established Fernwood Records as a real label. As for Slim, he wisely kept his day job as a truck driver. One day he was trucking out West and he stopped in a diner to eat. "Tragedy" came on the radio. He exclaimed to a waitress, "That's my record!" She just smiled and politely kept her mouth shut. Most people snickered. Back at the Fernwood office on Fernwood Avenue, his wife was the only employee for a while. Her job was to answer the phone. It rang often, with record distributors and big-shots calling for Slim. Someone asked to speak to the president of Fernwood Records. She said, with a straight face, "I'm sorry, sir, but Mr. Wallace is on the road right now."

Message Songs

In the early 1960s, people in the music business coined a name for songs that sent a particular message to listeners. As *Cashbox* noted, "The 'message' song, as we see it, is that type of pop effort that displays a certain awareness and concern over some social situation or problem that exists in today's society." Examples included "Where Have All the Flowers Gone?" by the Kingston Trio, "Blowin' in the Wind" by Peter, Paul and Mary. The magazine's editorial writer noted that a message song could be more subtle and less political, as in "Up on the Roof" by the Drifters. Why? People were fed up with life in the city.

Microgroove

It changed the way people listened to music. In 1948, Columbia Records introduced its LP (a trademarked project), ten- and twelve-inch discs that played at 33⅓-rpm. The term microgroove evolved because its fine groove widths were only about half the size of conventional 78-rpm grooves—less than one thousandth of an inch on the microgroove bottom. The new LP was made of "unbreakable" Vinylite. Columbia's LP was developed by Dr. Peter Goldmark, the director of engineering research and development for the Columbia Broadcasting System, owner of Columbia Records. He was also the developer of CBS color television. His new LP could hold 43 minutes—"a whole symphony, an entire concerto, or any given combination of music lasting that long," Newsweek reported, "recordings which took up approximately eight-plus inches [on a 78-rpm disc] may now occupy only one-plus inches." Without the microgroove, rock 'n' roll albums of a decade or two later would have hardly been possible.

Micro-Verter

Described by *Newsweek* as a gadget for converting the conventional 78-rpm turntables to handling LPs. In 1949, Columbia Records introduced the Micro-Verter. "It consists of a smaller planetary turntable, with ball-bearing differential—which is placed over the regular spindle," the magazine said. "An astatic pickup is placed on the opposite side of the turntable base from the regular tone arm. To achieve 33⅓-rpm, a lever catches against a switch bar and slows down the planetary mechanism."

The Micro-Verter, which retailed at $24.95, eliminated the need for a separate LP player to be jacked into old sets. Some Micro-Verters were made to accommodate all three major speeds.

Mike Hog

A singer obsessed with being in front of a microphone, even when background singers needed to get closer to it. Spelled mike hog originally, instead of the modern version, mic. This term came from the days of acetate recording when records were often made with one mic for all the vocalists together. Some engineers continued to use the name into the 1960s.

Mini-Mini

Possibly the shortest 45-rpm disc in history. A "mini-mini single" is how record executives described it in 1968. White Whale Records of Los Angeles released the disc, which ran a whopping 32 seconds. (The average single of that time ran three minutes or less.) The single's A-side (and short side) was "Break of Dawn" by J.K. & Co., led by the sixteen-year-old son of Mary Kaye, the singer-guitarist of the Mary Kaye Trio. It featured a clap of thunder and electronic sounds. The flip side, "Little Children," ran the regular length. Despite "Break of Dawn's" brevity, White Whale still charged the regular single price for it. Both songs were also released on the group's LP, *Suddenly One Summer*, which musically depicts a man's life from birth to death. Perhaps the mini-mini was more of a marketing and promotional gimmick than a serious single. Some underground radio stations had begun playing the album and requested that the brief cut be issued as a single.

Miracle Surface

A trademarked anti-static compound known as 317X and developed by RCA Victor in the late 1950s. Its purpose was to help keep vinyl discs clean and free of dust. The company promoted Miracle Surface into the 1960s.

Mix

Final version of a recorded song. Years ago, mixing was a different kind of chore. It was difficult when you worked with one and two tracks. With one-track recorders, the band and singer recorded live. Microphones had to be at the proper levels; no room for mistakes. The mix had to be done on the spot, as sort of a pre-mix, before the tape started rolling. Once the proper volume levels were established for each instrument, including the voice, the engineer taped or cut the session and hoped that nobody made a mistake. When you hear some of those old tapes today, you realize how talented many of the engineers were. Just listen to the early Sun records. Traditionally, a sound engineer mixed the signals from each track and put them on a quarter-inch tape. During the process, he or she could dress up each track sonically, compressing sounds, equalizing, and doing just about anything but making a bad singer sound good. (See **Remix**.)

MOA

Chicago-based jukebox and coin machine operators' main trade association. Formed as Music Operators of America (MOA) in 1948. MOA. It had clout. Its founding came just in time for the beginning of R&B and rock 'n' roll. In 1969, the MOR sent a special mailing to record companies telling them that jukebox operators bought $60 million worth of records in 1967. These discs were played on half a million jukeboxes. These days, the MOA still operates, although the early emphasis on jukeboxes is now spread around to all types of coin-operated machines that you see in the lobbies of movie theaters and other places where young people congregate.

Money Music

A popular *Record World* column about rock and R&B singles, written by staff member Kal Rudman. The column often ran a full page and onto a second, and it was crammed with tips and tidbits on new records and recording artists. The name was appropriate; it was one of *Record World's* most-read columns. Rudman watched the new releases carefully and followed the charts and the varied distributors' reports on up-and-coming singles. The magazine gave him free reign to offer his opinions, as he did in the October 22, 1966, issue: "There are very few 'geniuses' among record company execs. Though we pick our share [of hit records], it is at best an educated guess. I know a lot of record execs who would have gladly paid $20,000 for 'Mind Excursion,' Trade Winds. This record is different, refreshing, and I predicted Top 3." The record was a hit in Washington, D.C., and went to No. 1 in Sacramento, he wrote, "but it sure isn't doing the great things most 'smart money' would have figured. And this is how 'winners and losers' get that way." Money music was just that—big money if you managed to get a hit.

Mono

One-channel sound. Many Top 40 hits were recorded in mono in the 1950s and '60s. In those times, it was mostly a monaural world out there—one track for all speakers and tape recorders. When you played a mono record over just one speaker, you lost nothing. Many of the Sun Records classics—early Elvis Presley and Carl Perkins and others—were recorded on one track. You can find the word mono at the top of many old album covers. If you listen closely to old mono recordings, you can hear musical mistakes now and then. Perhaps the engineer cared more about the live feel than the mistakes, but maybe it was the best take they could get. No matter how record companies tried to jazz up the term—monophonic, whatever—it was still one track. Recorders recorded across the tape, using all of it. Records were pressed monaurally. Even when multi-track recording arrived, records still lagged behind. Mono singles thrived until the late 1960s. Interestingly, a Capitol album from the mid-1960s noted in fine print at the bottom of the back cover: "This monophonic microgroove recording is playable on monophonic and stereo phonographs. It cannot become obsolete. It will continue to be a source of outstanding sound reproduction." Though sales of mono LPs had been declining slowly, but not radically, through the 1960s, they were still the king of the album domain. In 1966, the sale of mono LPs surpassed stereo, 61.4 million to 38.6 million copies. Then in 1967, the turntables turned against mono. Units sold: stereo, 54.1 million; mono, 45.9. The record companies were behind the coup. In 1967, they increased the prices of mono LPs to those of stereo versions. The companies knew that buyers would choose stereo albums over mono—if the price were the same. The companies wanted an all-stereo market. Their strategy worked. A year later, in 1968, 94.2 million stereo records were sold, compared with 5.8 million mono. The LP's mono world had ended. But for singles, mono would continue for a few years. Old habits do not end easily. Many recording engineers liked mono, and so did some radio stations. Despite losing the war, mono battled on until the mid-1970s.

MOR

Synonymous with adult contemporary in the 1960s. MOR was a record industry abbreviation for middle-of-the-road music. MOR was synonymous with adult programming. In the 1960s, Andy Williams, Johnny Mathis, and Jerry Vale were three famous MOR singers on Columbia Records. Their records popped up frequently on the MOR charts.

Mother

A metal copy of the acetate. Stampers are made from the mother. (See **Stamper** and **Iron Mothers**.)

Muirized

Blacklisted. Intimidated. Anyone in the entertainment business in 1950 probably knew what "muirized" meant. And it was not healthy for a career. In short, "muirized" meant the story of Jean Muir, a television and movie actress who began a film career in the 1930s. She was removed from the set of NBC's *Aldrich Family* only minutes before show time after a sponsor, General Foods, feared she might be a "controversial personality." The company had just discovered that her name had recently appeared in an anti-communist publication that was known for "outing" leftists in the movie industry. This happened in the post-war years when Americans were learning that some communists, fellow travelers, and dupes were working in everything from Hollywood studios to the State Department—even in the record business. While the war in Korea was raging, *Billboard* devoted several pages to the Muir incident and its ramifications for the entertainment industry. (The magazine then covered television and other forms of media.) A headline blared, "Hysteria Hits." Though the magazine sympathized with the plight of liberal entertainers, it printed a piece listing steps that liberal groups should take to avoid being taken over by what the publication called "commies." In this respect the magazine showed that it was tough on communism. Muir's husband vehemently defended her, but she was blacklisted. She retired. Later, she became a college drama teacher. A number of record-business people with leftist ties worried that they might be caught up in the furor. Folk singer Josh White received his share of *Billboard* coverage that year. He testified before the House Un-American Activities Committee that he was naïve and didn't know that some causes he supported were infiltrated by reds and radicals. As *Billboard* put it: "Played for Sucker, Says Folk Singer."

Multiplying Records

Manufacturing master recordings the hard way. In the late 1800s and early 1900s, before durable, high-quality master recordings were made for copying cylinder recordings, recording laboratory employees would sit behind several recording machines and "multiply records"—that is, they would record copies from very breakable master cylinders. A finite number of successful copies could be made—usually no more than a few dozen. When they went bad, the record company had to bring in the singer and musicians to re-record a new master cylinder. From it new copies could be made.

Multi-Track Recorder

The savior of 1960s rock 'n' roll. Multi-track machines—with more than two tracks—were not widely used until those early years when the

Beatles recorded their early masterpieces on four tracks. In the hinterlands, many little studios still used two- or three-track machines. Technology leaped forward quickly. Eight-track machines dominated briefly in the late 1960s before giving way to sixteen tracks in the early '70s. Multi-track mania set in, as productions grew more elaborate. Drums alone might occupy six tracks. By coupling two or more recorders, tracks expanded to forty-eight and then sixty-four.

Muscle Shoals Sound

It happened in Alabama in the early 1960s and continued deep into the 1980s. Sounds emanating from Muscle Shoals—pop and commercial R&B—came from some of the nation's best studio musicians. Radio programmers looked twice at singles bearing the words: "Recorded in Muscle Shoals," then often slapped them on the turntables. The hits first started flowing from a studio owned by Rick Hall, who operated FAME Recording (Florence Alabama Music Enterprises). In the early 1960s, he produced "You Better Move On" by Arthur Alexander. Soon came more hits, including "Mustang Sally," "Funky Broadway," and "In the Midnight Hour." All by Wilson Pickett. Aretha Franklin came in. So did Clarence Carter and his "Funky Fever." The locals greeted visitors with a sign that summed it up: "Welcome to Muscle Shoals, Hit Recording Capital of the World." The rhythm section consisted of four white men who were entrenched in the community. They had wives, kids, and mortgages. In a dispute with Hall over pay, the four quit and opened their own place, Muscle Shoals Sound Studio, in a funky little building on Jackson Highway. They called themselves the Swampers: David Hood, bass; Jimmy Johnson, guitar; Barry Beckett, piano; and Roger Hawkins, drums. They started playing on hits for Atlantic Records, including "Take a Letter, Maria" and "There's Always Something There to Remind Me" by R.B. Greaves. Through the 1970s, their fame—not FAME—spread throughout the world. Paul Simon arrived. Bob Seger cut "Old Time Rock 'n' Roll." Delbert McClinton recorded "Giving It Up for Your Love." When the Swampers moved into a larger studio, the hits continued. Record companies came in to get the special sound—a special feeling—that the Swampers brought to any record. Meanwhile, Rick Hall was still cooking too, with a new rhythm band. He went into pop music too, recording the Osmonds, Paul Anka, and other singers. More studios, not as well known, opened. The record business couldn't get any hotter than the scene in Muscle Shoals. Then came a sea change: Digital recording. Less emphasis on a studio-band sound. Home studios. By the late 1980s, things had slowed down in the "Hit Recording Capital of the World." It continues to function, but today the name Muscle Shoals is not on the lips of record label owners, radio executives, and musicians. Most young musicians don't even know that the Hit Capital existed.

Music Business

A New York–based magazine that reached its summit in the mid-1960s. *Music Business* published its own charts, columns, feature stories, and industry news. It was a nominal competitor of *Record World*. By late 1964, *MB* had absorbed Charlie Lamb's *Music Reporter* magazine, a smaller but similar trade publication. Lamb became a writer for *MB*. At *MB*'s peak in 1964, it carried a special section on the seventy-fifth anniversary of the founding of Columbia Records. In the mid-1960s, *Record World* bought Music Business, thereby increasing *Record World*'s sagging advertising base. If Record World hadn't connected with Music Business, it would have folded under the weight of the Big Three trades—*Billboard*, *Cash Box*, and *Record World*.

Music Director

The radio station music director, the person instrumental in breaking so many hit records, was one of the most important cogs in the record business from the 1950s through the 1970s. Record promotion men sought out the directors in an effort to convince them to play records. By 1968, however, things were changing in radio. "The music director," wrote Claude Hall of *Billboard*, "is becoming a dodo bird." By then, Hall said, the full-time music director had been replaced at many stations with a DJ who had no real interest in the music nor the time to objectively listen to incoming records. He was music director in name only. This brought a big change, and it hurt the independent labels and their unknown artists. Often the full-time music directors would discover obscure gems among the hundreds of records sent to stations every week. And if they liked them, they would place those records on their stations' playlists. They would also take time to turn over records and try the B sides, which sometimes became hits as well. Harry Carlson of Cincinnati's Fraternity Records used to tell the story of how "Memphis," the guitar instrumental by Lonnie Mack, became a hit in 1963. He said he did not receive any interest when he mailed the record to radio stations. So he called a friendly music director and told him that if he would play "Memphis" regularly for several weeks, and if it did not become a hit for the station, he would never bother the director again. The director played it. The record caught on with his audience, then exploded to other stations, and finally "Memphis" hit the national top ten. So what killed the music director's position? Financial constraints, for one thing. Stations saved money by cutting loose their directors. Also, stations across the country were being purchased increasingly by chain radio companies, who preferred to program all their stations' music from the companies' headquarters. There was no need for a local expert who loved music and knew the workings of the record business and the reputations of its hit-makers. *Billboard* conducted a poll in the spring of 1968 and concluded that "an alarming number of music directors do not listen to all records and others have a closed mind," Hall wrote. The decline of the real music director was a sad trend.

Music Guild

In 1948 the Music Guild of America, a jukebox operators' association, founded a small publication initially called the *Music Guild*. In only a few pages the magazine covered the jukebox industry. With help from the operators, record companies broke records and juiced up their sales from the boxes. The magazine was definitely a juke trade publication, a rather boring publication if you were in radio and other businesses. It evolved into the *Music Vendor* magazine. (See **Music Vendor**.)

Music Guild of America

Trade association for jukebox outlet owners. Its purpose was to promote, defend, and inform members. By the late 1950s, they felt pressure from all sides. "Your jukeboxes are competing with background music and television," noted the editors of *Music Vendor*. Based in New Jersey, the Music Guild of America—commonly referred to as the MOA—continued to represent the jukebox business until it began to lose its once-impressive share of the music-business market in the 1980s. Through its trade magazine, the MOA reached juke operators, one-stops, DJs, and retailers.

Music Machine

Originally, it meant the jukebox. This was before the name jukebox arrived in the 1930s and 1940s. (The Music Machine was also the name of a rock band that recorded the hit "Talk, Talk" on the Original Sound label in 1966.) The name Music Machine began to fade after World War II, and today the reference is obscure.

Music Mite

Small, coin-operated jukebox that played ten records. Most of the Mite boxes that have survived are equipped with a large spindle to play 45s. Each box is made of attractive wood, with several 78s painted on the sides. The boxes could be mounted on tabletops or on top of special stands to make the machines more accessible to customers. The Mite was made in Chicago by the Williams Manufacturing Company from 1944 to 1958. Some jukebox clubs sell repair manuals for the mighty Music Mite. The machine evokes images of teenagers popping a nickel into the slot and dancing the jitterbug.

Music Publishers' Protective Association

A clearance organization begun in the 1940s when the government was sending thousands of records and pieces of sheet music overseas to boost troop morale. During World War II, when fewer advocates and protections existed for music publishers and composers, two groups were formed to monitor the use of music. Though not intended to be the junkyard pit bulls of the music industry, the groups did take their roles and their best interests seriously. They genuinely wanted to help do their part to win the war. The Music Publishers' Protective Association (MPPA) had a lot to accomplish. The army was distributing to troops what it called the Hit Kit, made up of lyrics and music, and V Disc 78-rpm records. (The MPPA was not a part of ASCAP.) The MPPA also oversaw wartime orders for music productions and generally kept a collective eye open for any misuse of members' copyrights and sales. A similar group, the Songwriters' Protection Association (SPA), provided similar safeguards for writers. It brought its own interesting aspect to the war: Songwriters went overseas and across the country to entertain and perform. The group felt that the public knew the big singing stars, but not the songwriters. It gave the composers an opportunity to do what many of them had wanted to do all their lives: sing and play before an audience. After the war ended, privately-run organizations popped up to resume some of the functions of the MPPA and SPA in the peace-time market.

Music Reporter

Founded in the early 1960s by Nashville music operative Charlie Lamb. *Music Reporter* was a weekly trade magazine for which Lamb served as president, publisher, and managing editor. His goal: Compete with *Billboard*, *Cash Box*, and *Record World*. All three were based in New York and had bureaus in Nashville and Los Angeles. Lamb wanted to mine the advertising from Nashville's Music Row, where he had spent his career, yet provide a nationwide focus. The small magazine reached its zenith in the mid-'60s. He offered a whole page of briefs called "Dateline Music City," that included the country market. In time, the magazine faded, but not until it had risen to the No. 4 position in circulation among the major record-industry trade magazines. And as far as credibility, the *Music Reporter* ranked with *Billboard*.

Music Vendor

Published as a simple jukebox trade magazine named *Music Guild* in the late 1950s. Soon the *Music Guild* changed its name to *Music Vendor* and devoted itself to predicting hits, reviewing records, and listing them. But the focus was still on jukebox operators. The *Vendor* was much smaller than its competitors, *Billboard* and *Cash Box*. In 1964, *Music Vendor* changed its name to *Record World*. *Music Vendor* was roughly the dimensions of the original *Reader's Digest*. The parent company also owned the rights to a half a dozen other music publications, including *Hit Parade*, *Harlem Hit Parade*, and *Holiday Hit Parade*. Seeking to expand its reading audience, the magazine started accepting advertisements. Its charts were designed to guide vendors in programming jukeboxes and purchasing records for their routes. By 1958, disc jockeys had taken an interest in the magazine, and it began to run more stories about the record industry. *Music Vendor* was known for its strong page-one editorials and its "Top 200" hits—100 popular, fifty R&B, and fifty country-and-western. It also carried one-stop charts and advance record releases. Long-time editor David Steinberg called the magazine "primarily a service publication." It began to decline when advertising became more difficult to obtain in the second half of the 1960s.

N

National Breakout

A record on its way up—fast. *Billboard* magazine once listed the single records that were breaking nationally, usually, in many markets. Such records jumped up the charts by large leaps in their first week. They were regional breakouts. Many of them would go on to be hits in some form, sort of like minor-league baseball's phenoms. Some were busts, too.

Needle

They hugged the grooves with the strength of tungsten. They were sharp, too. No wonder those old 78s didn't last too long with that thick needle digging into the grooves. By the 1950s, the "needle" no longer had a sharp tip, yet people couldn't stop using the old name. "Rather it is a cone with a smooth ball-shaped tip," as 1950s Columbia engineers described it. "When playing records, the needle vibrates in the grooves at an astonishing rate to produce dynamic forces, and only a first-class needle can give first-class reproduction." Columbia, which also manufactured phonographs, made certain that customers understood the temporary nature of needles. "A permanent needle," the company told them, "is 'permanent' only in the sense that a permanent wave is." How can you tell if your needle is worn out? Today, you will know when your needle tells you: Your record skips (needle jumps out of the grooves) and the sound deteriorates. Those pioneer Columbia sound engineers recommended two kinds of needles. A diamond needle is the finest made and most expensive, but more economical over time. It outlasts ten to twenty-five sapphire needles and will play about 1,000 hours. A sapphire needle, with a standard-grade tip, lasts three to ten times longer than lower-priced osmium needle, Sapphires usually wear out after fifty hours of play, while the lower-quality osmium needle will last only about fifteen hours. The osmium needle wore out records quickly, if it was not changed in time. I find it interesting that some of these record terms date back to the early 1900s. The definitions just don't want to give up the ghost. So it is with the venerable needle. At the phonograph's peak time, the 1960s, there were some twenty major "needle" manufacturers, including Pfanstiehl near Chicago, Fidelitone of Chicago and Fine-Tone in Brooklyn. When the entire phonograph industry went into a tailspin in the 1990s, many of the needle manufacturers closed or started making something else.

New Orleans Sound

Originality at its best. Record executives called it the New Orleans Sound because it was. Most regional music capitals didn't define themselves by one dominant sound, but New Orleans did. Executives could listen to a record and tell that it was cut in New Orleans. The Sound was most successful on the national pop charts in the 1950s and '60s, when a lot of black hits came out of the Crescent City. Like its most famous singer, Fats Domino, the music had a party feel. It felt happy and loose, reminding one of a band playing down in the French Quarter. The city and its music were filled with life and laughter. New Orleans is where jazz met R&B and flourished in a commercial way that could be appreciated by kids across the country. The sound was achieved and spread around the world because many of the hits from New Orleans were made with local musicians. When rock 'n' roll began in the mid–1950s, many vocalists and groups didn't know which songs to sing. They had grown up listening to Sinatra. In New Orleans, Frankie Ford didn't have such a problem. "I was one of the more polished acts [in 1959]. Some performers could sing only two songs during the transition from early rock to the Beatles. Everything was turned inside out, and nobody knew where the business was going." His hit "Sea Cruise," is now considered a classic New Orleans early rocker. Who can forget its fog horn? Recording for the Ace and Imperial labels, Ford cut four more nationally charted records, but he never returned to the top fifteen where "Sea Cruise" landed in early 1959.

The marginal records didn't seem to bother him. Music was all that mattered. He turned his one hit into a lifelong career in music—and in the unmistakable New Orleans sound. Other cities had players and singers from all over the country, but not the town of the Basin Street Beat. Memphis is known for the Memphis Sound, but that is a generic one. Historically, blues was its real sound. Yet to most young record buyers in the 1960s, Memphis meant Elvis Presley, Johnny Cash, Jerry Lee Lewis, and the Sun Records roster—mainly rockabilly and country. Yet ask people who grew up listening to Top 40 music in the 1960s, and they will name other Memphis hits, including "Suspicious Minds" by Elvis, "Hooked on a Feeling" by B.J. Thomas, and "The Letter" by the Box Tops. In other words, Memphis was more of a potpourri of sounds. In New Orleans, the players and musicians were a

Lee Dorsey exuded the New Orleans sound. His collaboration with songwriter-producer Allen Toussaint took the party feel of the Crescent City nationally and globally. Dorsey was born in 1926 in New Orleans, and he never deviated from his roots. In 1959, he began recording for the local Rex label, then signed with several national labels until he landed with Fury, which gave him "Ya Ya," a big hit in 1961. He named his band the Ya Ya Band and recorded steadily for five years, always gaining local airplay. Finally, he landed at Amy Records in New York. This arrangement resulted in "Ride Your Pony" and in 1966 the hit "Working in the Coal Mine." Lee Dorsey died in New Orleans in 1986.

more tight-knit group. Band leader and songwriter Dave Bartholomew and producer-writer Allen Toussaint cut many of the hits over at audio engineer Cosimo Matassa's little studio with its outdated equipment. Cosimo's studio was about the only one in town for years in those early days. He cut records such as "Working in a Coal Mine" by Lee Dorsey, "Mother-in-Law" by Ernie K-Doe, "Barefootin'" by Robert Parker, and, the New Orleans' masterpiece, "Tell It Like It Is" by Aaron Neville. There's always a story behind a hit, and

Ernie K-Doe had one about "Mother-In-Law." When Allen Toussaint was working as a staff producer at Minit Records in New Orleans in 1963, just before the Beatles arrived, he wrote the song, but didn't like it. So he tossed his lyric sheet in a trash can. But vocalist K-Doe (real name Ernest Kadore, Jr.) picked it out of the can and told Toussaint he wanted to cut it because the song's message was universal. "Everybody will have a mother-in-law," K-Doe told writer Bill Griggs twenty-five years later. "Do you dig where I'm comin' from? Someone is getting married every second of every day." And twenty-five years later, K-Doe was still singing "Mother-In-Law" in clubs across the country and in New Orleans. As for Lee Dorsey, his lucky day came while he was at work in a body shop owned by disc jockey Ernie the Whip. Dorsey was singing while working underneath a car. In came record producer Reynauld Richard, who had strolled in to pick up his vehicle. Suddenly he heard a voice, a soulful, wonderful voice. He liked the sound and traced it to the car that was being repaired. Dorsey's voice echoed from underneath. Without seeing Dorsey, Richard yelled, "Hey, you wanna make a record?" The unseen voice replied, "Of course I do!" That forgotten song under the car started a long recording career for a true Crescent City original. Toussaint would write and produce Dorsey's 1966 hit "Working in a Coal Mine." The happy soul records brought the New Orleans Sound to the Hot 100.

New 600

A musical workhorse. In 1954, Ampex introduced its *600* model tape recorder, which would become a staple of the music business. At first, people called it the New *600*. The *600* was sold as a professional recorder aimed at the home hi-fi market. Ampex assumed that buyers of this caliber of recorder would not need editing facilities, so they built a single synchronous motor to run at seven-and-a-half inches per second instead of fifteen, which was normally used to make studio recordings. However, the *600* would be used in the offices of record companies and song publishers for years. It also would be used in the field to record radio-station commercials. In some cases, record producers would make recordings with it in clubs and even in makeshift studios. Remember, those were the days when mono and AM radio still reigned. So in some cases records could still be made "on the cheap," particularly by traveling producers who were recording old-time country, blues, and some R&B. But the single-speed *600* was not expressly meant for making records. It was intended for exactly what it came to be used for: office use and sophisticated home use. *Radio & Television* magazine, a trade publication, loved the *600*. "Like all professional-type recorders the 600 does not incorporate a speaker or audio amplifier," the magazine explained in a review and introductory story. "A separate amplifier-speaker unit, the Model 620, in a matching portable case, is available for those who want a single-package unit." In the offices of A&R men and song publishers, the venerable *600* played many mix-down masters for aspiring producers and artists. It was a classic.

Newies

New releases. In 1973, *Cash Box* ran an editorial titled "Radio: What about Newies Slots?" The magazine urged radio to play more new records to help the record industry break more, well, newies. This irked one Neil McIntyre, program director of WPIX, a New York FM station that was already devoting a whole program, called "PIX Newies," to new records. He wrote a letter to *Cash Box*, chastising the magazine for claiming that newies was a newly arrived word in the jargon of the radio and record domain. His admirable interest in newies seems misplaced. Even in that somewhat less competitive era, it seems hard to believe that radio stations could afford to devote an entire program to playing only new records. Labels had a hard enough time convincing program directors to play one new record, especially one by an unknown act. Anyhow, *Cash Box* printed his letter inside a new story on the subject. Mr. McIntyre, in a nah-nah-nah moment, ended his missive with this admonition: "P.S. You're not spelling New-ies right!" *Cash Box* responded by titling its story, "What about the 'Newies?' Some Stations Have Got 'Em!" Now, all those newies—New-ies—are all oldies.

Nipper

The canine symbol of the Victor Talking Machine Company of Camden, New Jersey, in the early 1900s. The dog is now intertwined with its owner, RCA Victor. The company used the Nipper figure for decades. First appearing in magazine advertisements of the period, the dog was cocking its head when its master was playing a talking machine record. Accompanying Nipper was an unforgettable slogan, "His Master's Voice." Nipper became so popular that by the late teens Victor was distributing white canine figurines with its machines. At record stores in the 1950s, large Nippers sat outside the door, enticing customers to enter. Nipper is a true record-business icon.

No Hole

A jukebox operator's term used to describe defective discs, usually seven-inchers, without a hole. The pressing plant failed to punch them out.

No Label

Another jukebox term to describe discs, usually seven-inchers, without labels. The pressing plant forgot to put them on.

Novelty Records, Acoustic Era

A staple of the record industry at the end of the nineteenth and the beginning of the twentieth century. The novelty recording evolved over the decades as people became more accustomed to phonographs. In the earliest acoustic days, of course, nearly everything was a novelty: people laughing, imitations of birds and chimes, funny songs, monologues, ethnic humor, and country humor. Like other contemporary recordings of the day, the novelty was boosted by eager listeners who had never experienced recorded sound. The discs and cylinders carried descriptions such as "comic song," "comic selection," and "laughing song." In its June 1897 catalog, Columbia Records listed banjo solos, xylophone solos, "artistic whistling" by John Yorke Atlee, "negro specialties" by white comedians Billy Golden and Len Spencer, and a new series by W.O. Beckenbaugh, "the leather-lunged auctioneer." Monologist Russell Hunting, originator of the famous Casey series of recordings, became another popular performer, entertaining with the antics of Mr. Casey, an Irish character. Another Irishman, Pat Brady, came to life through Dan Kelly, who recorded for the Ohio Phonograph Company. As the immediacy of the phonograph waned in the early 1900s, the novelty record held its ground, even when, in 1925, the electric microphone arrived, bringing more varied records. Record companies' back lists, consisting of their older records, became passe, however, for they were limited in comparison to the better, more recently recorded electrical performances. As the phonograph evolved further in the early 1920s, it nurtured all kinds of music and spoken performances, as well as the novelty record.

Novelty Records, Radio Era

Blossomed in a small but fertile corner of radio. Veteran DJ and record producer Shad O'Shea, who produced hundreds of novelties for himself and other acts, summed up the novelty disc in just two sentences. "It's the biggest gamble in the record business. It'll make a fortune or be so obscure that even your mother never heard of it." To some record-business operators, novelties of the radio era fell under a broad umbrella, encompassing more than just funny records. To other A&R men, novelties were strictly humorous. In the '60s, there were serious spoken "novelties" such as "An Open Letter to My Teen-Age Son" by Victor Lundberg, patriotic novelties such as "The Battle Hymn of Lt. Calley" by C Company and Terry

Nelson, generic novelty songs such as "Little Arrows" by Leapy Lee, Christmas novelties (a later one was "Grandma Got Run Over by a Reindeer"), and other types of novelties that radio stations played. Some, like Lunberg's hit, were also in other categories, such as the recitation record. Perhaps back in radio's earlier years, some music directors conveniently started

When the Chipmunks, a novelty group developed by Ross Bagdasarian, hit in 1958, jazz players Don Elliott and Granville Burland created the Nutty Squirrels. The novelty record was in full bloom then, and the Squirrels made it to television with an animated series in 1960. Their two charted records were "Uh-Oh (Part 1)" and "Uh-Oh (Part 2)," the latter hitting the national top fifteen in 1959. Americans had a sense of humor then.

lumping these varied kinds of records together, despite their incongruous nature. Back then, a novelty was anything that didn't fit into the conventional record or radio categories. All this craziness began to flourish in the early 1900s and continued into the 1920s. Then came the Great Depression. Slowly, the need for recorded music increased again as the economy limped into the 1940s—and into war. Despite shellac rationing, which limited disc manufacturing, novelty records persisted, mostly with cute post-war songs like "The Thing," recorded about 1950 by Phil Harris and others. In the post-war years of the late 1940s, people were feeling good about themselves and their country. The baby boom had started and, coincidentally, in 1949 RCA Victor introduced the 45-rpm disc. When coupled with a new youthful music, first called rhythm and blues and later rock 'n' roll, the 45 took on new meaning. It became a symbol of the new youthful music. As the 45 helped boost rock, the novelty received a free ride. Dickie Goodman and Bill Buchanan, young New York songwriters, developed the cut-in (or break-in) record, on which they spliced a recorded narrative to brief lines from currently popular records. They hit first with "The Flying Saucer (Part 1)" on Luniverse Records, then came back with more cut-ins, including "Buchanan and Goodman on Trial." The cut-in was made purely for fun, and it was enthusiastically received by its young fans. Goodman established a career with it, becoming the cut-in champion and its most well-known practitioner. With the cut-in came other kinds of novelty singles. By the mid-1950s, the heyday of the modern novelty record had begun. Radio was receptive; that was the key. Novelties became outrageous, leaving behind the typical novelty song of prior years for crazy stories or songs meant to grab the listener by the ears for no longer than two-and-a-half minutes. It worked, too. Disc jockeys would jump on a novelty and play it until the public could take no more of it. Then it would be relegated to the junk pile of modern sounds, rarely to be heard again unless it was tied to a holiday (Christmas and Halloween, for example.) A hit songwriter named Ross Bagdasarian changed his name to David Seville, in honor of Seville, Spain, where he had served in the U.S. Air Force. He recorded "The Witch Doctor" smash for Liberty Records in 1958. It hit number one. Later that year, he developed the high-pitched, fast-talking record "The Chipmunk Song" for Christmas. The good doctor's voice came by accident, while Bagdasarian played back a tape on the recorder at a faster speed. That year he conceived the Chipmunk characters while on vacation at Yosemite National Park. He saw a chipmunk walk across the road, and suddenly he knew what to do. His next record featured the Chipmunks—Alvin, Simon, and Theodore—singing "The Chipmunk Song." It sold nearly five million copies and established a separate enterprise for Seville. He set up licensing agreements and continued to make more hit records as the Chipmunks. Encouraged by his reception, Seville developed other novelty characters, although none of them were met with such enthusiasm and popularity as the Chipmunks. Seville's personal financial success occurred in part because radio stations played novelty records. Radio offered the ultimate diversity with everything from country to folk to novelties. In 1958, country singer Sheb Wooley, later known for his acting role in *Rawhide*, wrote and recorded "The Purple People Eater," a huge hit for MGM. But not all novelties were silly. By the early 1960s, some novelty records were, well, beyond silly. They were plain weird. In 1962, "Mr. Custer" by Larry Verne told the story of a soldier lamenting his impending death at Custer's Last Stand. Also that year Ray Stevens, a great novelty man but also a terrific singer of straight songs, brought out "Ahab the Arab." The Hollywood Argyles—actually, producer Gary Paxton—gave the world "Alley Oop" in 1960, and in 1963 Australian Rolf Harris came along with the infectious song "Tie Me Kangaroo Down, Sport." A year earlier, popular horror films mated with the novelty record when Bobby "Boris" Pickett and the Crypt Kickers imitated actor Boris Karloff for "The Monster Mash," which unleashed many horror-themed novelties. (The mash in "The Monster Mash" referred to the popular dance of the period.) In 1966, New York recording engineer Jerry Samuels wrote and performed perhaps the ultimate insane novelty with "They're Coming to Take Me Away, Ha-Haaa!" It became one of the best-selling of its genre. He did it for fun while his boss, the studio owner, wasn't around to monitor him. Because Samuels' voice became increasingly fast and zany by the record's end, mental health advocates demanded the song be banned. While all this was happening on Top 40 radio, country and rock music were not to be outdone by the basic novelty. Over the years they developed their own novelty songs. There were Brian Hyland's "Itsy Bitsy Teenie Weenie Yellow Polka Dot Bikini" in 1960, "Surfin' Bird" (mostly an instrumental novelty, no less) in 1964, and "Yakety Yak" by the Coasters R&B group in 1958. As country music joined the craze, Homer and Jethro provided laughs on their RCA Victor discs in the 1950s and early 1960s, including "That Hound Dog in the Window." And Sheb Wooley returned—as Ben Colder—with "Don't Go Near the Eskimos," "Hello Walls No. 2," "Harper Valley PTA (Later that Same Day)," and "Little Green Apples No. 2." The 1970s brought more topical novelties. C.W. McCall arrived with a giant hit, "Convoy," which mirrored the public's brief obsession with the citizens band radio. Meri Wilson hit with "Telephone Man" in 1977 and Rick Dees, the Los Angeles disc jockey, came along with "Disco Duck" in 1976. The 1980s inspired another topical hit, "Pac-Man Fever" by jingles writers Jerry Buckner and Gary Garcia, and a Michael Jackson spoof called "Eat It" by "Weird Al" Yankovic, an accordionist who has forged a career from such records. By then, however, radio had begun to lose interest in novelties, although record producers had not. Lacking sustained radio play, most of the novelty records became just that—a real novelty on the radio. They were relegated to jukeboxes and parties. It is only fitting that this happened as the 45-rpm disc was declining and the compact disc was gaining popularity. The main years of the modern novelty occurred at the beginning of the rock era, 1955–1970, when radio was still receptive to the offbeat singles. Now, the definition of novelty record means anything out of the ordinary in the record business.

O

Obscene Records

Over-the-top sexual humor, and downright dirty discs that were, in many places, illegal to sell. There seems little difference between party records and "obscene records" of the 1950s. To avoid prosecution, labels often used the words "party record" on their LP covers. Fine lines separated party records, risqué records, and obscene records. Party and risqué were often lumped together, but obscene ones were the untouchables of the business. Today, obscene records are passe. Perhaps someone is cutting them in some format, but the need to get a laugh from a dirty record is no longer as prevalent in the time of Internet pornography and bawdy humor on television. In the early days of vinyl and into the 1970s, a record company chief could record, press, and release a party record without running into the local constable or being ostracized by fellow record executives. In fact, larger independents such as Jubilee and King did it without incurring censure. Other labels tried it, too. However, if someone cut and released an *obscene* record, he or she might end up in jail and shunned by the industry. Mainstream pressing plants pressed party records, but only the smaller studios and plants dared record and press obscene records. Their owners had to keep one eye cocked toward the parking lot in the dead of night. They knew the police might arrest them. Nonetheless, *proving* the difference between a party record and an obscene one was difficult. In Cincinnati in 1953, a young record store employee and part-time songwriter was busted in a raid at a small, local pressing plant that was producing obscene records on the sly. During daylight hours, the company made country records. Most likely the company's studio did the raunchy recording, too. Police charged the kid with "possession of obscene recordings," and seized 5,000 discs. He claimed he was only working there part time one night while the owner, who had approved the pressings, was vacationing in Texas. No matter. The FBI got involved in the case. The Feds wanted to see if this little pressing plant was a part of a regional or national ring. A federal judge sentenced the kid to a year and a day in prison. By then, the plant owner had returned home, and he must have worked out a deal. The kid—who would later become one of the best recording engineers in the country—ended up avoiding a prison sentence. But the act of pressing obscene records was not as minor as jaywalking. Few record men with any reputation ever admitted to recording, pressing, or even listening to truly obscene records. (See **Risque Records** and **Party Records**.)

O.C. Center

Trademarked name by Capitol Records, Hollywood, to describe the firm's Optional Center 45, a disc with a ready-made spindle inside the record hole so that it could be played on three-speed phonographs. Owners could punch out the center to play the disc on the new 45 changers.

Off-Centered

Discs pressed with holes positioned improperly. They were referred to as "off-centered." The affected products were usually 45-rpm discs. The problem originated in the pressing plants, which pressed holes where they shouldn't be—sometimes in the middle of grooves. Other times, the holes were centered but the paper label was not. Disc manufacturers blamed the problem on the labor force.

Oldies

Began in the late 1950s when fans sought records from the beginning of rock 'n' roll. Oddly enough, the early days had happened only five or six years earlier. No matter. The desire was there. The original term oldies meant something specific: doo-wop singles. Soon the demand for oldie LPs increased too. As *Music Business* magazine put it in 1964: "The evolution of the term oldie in recent years is comparable to what has happened to such originally specific terms as folk and hootenanny. They tended to take on a broader meaning than originally and as this pattern developed the trend itself became diluted and less clear-cut." In New York, Irving "Slim" Rose opened what is considered one of the first oldies-only record shops in the nation, Times Square Records. Rose referred to oldies as those made from 1953 to 1959. His customers were mainly in their teens to early twenties. Rose sold original 45- and 78-rpm discs. Soon he started releasing original doo-wop masters on his own label. Some DJs began playing them on oldies radio programs. Noticing the trend, the original record labels started re-releasing some of their old hits. In the late '60s, the oldies market picked up considerably, blossoming in the era of hipness, hippies, and psychedelia. Companies kept up with the times by re-releasing songs from the early

'60s. Meanwhile, the '50s oldies market remained strong, sparking a modest career comeback for singer Bill Haley. And so the market drifted into the future. Old being a relative term, the oldies expanded to include classic hits a decade ago. To meet the demand, an increasing number of the original record labels began publishing catalogs exclusively devoted to their re-issue discs. By 1971, Sterling, the title-strip maker for jukebox records, counted forty-one record companies with oldies catalogs. From 1970 to 1971, the number of labels offering oldies catalogs doubled, according to *Billboard*. One beneficiary of the oldie was the jukebox industry. When labels realized the oldie was not a fad, they started forming their own special imprints for oldies. One of them was Starday's Country Jukebox Oldies. Others included RCA's Gold Standard and Decca's Original Performance. Elektra introduced its Spun Gold series in 1971. In that period, the favorite oldies were by big-name acts in various genres, including Ray Price in country and Creedence Clearwater Revival in rock. Obviously, not all kids were dipping into the past for their music fix. These days, oldies are taken for granted as a part of the record business. They are often called re-issues. Perhaps the 45 oldie will come back stronger now that people have rediscovered vinyl.

One-Siders

Single-face records, or those with only one side recorded. They were from the early 1900s.

One-Stop

Carried so many different records and labels that it became known as the place to get everything—thus, one-stop shopping for record stores and other music outlets. One-stops reached the zenith of their popularity in the 1960s. Their origins date to the late 1940s, when Syd Nathan of King Records in Cincinnati opened company offices in thirty-some cities across the nation. At some of his branches King often sold other labels' records as well as its own. The one-stop idea started catching on; operators were affiliated with no labels of their own. One-stops sold much of their product to local jukebox operators, and in doing so they helped establish the 45. Sometimes traditional record distributors had to buy their records from one-stops, putting one more company in the transaction. One-stops also served the growing numbers of discount stores. One-stops still operate, but not as predominately as they did in the late 1960s, when the jukebox business and the 45-rpm record thrived. In the mid–1960s, *Record World* carried a chart called One Stop Top Ten, reporting the top ten singles from important one stops across America. On a rotating basis the reporting businesses included Poplar Tunes in Memphis, New Deal Record Service in Detroit, Musical Sales in Baltimore, One-Stop Record Service in St. Louis, Martin & Snyder in Dearborn, J&S in Philadelphia, Beacon Record Distribution in Providence, and Real Record One-Stop in Pittsburgh.

One-Track Recorder

Everything went on one track. This was no easy chore in the 1940s and early 1950s, when studios used only one-track recorders—either acetate or tape. So if a singer or musician fouled up, the entire song had to be recut. Some of the best culture-changing record men preferred to keep the track that had the most feeling to it, despite minor errors. They included Sam Phillips, owner of Sun Records, and Syd Nathan, owner of King Records. They both believed in getting as much emotion out of a session as they could. What good was a song that was technically correct but lacking in feeling? Some of the biggest hits in country, R&B, and rockabilly were recorded on the one-track magnetic tape recorder in the 1950s. The most popular recorder one in the late '40s was made by the Ampex company. The Ampex 200 became an innovation in sound recording. Soon it was followed by the 300 model. Still, early tape engineers had to record everything at once—vocals, instruments, and background singers. Often this method required multiple takes because there was only one working track. One of the early one-track studios was the Castle Recording Laboratory at Eighth Avenue South at Church Street in Nashville's Tulane Hotel. The Castle recorded many of Hank Williams' hits, including "Hey, Good Lookin'." As recording technology progressed, two-track recorders came along and simplified the recording process. Then came three tracks, four tracks, eight tracks, sixteen, twenty-four, etc. When two-track tape recorders arrived a few years later, the producer had more leeway to place various instruments on one track and vocals on the other. Fixing a mistake was easier. As the 1950s continued, two-track machines dominated.

Open-End Interview

Appeared on both 45-rpm and 33⅓-rpm discs. The recordings were made for radio stations, which filled the discs' "open ends" with their own questions at the beginning of each interview. To listeners, it appeared the DJ was actually interviewing the performer. Examples include a 1963 interview LP with Ann-Margret recorded by *The Saturday Evening Post*, and a couple of 45 discs featuring Mrs. Miller, the middle-age vocalist known for her humorous pop vocals in the 1960s, on Capitol Records.

Open Reel

Record companies' commercial albums made on reel-to-reel tapes. The category didn't sell nearly as well as audio cassettes and eight-track tapes because the buyer had to play the open-reel tapes on reel-to-reel player/recorders, which more often were owned by adult audiophiles. Young people tended to go for cassettes and eight-tracks. The open-reel albums hit their peak in the 1960s.

Ops

Jukebox outlet operators. Slang used in the 1950s and '60s by record industry people. In the summer of 1961, the Ops wanted to turn around what they believed to be a slow decline in jukebox operations. Ops renewed a push to regain the strength they once had—and to a degree still had—with record companies. In New York, operators were hopeful because labels offered to renew their emphasis on the jukebox trade. Ops wanted records intended for adults, not teens, because so many jukeboxes were located in taverns and other adult venues. Columbia, Decca, and United Artists agreed to cooperate and send adult records to the outlets. Columbia and Decca had a large backlist form which to choose older recordings. UA, though a larger independent, had not been in business long enough to accumulate older recordings in its catalog. *Music Vendor*, the trade magazine for Ops and radio, noted in an editorial: "Rarely do charts reflect jukebox reaction to singles product. *Music Vendor* offers one of the few charts in the country which has consistently mirrored coin machine play through the years." Editors pointed out that Ops frequently ordered discs from one-stops, and those records did not count when charts were compiled by the trades.

Orange Peel

A rectangular series of bumps on vinyl discs. They were called orange peels because they looked something like the bumpy surface of an orange. The vinyl bumps came from an improper pressing job. Because platen surfaces were not smooth, tiny raised places were imprinted into the vinyl disc.

Orchestras

From five-piece combos and more. Today we think of an orchestra as a large symphony with a huge, lush sound. This was also true at the dawn of rock 'n' roll in the mid-'50s, but the definition became blurry. Labels released records by solo rock vocalists and rock combos, but the labels' A&R staffs didn't know how to describe the new music to the public. So the discs came listed with names such as Joe Smith, backed by Tom Duffy's Orchestra. That "orchestra" was only a five-piece group. Once the '50s ended, however, record companies got this odd description out of the way and knew how to describe the combo. Interestingly, trade-magazine shorthand referred to orchestras as "orks."

Originals

The first-recorded and first-released versions of a song. Many recordings that listeners considered originals were not. Take "Rock Around the Clock," for instance. Though the song is closely identified with Bill Haley, it was first cut by a group named Sonny Dae and His Knights, according to a 1998 *Discoveries* magazine story written by Dick Rosemont. Dick, an expert on such matters, noted that many later versions of songs are more recognized than the originals. For example, the Kingston Trio cut "It Was a Very Good Year" in 1961, several years before Frank Sinatra made the piece his signature song. In 1959, rockabilly Marvin Rainwater recorded Don Fardon's "The Lament of the Cherokee (Indian Reservation)." Later, the Raiders cut it. An original is neither a cover nor a remake. The term original was used by record industry personnel as well as record collectors.

Orthophonic Victrola

A forerunner of the modern-era phonograph of the 1950s and one of the more popular of the old internal horn phonographs, particularly because of its beautiful wooden case that looked similar to the console phonograph of the 1960s. The Victor Orthophonic Credenza, introduced in 1925, represented a new phonograph era because it was the first model to use an improved reproducer to play new electrically recorded discs. When Victor executives heard about a new electric recording technology being developed by Bell Telephone Laboratories and Western Electric Company, they arranged for it to be compatible with their new Orthophonic phonograph. Columbia also obtained rights for its new—and competing—Viva Tonal phonograph. Both were forerunners of later phonographs.

"Out of the Groove"

Newsweek's timely description of the new 45 single versus the competing LP and the stodgy 78. In this case, if anything was out of the groove, or the ordinary, it was the jumbled phonograph record scene of 1949. Predictably, *Newsweek's* catchy line did mean anything out of the ordinary, including the impact that the new vinyl record was having on confused buyers. They were being clobbered with information, misinformation, and complicated advice from elite audiophiles in the print media. In January of that year, the magazine's staff analyzed the competitive audio market and predicted that the 45 would have an advantage over the larger LP because it would sell for considerably less than both the new LP and the old-style 78. Take the singles market, for example. For popular records, the magazine noted that the 45 would sell for sixty-three cents versus seventy-nine cents for the 78. For classical records, the price was ninety-five cents for the single 45 versus $1.25 for the 78-rpm single. Out of the groove? Yes. Out of style? Indeed. The old 78 was beginning its journey to the antique shop. Welcome to the vinyl era.

Over Music

A noun that described vocals coming in over a music track. The words came from the early days of tape recording.

Overdub

Vocals and instruments onto multi-track recording tape revolutionized the music business and its records. When overdubbing came into use in the mid–1950s, studio engineers suddenly had the luxury of using two tracks (then three, then four, etc.) On the earliest recordings, however, there was no overdubbing. Acoustically recorded discs were made at once, as were early electrically recorded discs. The band played and the vocalist sang simultaneously—a live presentation. If someone made a mistake, the record company had to issue the song that way or cut another version. Though one-track recorders of the late 1940s and early '50s looked like basic washing machines, they opened a new vista in sound with magnetic audio tape. Despite having only one track to work with, recording engineers of that period made records that had energy and verve. This is because they were done live, on one track and in monaural. One take, one track. The overdubbing in later years made it possible to make records over a period of time at the leisure of the producer.

P

Pantomime Records

The father of lip syncing. In the early 1950s, when television took hold, pantomiming popular records became an easy way to entertain eager viewers. It differed from modern-day lip syncing because it allowed "singers" to mouth the voices of hit vocalists. The fake approach didn't matter to the audience, for pantomiming was accepted and enjoyed in any form then.

In fact, the act of pantomiming became so well-accepted that the word became a noun and a verb. Originating from the word mime, an early version of pantomiming started as entertainment in ancient times, and by the early 1900s had made its way into everything from burlesque to Christmas plays. When the quality of recording and record-pressing reached a new high, the pantomiming of someone else's hit records became mainstream entertainment. Its heyday was the late 1940s to the mid–1950s, but the practice continued on into the early 1960s. The best part was, a TV personality didn't have to be a vocalist to pantomime a hit song. Popular hosts stood on simple sets and "pantomimed" songs of the past and present. Sinatra? Como? Patti Page? Who needed them when a staff member could pantomime their hit records? Though modern audiences would find this laughable, early viewers found it entertaining. They were starving for anything on the tube. In Cincinnati, a local show called *Pantomime Hit Parade* featured TV personalities Dotty Mack and Colin Male, and a popular local singer named Bob Braun. Even though he got paid for it, pantomiming some other singer's record must have frustrated Braun, who got his revenge finally with "Till Death Do Us Part," on Decca Records in 1962. Mack became Cincinnati's, and later America's, Queen of Pantomime. Dorothy "Dotty" Macaluso was born in Cincinnati in 1930. She began her career in 1948 as a live model—another oddity today—in a Cincinnati department store window, where she was discovered by someone from the new WCPO-TV. She changed her surname to Mack and joined the station's staff of announcer-hosts. The station was so new that Mack performed her first live pantomime show only two hours after WCPO went on the air for the first time. Pantomiming was easy programming, and the public liked it, so she continued "singing" the hits. A part of Mack's immediate appeal was physical. She was a looker, and a natural entertainer. Braun was the male version. As an early TV spinoff, Dotty's own national pantomime program, *The Dotty Mack Show*, started on the American Broadcasting Network (ABC) in 1953. It ran for three years—first on ABC and later on the Dumont Network. Similar pantomime shows were broadcast locally in other cities across the nation. Technically, the TV definition of pantomiming was different from today's lip-syncing, which is often performed by a singer who fakes singing his or her own songs. Lip-syncing on TV might be done out of necessity, such as when fast songs are accompanied by vigorous dancing. Conversely, in its heyday, pantomiming was associated with slower songs. You could see the "singers" lips move as the records played. As TV sound production and audiences grew more sophisticated in the late 1950s, Dotty Mack's TV pantomiming lost favor and all but died. Singers lip-syncing their own records would continue, however, on *American Bandstand* and other shows. It is still done. As for Dotty Mack, the Queen of Pantomime continued to work, hosting Cincinnati television shows. Though she could "croon" exactly like Patti Page and Rosemary Clooney, she didn't do it much anymore. She once joked that she invented MTV.

Paper Add

A record added—on paper only—to a radio station's rotation or official play list. This not-so-rare practice tricked inquiring trade magazines into believing that the record was receiving regular airplay when it was not. The paper add was usually done as a favor for a friendly promotion man or label. The practice was largely discontinued in the 1980s. Most paper adds probably never developed into national hits, but nonetheless they were often coveted by labels just to see if distributors, larger labels, and the trade magazines might take notice of them.

Paper Labels

Paper labels pasted to discs. The practice began as early as 1890. Victor Records was a leader in the development of paper labels in the early 1900s. When discs first appeared, many carried rectangular pieces of paper that were glued to the smooth, groove-less backs of the records. Their purpose was to identify the artists and songs or recitations. On cylinder records, such pieces of paper were rolled up and stuck into the cardboard boxes that housed the cylinders. Some even included the complete lyrics or words to recitation pieces. On the top of the lid or on the box front, paper labels sometimes listed the issuing company, the artist's name, the song or piece, and other information. Today, researchers and collectors use paper labels information to compile company histories, lists of artists, and musical information. The printed material can be found on the backs of LPs and on compact-disc booklets.

Paperless Labels

Manufacturers achieved this effect by using injection molding instead of the usual compression molding pressing techniques. The public wasn't used to seeing a record without a paper label glued to it. Polygram started using paperless labels on 45s in the mid–1970s, but the idea wasn't new. Edison Diamond Discs had paperless labels in the early 1900s. Earlier, Berliner had done it.

Parent Songs

Important in making answer records. Throughout the first six decades of the twentieth century, songwriters sometimes "borrowed" from popular commercial songs to create new songs. The writers either imitated the melodies or wrote answers to the lyrics. In 1960, *Music Vendor*, a trade publication, ran this headline: "Answer Discs Gain Momentum." The magazine noted that "the lyrics assume a familiarity with the 'parent song,' on the listener's part ... the answer discs are becoming increasingly popular with the teens, and a growing number of manufacturers, aware of this, are rapidly preparing to answer some of the songs on top of the charts." In modern, and more competitive times, few listeners would want to hear songs that borrow from originals. Besides, predatory lawyers would jump into the mix to "answer" one another with lawsuits.

Party Records

Sold from under the counter in the 1940s and '50s. They were more embarrassing than they were obscene. Before the Internet, DVDs, and a more open society, party records—on 78-rpm discs, 45s, and LPs—were an underground favorite. Early party records had no label or artist name listed, only the title. Some early ones can be found on YouTube. The include ditties such as "The Urinal," "Confusious [sic] Say," "I Took My Organ to a Party, but Nobody Asked Me to Play," and "Klondike Kate." They used some foul language, sexual situations, racist comments, and any offensive remarks they could dream up. While men's magazines and hipsters called them *party* records, sometimes the authorities tried to call them *obscene*. That tactic didn't work when the record companies' lawyers pulled out a *real* obscene record. Then came the arrival of vinyl records, and definitions got interesting. People in the music industry started referring to an increasing number of blue comedy records as real party records. Many of these records featured comedians doing club performances that featured the double entendre galore, dirty jokes, and risqué stories about traveling salesmen. In the modern perspective, usually it was the kind of naughty comedy that people heard in nightclubs. Today, more provocative material is aired on television. The heyday of the party record came in the mid–1960s, when the LP ruled the adult world. Race didn't matter. The Dooto label in Los Angeles made many of these discs for the African American audience. Red Foxx was a star in the field. About 1970, he also recorded for King Records in Cincinnati. Another black LP man was Wild Man Steve, who pushed the genre to its bare limits. Jubilee Records in New York promoted a white club comic named Rusty Warren, who performed her "classic" naughty album, *Knockers Up!* Then there was Ruth Wallis, another good-looking club act who recorded for DeLuxe and later for King. She was the self-described Queen of the Party Record, aimed at "the genteely [sic] risqué." The records were obscene, and almost everyone knew it when they heard them. As for

Warren, in later years she was still telling women in her audiences to put their "knockers up." She has released videos of her club performances on DVD. Warren—real name Ilene Goldman—is the undisputed queen of blue comedy. Jubilee presented her with gold albums for *Knockers Up!*, *Rusty Warren in Orbit*, *Rusty Warren Bounces Back*, and *Banned in Boston*. These days, the "glory times" of party records have come and gone. They're still around on CD, but in the era of streaming it just doesn't seem hip for couples to sit around listening to older performers telling jokes about women's breasts. (See **Obscene Records** and **Risque Records**.)

Payola

Supposedly the word payola is a cross between the words payment and Victrola. Giving money or something of value in exchange for radio airplay or superior placement of sheet music or some other product is a practice as old as Tin Pan Alley, radio, and the record business. Payola is, simply, payment to a disc jockey or a radio station employee in return for playing records. The difference between today's payola and yesterday's is simple: It wasn't illegal then. Payola first came to the public's attention in the mid- to late 1950s, when a number of prominent DJs were accused of accepting money to play rock 'n' roll records. Top rock DJ Alan Freed eventually plead guilty to a commercial bribery charge and paid a $300 fine. The scandal ruined his career. In congressional hearings, meanwhile, label chiefs, most of them independents, testified how they had given payola to get their records on the air. In more recent years, payola has taken other forms—drugs, sex, etc. It always did include this element, but often the radio people preferred cash. You don't hear much about payola these days, but it still lurks. It has been around for at least a century, and it will continue so long as someone wants to be a star.

Pellets

Sent into pressing machines by chutes. They melted in the heat of the press, creating a substance to mold the vinyl records.

Personal Records

A single recording made for personal use. The term dates to the early days of the talking machine, when recording artists frequently made personal records for individuals and companies. They were recorded on cylinder machines, which could record as well as play. Stores (frequently furniture stores that sold phonographs and records) invited recording artists to visit and make personal records for customers. Performers greeted the customer, used his or her name as a character in a famous song or monologue, and continued with a story. Performers did this for dozens of customers in one afternoon. Few personal records remain because of the fragility of the wax cylinders and the rigorous play. As the phonograph developed in mid-century, personal records became the kind that people could record in booths at amusement parks—little floppy records for your parents or friends. Before he was discovered, Elvis recorded a personal disc for his mother.

Personality DJ

One of the radio industry's more important figures from the 1940s to the 1960s. The DJ was typically a well-paid man. He dominated a radio market with his strong and appealing air personality, as well as with his own choice of records, which he programmed and plugged on his whim and expertise. While his colleagues at the station played records chosen by the music or program director, the personality DJ's choice of records made him a local king. Often the records complemented his image. Though the rock 'n' roll personality "spinners" are more often remembered these days, personality jocks operated in other genres too, particularly pop. The personality DJ concept was pioneered by Ted Cott when he was the program director of WNEW in New York in the '40s. The idea caught on quickly. Unfortunately, the growing controversy over payola, participation in record industry operations, rising salaries, and the arrival of the Top 40 format killed the personality DJ concept by the early '60s. But Top 40 was the early culprit. Nowadays, with many stations being automated and many others adhering to strict programming from corporate headquarters, the personality DJ seems like one from an old movie. And indeed, he is. The idea of a personality DJ began in the 1940s, when a few larger-city DJs began to develop cult audiences, who tuned in to a program because of the notoriety of the DJs, such as the funny Paul Dixon at WCPO in Cincinnati. He and some others even got their pictures placed on the covers of sheet music, which must have galled the singers. The shock waves against the personality jocks began in full force in 1958, when *Billboard* ran a cover story on how the Top 40 format was killing off the kings of radio. Among the early departures were Denver DJs Joe Flood of KTLN, Ray Persons of KIMN, and Ed Scott of KMYR. Perkins was the first to leave in the fall of 1957. He did it to protest his station's switch to Top 40. The other guys soon left. Flood was being paid $32,000 a year. That was a good salary in the late '50s, when a working man was thrilled to bring home $10,000 annually. New York's big dominoes soon fell, too. Alan Freed, the Big Beat man himself who practically invented the marketing and promoting of rock 'n' roll, resigned from

WIN, and soon Art Ford left WNEW and Ted Steele departed WOR-TV's record-hop show. *Billboard's* headline summed it up accurately: "N.Y. Deejays Spin Faster Than Disks." As everyone knew, Freed had other problems—a bribery indictment being the most immediate. Meanwhile, Top 40 rolled on to higher and higher ratings. Kids wanted more records. Cott maintained that kids should not dictate radio programming. "Radio is making a terrible mistake," he told *Billboard* in May of 1958. "Formulized radio is Muzak with commercials." Goodbyes also went to Don Bell of KIOA in Des Moines and Peter Porter of KLAC, who on his way out predicted that a totally automated radio world would come soon. Perhaps the biggest purge came at Hollywood's KLAC, where in addition to Porter the station had Dick Haynes, Gene Norman, Earl McDaniel, Duke Norton, and Jack Smith. All went into the radio void that came with the death of the personality DJ.

Personals

Used by music-business agents and managers in the 1950s and early 1960s. It was short for personal appearances.

Phonograph

Its obituary is now its calling card. In 1994, reporter Clara Herrera wrote, "Where has our vinyl heritage gone, and how can we get it back if we want it?" The phonograph had all but died, and replacement parts were in short supply. The compact disc had put the phonograph on the scrap heap. Now, the compact disc is dying and the phonograph is coming back. It has a long history in the music business. In the record industry's infancy, during the 1880s, the phonograph meant something specific: talking machines (with cylinders) manufactured by Edison. But soon people started calling all talking machines phonographs. By the early 1900s, phonograph meant any kind of talking machine. Emile Berliner's Gramophone, a disc-playing talking machine invented toward the end of the nineteenth century, should not be confused with the Thomas Edison's cylinder-playing machine. The two competed for decades before the Gramophone—now known as the phonograph—won the battle. The champion of the early disc machine was the Victor Talking Machine Company, a maker of players and discs and one of the major labels of the day. A half-century later, a sales boom occurred when the LP and 45-rpm disc became popular. In 1950, only 16.8 million phonographs blared in American homes. (There were more car radios than phonographs.) By 1968, that number had increased to 53.8 million. In that eighteen-year span, the number of phonographs had continued to increase each year. A major force behind the continued increase was youth.

Teenagers bought phonographs—or record players, as they called them. Some were small. This was not a new innovation; small, portable players had been around for decades. By the mid–1950s, phonographs also came in bright colors, leaving behind the staid black and wood looks. In 1955, Philco introduced a self-powered, completely transistorized portable phonograph. The company claimed you could play it for 150 hours before the batteries drained. In the 1960s, phonographs took on all sizes, shapes, and appearances. Phonographs was made for varied budgets and tastes. These days, phonographs again can be purchased in all sorts of stores. Reports of vinyl's demise were premature.

Phonograph Furniture

Upright, high quality cabinet models, often made of oak or walnut, that were sold by Columbia, Edison, Victor, and smaller companies. As the 1920s and electric phonographs arrived, furniture models began to look more like other horizontal living-room furniture. This led to the family phonograph concept of the 1960s. The popular stereo phonograph had evolved into beautiful furniture that just happened to have a radio and phonograph inside, and maybe an eight-track tape player as well. The big, heavy pieces were obviously aimed at middle-aged homeowners who wanted both attractive furniture and a phonograph. At this time, television manufacturers were trying the same marketing technique. Phonograph furniture of that era was often more of a decorative piece than hi-tech audio equipment, but those big boys could belt out the sound as well as any other phonographs.

Phonograph Tins

Contained needles. During the days of new acoustic talking machines, from the 1880s to the mid–1920s, disc machines used metal "needles" that came in small metal cases with highly decorated lids. They were small enough to be placed in the pants pocket. Tins are collectible items today.

Phonographic Studio

Recording laboratory of the early 1900s. In the era of acoustic recording, from around 1880 into the first decades of the twentieth century, the term phonographic studio was used interchangeably with recording laboratory. In 1899, the writer E.W. Mayo explained in *Quaker* Magazine: "It has the appearance of a studio, being hung all about with pictures and mementoes of great singers and writers … the 'record room' or 'phonographic laboratory,' where all these various forms of entertainment or instruction are prepared for use of the [recording] machines, is a curious place. In appearance it is something between the rear of a theater stage and a machine shop. At one end is a small platform that holds a piano. [When] playing [on] a record the piano player faces the machines, and the top of the instrument is raised so that the full volume of sound may be caught. When piano and voice are to be 'taken' together, the singer stands between the piano and the machines and sings directly into the recording instruments. About the sides of the room are a number of odd-looking machines. Their purpose is to test and 'trim' the records, and to prepare them for actual use. All these machines are run by electricity and all unnecessary noise is carefully excluded from the rooms."

Pick-Up

Record purchased by a larger label based on the record's local popularity. A pick-up was a favorite term of record distributors, and occasionally by record chiefs. The thinking was that if the record was a strong seller in a major market or across several medium-size markets, it could be a national hit, too. A local label test-marketed a record for a larger indie company. An example is "96 Tears" by Question Mark and the Mysterians on the Pa-Go-Go label in San Antonio, Texas, in 1966. This is an unusual case. The label was known in Texas for its Mexican-style music. Through an arrangement with the Michigan-based band, "96 Tears" was cut on a four-track recorder in a Michigan studio with no frills. Pa-Go-Go released the disc. The band then promoted its record in Michigan, where "96 Tears" first hit in Saginaw and soon spread across the entire state. Neil Bogart of Cameo Records in Philadelphia, the label that produced many teen dance records, leased the master. Another example of a pick-up was Tommy James and the Shondells' "Hanky Panky," which James recorded in 1964 at WNIL radio in Niles, Michigan. A local label, Snap, released the record. Not much happened. Then in 1966 a rock station in Pittsburgh discovered "Hanky Panky" and started playing it. The record caught on in Pittsburgh. The indie Roulette Records in New York obtained the master and started a long career for James and the group. Oddly enough, the song was first recorded as a B-side for the Raindrops group in 1963. Composers Jeff Barry and Ellie Greenwich didn't think "Hanky Panky" was worthy of an A-side. (See **Master Acquisition**.)

Picture Disc

A record with a colorful picture on it. Most memorable are the Vogue Records discs of the 1930s. Today, some sell for anywhere from $40 to $100, depending on the artist. Picture records made a revival in the 1960s and

1970s, when special-issue rock LPs used colorful artwork. In the 1980s, collector records featured black and white photographs of historic rock pioneers—Buddy Holly, Carl Perkins, Eddie Cochran, etc. Now that fewer LPs are pressed, the picture disc itself has faded into history.

Picture Sleeve

Paper envelope for a 45-rpm single that features a photograph of an artist or artwork. Its peak came in the 1960s and 1970s. Not all singles came with a picture sleeve. They were usually reserved for the more well-known acts. Often the artists' photos appeared on the sleeves. Others were colorful, often garish; others were in black and white line drawings and other styles. All kinds of picture sleeves were made. By the 1980s, however, they had become slick. The most collectible sleeves were made in the 1950s and 1960s. The sleeves are making a small comeback today as vinyl 45s have returned.

Piledriver

A 1960s reviewer's term for a 45-rpm record with a strong, steady beat.

Piracy

A term technically used to describe illegal duplication of copyrighted tapes and records, often sold with plain sleeves or album covers. But often people in the record industry considered piracy *any* illegal duplicating, including the counterfeiting of records that looked almost exactly like the real thing. Record pirates operated at full force in the 1960s, when they could easily master a record, directly from the vinyl disc, then press their own versions of it. They copied the parent company's logo, and sent the pirated copies into the distribution network. Obviously, this hurt the parent companies, which were often independents. Even if a record hit big, it wouldn't do as well as it should have because of all the pirated copies. A major break for the Recording Industry Association of America came in the summer of 1970, when a federal district court in California ruled that the state's strong anti-piracy law was constitutional. *Record World* called the practice of piracy "evil" and "pernicious." Allied in the cause against the pirates were the Harry Fox Agency, the National Association of Record Merchandisers, and the American Federation of Musicians. In later years, authorities continued to seek out and arrest the pirates, making it harder for them to set up shop. Many turned to pirating cassette tapes because they knew teens didn't care much about fidelity. There was no good way to identify, track, and prosecute tape pirates. By 1970, they had hit the four-track market, and were marching into the eight-track.

Pirate Editions

By the 1960s, so-called pirate editions of popular singers' albums were popping up in abundance on both vinyl and audio tape. The pirates would obtain or record a performance, then duplicate it and sell it. In 1970, *Billboard* headlines labeled Asia as the "pirate playground," and "U.S. Is Child's Play as Pirates Run Rampant in Asia-Pacific." Anyone caught with more than five copies of an illegally duplicated record was considered a pirate and could be prosecuted.

Plates

Slang for disc records from the late 1800s. An advertisement by the United States Gramophone Co., 1410 Pennsylvania Ave., Washington, D.C., on April 20, 1895, announced: "Advance List of New Plates made with the Latest Improvements regarding Articulation and freedom from friction. Now Being Duplicated in Hard Rubber." Plates evolved into platters. As with so many of these old terms, plates survived into the vinyl era of the late 1940s and even later.

Platter

Disc records. Recording engineers surmise that the black stacks of 78-rpm discs resembled plates, and thus, the name platters was born. Industry workers also used the word platters to describe the transcriptions or recordings used for the audio portions of otherwise silent-film commercials in television's earliest days. The word platter might be one of the few slang terms used by industry insiders. Syd Nathan, president of the legendary King label, occasionally referred to his singles and albums as platters. Because his label once recorded the Platters, he could safely say he produced the Platters' platters. (See **Plates**.)

Platter Chatter

A disc jockey talking about records on the air. Term originated in the 1950s, and continued into the '60s, when it became the name of a music column in the trades.

Platter Turners

Club DJs who threatened livelihoods of jukebox operators in Chicago in the early 1960s. The "platter turners" had expensive hi-fi equipment, and they moved it into jazz and R&B taverns on the South Side in 1961. Naturally, this was one more problem that the jukebox operators didn't need.

They were afraid that platter turners would put them out of business by eliminating the playing of jukeboxes. Two years later, the issue had become so prevalent that *Billboard* ran a story. Reporter Nick Biro wrote, "A platter turner is a cat knowledgeable in music." The turner played a record, and then interpreted the music to the crowd. As the 1960s wore on, the platter turners obviously didn't run the ops out of business. But they did land one more blow toward the decline of the jukebox business. Perhaps the people in Chicago used the term platter turner because they were familiar with it. It dated to the mid–1940s, when NBC in New York felt pressured to hire platter turners—employees who placed the records on the turntables. The National Association of Broadcast Engineers and Technicians (NABET) insisted on the platter turners. Later, when NBC's contract with NABET was ready to expire, James Petrillo inserted himself into the picture. He was the heavy-handed chief of the American Federation of Musicians, and he lived in Chicago. When Petrillo spoke, people listened. He had talked his membership into approving nationwide strikes before, and he could do it again. This time, he claimed anyone who turned the platters should be a member of the musicians' union. The issue went to the National Labor Relations Board, whose members ruled that the platter turners could be "engineers and technicians" in New York and "musicians" in Chicago. A newspaper reporter wryly observed, "All this to-do over a child's task to be done for a man's pay."

Plattery

Trade magazine euphemism for record company.

Playtape

Another ghost of the tape days. Playtape was a late-1960s tape company that sold players and tapes aimed at the youth market. Playtape issued hits on lower-cost audio cassette tapes to compete with the eight-track market. In 1969, the New York company issued ninety-nine-cent cartridges featuring hit songs from the company's own top 100. By then the worldwide firm, especially popular in Japan, was developing a playback adapter that would enable consumers to use Playtapes and eight-track tapes on their eight-track players. The company also received a contract to make Playtape cartridge machines for the 1968–1969 Volkswagens. Playtape was also working on a machine that could play two-, four-, and eight-track tapes.

Pluggers

Another name for song publishers who promoted their songs to record labels. In use by trade magazine reporters in the 1940s and 1950s. (See **Song Plugger**.)

Plugola

Illegal payments from record companies to press agents, publishers, promotion men, and advertising agencies. Plugola's sister, Payola, wanted the same thing—attention for records. The names were used interchangeably in the early 1960s, but the name plugola usually meant illegal activity from people other than DJs, who got into trouble for accepting payment for playing certain records. Plugola's situation was similar, depending on what the pluggers specifically wanted. After the 1959–1960 payola scandal, in which DJ Alan Freed was accused of accepting payments, the Feds amended section 317 of the Federal Communications Act. This allowed the Federal Communication Commission to prosecute anyone who in any way paid to help boost a record's chances. In 1961, word got around the radio and record worlds that the Feds were looking into violations of the law. By then, many DJs, record librarians, and program directors were required to sign documents that stated that neither they nor any family members owned an interest in song-publishing firms, record companies, distributorships, or any other recording institutions. June Bundy, Radio and TV columnist for *Music Business*, wrote that the rumor set the industry into a state of "Panicsville." She wrote, "Dee-jays, network execs, and package producers are all certain that the probe will focus mainly their area of operations.... While we certainly don't condone this, we do fervently hope the investigators won't smear the vast honest majority of the industry." Apparently, the investigation did not result in any major busts, for today no one remembers Panicsville. Only the big DJ busts of 1959–1960 remain in the public's mind.

Pocketdisc

Ill-fated four-inch single available in vending machines in the late 1960s. It was introduced by its maker as the industry savior. It came at a time when singles has taken another dip in sales. Some people called the Pocketdisc a miniature single. Made by the Americom Corp., the new record debuted September 16, 1968, in Seattle, a test market. Initially, twenty selections of the current and varied top 100 single hits included "People Got to Be Free," by the Rascals; "House That Jack Built," Aretha Franklin; "1, 2, 3 Red Light," the 1910 Fruitgum Company; and "Sunshine of Your Love," Cream. In the next few months, many distributors and record store managers around the country reported a positive reception to the Pocketdisc; in fact, some even predicted it would rival the seven-inch single. But, it did not. The 45 single had become entrenched in people's minds for nearly twenty years. More importantly, the major labels still wanted it.

Political Satire Records

These vinyl discs—singles and LPs—were not hard to spot. They concerned politics. Some featured sophisticated humor, and others were corny. They usually boomed in sales after political scandals, but they were on the market most of the time. Political satire records date back to the turn of the twentieth century, when comedians such as Cal Stewart poked fun at various politicians, including Woodrow Wilson. Like politics, the political satire record was always around, lurking in the shadows of American history. According to *Cash Box* magazine, the "modern-age political satire on records began in 1961 with Cadence's [Cadence Records] *First Family* LP starring Vaughn Meader. Kidding the Kennedy administration, the LP went on to sell more than six million copies." Subsequent LPs exploited—using *Cash Box's* word—the personalities of presidents Lyndon Johnson and Richard Nixon, but they didn't sell as robustly as Meader's album. When Nixon's Watergate Hotel problems mounted in the late spring of 1973, however, the satire crowd went bonkers. A number of satirical singles and LPs arrived at radio stations. They included "Watergate" by Dickey Goodman, king of the cut-in novelty; "Son of Checkers" by Don Imus, the New York DJ; and country singer David Allen Coe's "How High's the Watergate, Martha." Meanwhile, Capitol Records shipped 500,000 copies of its new *Watergate Comedy Album* by comedians Burns and Schreiber. In June of '73 the label held a press party at the Troubadour, which was made up to look like the Watergate. (See **Novelty Records, Radio Era**.)

Pops and Clicks

An inadvertent byproduct of the vinyl manufacturing process. Interestingly, some modern recording software come equipped to add these old, familiar sounds to digital recordings to make them sound like a vinyl record.

Portable Phonographs

Came with a handle and were relatively lightweight for carrying. (Although some smaller tabletop phonographs may be portable, they are not true portables.) By the mid–1950s, portables began to look more modern—manufacturers used red and other colors. In the 1960s, some of them took on the look of the times. Sears made one covered with white and red checkered "pop art." The Kiddie Company issued numerous small phonographs for kids. They could play singles and LPs. The firm—and others—made portables with hit artists' color photographs on top and inside the lid. Ones with the Beatles and Elvis Presley are, naturally, highly sought after these days. These little phonographs evolved from the black hand-cranked portables of the early 1900s. They were made of wood and with metal handles and used for entertainment at picnics in the park. In 1934, RCA Victor introduced the first little phonograph to be marketed as a portable.

Porto-Playback

Popular brand-name machine used to play transcription discs. Porto-Plays were used mainly by radio stations in the late 1940s and early 1950s, and they could play sixteen-inch 78-rpm discs and 33⅓-rpm microgroove recordings. The unit weighed only twenty-six pounds, used a sapphire needle, and cost $125 in 1949. (See **Transcriptions**.)

Postcard Records

Grooves imprinted into the color picture, nearly undetectable to the eye. The records came in both the standard and larger postcard format, and played at 33⅓, 78, and 45 revolutions per minute. Some firms used the same technology to make other cards (not for mailing) of various shapes, including round. They were laminated on thin pieces of cardboard. Some depicted baseball stars and featured audio from games. Though never extremely popular, the picture postcard record did sell well enough in the late 1940s and the 1950s.

Premiums

Recordings used in direct-mail campaigns and as magazine inserts. They became popular in the late 1950s. Columbia Transcriptions manufactured many of them. (See **Auravision**.)

Pre-Packs

Promotion-record packages. Columbia's pre-packs were sent to radio programming managers. Sample packs usually preceded the release of a forthcoming album or perennial holiday albums. Decca Records specialized in using pre-packs for Christmas music, both pop and country.

Pre-Production Single

Reserved for rush releases on important discs. Phillips Records (USA) and some others sent pre-production singles—they were marked that way—to important radio stations across the country. Stark, with black letters on a white label, the single was nothing more than an acetate.

Pressing

Records were made with the same idea and purpose for decades. Only the technology changed. By the 1970s, records came from large machines that squeezed together melted vinyl. Some used the compression method, which shoots hot polyvinyl chloride into a pressing-machine cavity. The substance was hydraulically compressed in a stamper. Another pressing method, the injection method, used cheaper polystyrene to press 45-rpm discs and EPs. The method was faster but the results were not as good. Polystyrene discs became brittle with age and broke more easily. Surprisingly, disc-pressing technology did not change a lot in the twentieth century. It was started by German immigrant Emile Berliner for his Gramophone toward the end of the nineteenth century. He invented a method of playing and recording flat discs. Using electroplating, he etched sound vibrations into a zinc master, and stamped out records made with shellac. Soon after, Eldridge Johnson, a maker of spring motors for phonographs, invented a similar pressing method, this one using a soft-wax master instead of one made of zinc. Johnson concluded that the sound quality would be superior to the zinc method. His idea, supported by the courts, enabled him to acquire forty percent of Berliner's gramophone company. From it he built a new firm, the Victor Talking Machine Co. When vinyl declined in the 1990s, many pressing plants scrapped their machines. Today, with the demand for vinyl discs increasing, record presses are busy again.

Presto

A forgotten name in recording. Many hits in the early rock years were mastered on Presto machines. The company also made disc recorders. When magnetic audiotape recording arrived in the late 1940s, Presto started selling its own tape recorders for studio use. The Presto Recording Corporation of Hackensack, New Jersey, was known worldwide as one of the top makers of disc recorders and blank discs. Unfortunately, the company could not duplicate the success it had had in the disc recording field.

Prexy

Trade publication slang for a record company president.

Producer

Since the beginning of recording history, somebody had to take the lead during a recording session. Producers' names did not usually appear on records in number until about 1960. By the mid–1960s, producers had become well known for their sounds, and even production company logos appeared on singles and albums. The producer's job is to organize the session, select the material, and find the musicians, the arranger, the studio, and the audio engineer. Phil Spector, the most famous producer of the early 1960s, created the Wall of Sound on recordings by the Crystals, Bobby B. Soxx and the Blue Jeans, the Righteous Brothers, and the Ronettes. Though the term producer had been used earlier in the century, it wasn't until the heyday of rock music that it took on a real definition. The two types of producers were (and still are) the independent, who leased masters to labels, and the staff producer, who worked as a record company employee. (See **Independent Producers**.)

Production Song

Is much more effective as a holistic recording than as a stand-alone piece. In other words, the song and the recording are inextricably linked like a hand in a glove. A production song, as some record types referred to them in the 1960s and '70s, was—and still is—a potential hit. It just needs a nudge from the instrumentation to make it click. Many uptempo good rock songs wouldn't sound effective with only a vocalist and an acoustic guitar. It is difficult to imagine the production song and the recording as separate entities because they are so well linked. This in no way denigrates them, for some of the best records in rock 'n' roll history were production songs. In today's radio and records climate, production songs dominate. Unfortunately, many of them are poorly written and drenched in electronic and high-tech gimmickry, which becomes as important as the song—if not more important. Modern production songs constitute a disproportionate number of entries on Top 40 radio stations than they did even in the early 2000s. Examples: The Beatles' "Yesterday" is a *great* song, period. It sounds wonderful when a vocalist sings it with only a guitar accompaniment, and even better when done with appropriate background instrumentation. Thus, it stands alone with no instrumentation needed. In contrast, production songs such as Heatwave's "Boogie Nights" and the Jefferson Airplane's "White Rabbit" are also commercially terrific—but not for an "unplugged" record. They are effective overall as recordings. But "Yesterday" is effective with or without instrumentation.

Progressive Country

A name loosely and finally given in 1972 to the special sounds that Alabama's studio musicians were playing behind everyone from Aretha Franklin to Wilson Pickett to Lulu, the English pop singer. *Billboard* applied the tag of progressive country to a sound that had been around since the early 1960s, when producer Rick Hall established his FAME Recording. The music came out of the Muscle Shoals area in northern Alabama. He used a pool of pickers—the Southern version of L.A.'s Wrecking Crew—on the records he turned out there, including "I'm Your Puppet" by James and Bobby Purify. No matter what session players he was using and when, Hall seemed versatile enough to handle pop, country, R&B, and whatever else was thrown his way. In a '72 cover story in *Billboard*, reporter Nat Freedland described the sound as a "progressive country-pop picking and melody." To him, the sound they got on Franklin's hits and others was a "loose, fluent but uncluttered style of a new breed of Southern white musicians" who had been exposed to the Beatles, Nashville's pop-country, and the flashy guitar work of Jimi Hendrix. But the Alabama boys probably didn't analyze things quite so deeply. They just wanted to earn a living. About this time, Lynyrd Skynyrd, an Alabama rock band, was dubbed with the progressive country tag as well as the more generic Southern Rock. When Hall's studio band split with him to open their own place, Muscle Shoals Sound Studio, they brought "the sound" with them, like some kind of traveling ghost. That short-haired white band, nicknamed the Swampers, became the impetus for the progressive country tag. Though the group wasn't country per se, it incorporated a little country and a lot of soul into its licks and approach. Hence, the progressive tag came about some ten years after Hall had started gaining a big name in the studio and production game. Today, the name progressive country could be used to describe a lot of what is coming out of Nashville. (See **Muscle Shoals Sound**.)

Promo

Special DJ or radio station copies. When the 45-rpm vinyl disc established itself as the number one vehicle for radio play in the 1950s, promotion copies became more interesting. Usually labels pressed only a few thousand promo copies, so they are rarer than the store-bought versions of the records. By the 1980s, the larger labels often pressed their promo—also sometimes marked DJ or Audition—copies in the more expensive vinyl instead of the cheaper and less effective polystyrene, which wore out faster. Polystyrene was used for the mass-marketed 45s. More often the smaller independent labels pressed everything in one plant, and they did not switch plastics. Today, collectors buy promo copies for their interesting appearance.

Promo Play

Used portable transistor phonographs to promote new singles. The name Promo Play and its idea were conceived in 1961 by Irwin Zucker, a West Coast promotion man. By August of that year, Philadelphia-based promoter Ed Cothar had seen the light, or, rather, the turntable. He started carting his phonograph around to radio stations, hoping to attract another music director with the latest songs. As Cothar told *Music Vendor*, "I, too, can now corner deejays and P.D.'s [program directors], and no longer have to accept for an excuse their not having a phonograph available to preview the discs I am promoting." The idea saved him money on postage, too. Unfortunately, promo play did not receive widespread acceptance, possibly because promotion men had to carry a portable phonograph with them when they visited radio stations.

Promotion Man

Someone who pushes records. In the 1950s and '60s, radio and record executives believed that record-pushing was a job best suited to males. There were two kinds of promotion men: independent and staff. Independents handled many labels' releases and were paid per each title promoted. They helped build a bridge between rock and country radio stations and independent labels. In the mid–1970s, a controversy arose over the under-the-table methods used by some independents. Many larger labels began dropping the independent promotion men in favor of using their own staff promoters. Nevertheless, today the independents still wield power in the record business. But their presence is nothing like it was in the 1960s. Today, women have entered the field.

Promotion Records

Featured performers making personal ID tags and comments for radio stations. The name is easily confused with record labels' promotional copies. Recording artists' personal comments discs, usually on 45-rpm records, usually commented on the weather. Doug Hanners, the "45-rpm" columnist from Houston, has a record on which sultry April Stevens remarked about the weather—eleven cuts on one side alone! They featured her talking about fog, smog, cold, heat, hurricanes, hail, storms etc. Promotion records were a good way to enhance a station's status. The records also made listeners feel they had a personal connection to the artists.

Prophet

Sarcastic nickname for radio stations' program directors. A "prophet" is a sarcastic term. Prophets thought they could smell a hit record. Many bragged about their ability. Records deemed worthless were shoved back into the hands of the promotion men. To counteract the prophets' arrogance, the promotion men began carrying record charts with them. If a record reached number sixty with a bullet, the promo guys could point out that it was on the way up in a number of large markets. They could also use the charts for the same reason in record stores. By the summer of 1961, *Music Vendor* editorial writers noticed the trend of carrying charts: "While, obviously, this technique lacks the romance of the free-and-easy wheeling of yesterday, it should not inhibit the talented and the alert disc jockey in maintaining the glow he once projected so brashly and refreshingly over the air."

Pubbery

A music-publishing company. The ridiculous slang was used from the 1940s to about 1965. Trade writers also employed the verb "pubbing," or publishing a song. Using slang terms was considered attention-getting.

Punch-Out Hole

A seven-inch disc with a so-called punch-out center, which featured a small hole for use on the slim metal spindles that normally accommodated LPs and EPs. The center could be popped out to allow the record to be played with the larger 45-rpm spindles.

Q

Quadraphonic

A late-1960s name that popped up on all sorts of things, including a Nashville recording studio. Quad, as they called it, is a four-channel stereophonic system: two in the back, two in front. What happened to quad? Recording engineer Glenn D. White writes: "It did not provide the listener a convincing illusion of being immersed in a reverberant field; in short, it did not work."

Quality Zone

The part of the vinyl record where no distortion occurs. Any sound recorded beyond this zone falls into the distortion range, according to RCA Victor engineers of the early 1950s.

R

Race Records

Antiquated term that referred to recordings made by African American artists. It became a general, catch-all name for black recordings, though some African American pop groups on the major labels often did not receive the race tag. Once used interchangeably with sepia, the term dates back to the early days of recording. Some references appeared as early as the turn of the twentieth century when only a few blacks recorded. The closest that white record buyers could get to a "black" song was when white singers imitated African Americans, usually as a comedy or recitation novelty with sometimes a little singing. By the 1920s, record retailers and manufacturers used the terms race record and sepia record interchangeably. Though the term sepia started fading in the late 1940s, the name race record stuck and remained in frequent use into the mid-1950s, when labels and radio stations began using it interchangeably with rhythm and blues. Finally, recording executives believed that R&B more accurately represented a new type of music, without restricting it to any one race. As Bob Ellis, an A&R man King Records, wrote in liner notes for a R&B album: "In the early days of the phonograph industry almost every [black] artist was relegated to the various companies' 'Race' catalog, where comparatively few of this particular type of recording ever reached the popular record buyers' hands. There was always a great amount of talent in these so-called 'Race' catalogs. A few were fortunate enough to beat the barrier and become accepted by the general public." By the 1960s, R&B had eclipsed the race record appellation. A small number of retailers hung on to the old term until the end of the decade. (See **Sepia**.)

Rackers

A 1960s nickname that record executives gave to rack-jobbers. (See **Rack-Jobbers**.)

Rack-Jobbers

Sold records to discount stores and stocked their sales racks. Knick-name: Rackers. By the 1990s, the "rackers" were having tough times as vinyl discs were disappearing from stores. It had been a slow but steady decline as the survivors of the entire record-selling business fought over one life-saver. Things began going sour in 1963, when the Handleman Brothers Company, the nation's largest rack merchandiser, jumped into the distribution pool by forming Border City Sales. It would serve as MGM Records' major distributor in Detroit, but everyone knew Handleman wouldn't be satisfied to remain there. The traditional job of the distributor was to serve select label clients. One-stops carried many labels' products (thus the name) and bought records directly from distributors and labels. Rack-jobbers carried about anything they could find and served mainly department stores' record departments. They too bought records from multiple sources. Obviously, the presence of a big-time rack-jobber in the distributors' business niche upset old-line distributors and one-stops. On the other side of the story, distributors had been taking on rack-jobbing duties. In an editorial, *Billboard* noted, "There is no reason why a distributor cannot become a rack-jobber, if he has the time and energy to do so, nor any reason why a racker can't also open a separate distribution organization." Perhaps. The problem was, Handleman was an elephant jumping into a shrinking sales pool. A decade earlier, they all had their own niches. Rack-jobbers seemed content to serve the discount and department stores. In time, however, the large dinosaurs began dropping dead: K-Mart slowly declined. Sears withered. Woolworth, too. No doubt, rack-jobbers were an important force in the record industry when the national and regional department stores reigned. The rack-job heyday was the late 1950s through the 1980s. Rack-jobbers even had their own trade group, which decided the name rack-jobber sounded too industrial. So in 1963, the National Association of Recording Merchandizers (NARM) voted to change the name *rack-jobber* to *service distributor*. In changing the name, NARM members wanted to show the industry that the "service distributor" was as sophisticated as the venerable distributor. Despite the name change, most of the industry continued to use the name rack-jobber. H.W. Daily, the major Houston distributor, said in a 1976 advertisement: "A rack or sub-distributor [the one-stop] can do a marvelous job once an album has become a hit, but without these independent dealers [distributors] with store reports, in-store displays and in-store play, how does this album become a hit?" In time, many of the *s*ervice distributors would follow the other dinosaurs into the tar pits of record-industry history.

Radio Marathons

Exhaustion on the airways. In the 1950s, DJs tried to break records by staying on the air for days or playing an extraordinary number of records— just to get attention. In 1955, country DJ Jimmie Logsdon played records for fourteen straight hours at WKLO in Louisville. "We were crazy enough to try it," he said. "It almost killed us." At KTRM Radio in Beaumont, Texas, Jiles Perry Richardson, Jr., a 240-pound announcer who broadcast as the Big Bopper, set the world's record for continuous broadcasting by playing 1,821 records over six days and nights. He lost 35 pounds, and at times he had to be awakened by a coworker. He could do it because he had the enthusiasm and stamina of a twenty-seven-year-old. Later, he became a songwriter ("White Lightning" by George Jones), and a recording artist himself. He hit with his own "Chantilly Lace." At the height of his popularity, the Bopper died in the plane crash that killed Buddy Holly and Ritchie

Valens in 1959. The Bopper's six-day marathon lasted longer than some DJs' tenure.

Radio Spots

Records—usually 45-rpm discs—that carried 60-second commentaries by artists on various subjects. Example: Producer Bob Crewe sent out "A Special Message" to stations to solicit names for the new Bob Crewe Generation record, "Mini Skirts in Moscow or…." The winner was supposed to receive a trip to New York to meet the producer himself. Others featured interviews with artists to discuss their careers.

Radio Surveys

Local radio charts, primarily for country and Top 40 stations, were distributed free to record stores and at record hops. The larger stations in a radio market usually published the charts, reflecting how well records were selling locally. Often the charts featured the national hits plus a few regional records that weren't making the *Billboard* and *Cashbox* charts. Radio charts are gone now, lost with the regional hits.

Rapid Changer

A patented device introduced by RCA that enabled a 78-rpm phonograph to accommodate the smaller 45-rpm discs.

Raunchy Beat

Rock 'n' roll at its best. Veteran writers and reviewers at the trades in the early and mid–1960s had a good idea what that salacious beat was, and they didn't mind telling DJs and everyone else. It depended on the record. When someone at *Record World* and *Cashbox* heard it, they knew what it was. Reviewers didn't mean to imply that a raunchy beat was a bad thing. Actually, to them it meant good sales potential. One *Record World* review noted that "Kicks" by Paul Revere and the Raiders had the raunchy beat. But the raunchiness was more in their minds than in the vinyl.

Rebounder

A record or recording artist mounting a comeback after being absent from the charts. Rebounding was difficult to achieve. It took luck, planning, money, and total cooperation by the performers. They had built careers on their styles, songs, and music, so they were reluctant to change. Smooth singer Jerry Wallace had a rebounder. His first big hit was "Primrose

Lane," which went to the top ten in 1959. Though he had some nationally charted records after "Lane," he had to wait five years to hit big again, with "In the Misty Moonlight." It was especially difficult for him because he was a middle-of-the-road singer in a Top 40 world. Billy Joe Royal at least had a soulful, rocking voice when he hit the top ten with "Down in the Boondocks," in 1965, followed by a top-fifteen hit "I Knew You When." Then things slowed down. His follow-up that year, another Joe South song called "I've Got to Be Somebody," should have done equally as well, but reached a disappointing number thirty-eight. Like Wallace, Royal managed to land several more chart records over the next two years, but they fell far short of hitting in some of the major markets. As his career began to slide, his well-known manager, Bill Lowery of Atlanta, connected Royal with another Lowery associate, producer Buddy Buie. Columbia Records stuck with Royal through the lean times, perhaps knowing that Lowery's clients had plenty of clout behind them. Buie changed Royal's sound, producing a hard-driving, horn-driven and controversial record called "Cherry Hill Park." It fought its way up to number fifteen and might have done even better if not for the mildly salacious content of the song. Royal pulled it off with his powerful, soulful voice. After that, he had a couple of minor hits, but that was all until he turned to country music in the 1980s. "In the competitive world of radio, even back then you had to remain noticed," he said. "As they say, you are only as good as your next record. If you happen to stiff on two or sometimes even one, you might be finished. Soon the quality of your gigs go down. You go from playing Vegas to small clubs." Producer Sam Charters had the rebounder problem with the man who helped start rock music, Bill Haley. "It's always difficult to work with an artist whose career is not going," Charters told John Swenson, author of *Bill Haley: The Daddy of Rock 'n' Roll*. "You don't know whether to continue [in] the old direction or try something new. And Bill himself could never decide." In this quandary called the rebounder, Jerry Wallace opted to remain the same while Billy Joe Royal moved in a new direction. Both renewed their careers. Bill Haley tried once to change direction when he and Charters recorded the LP *Rock Around the Country*. When the country music experiment failed, Haley returned to his clunky brand of rock 'n' roll, in which he had an oldies following. Sadly, he continued in a downward spiral of more poor sales and alcoholism.

Recitations

The recitation record, on which an artist talked, gained popularity in the phonograph's infancy in the late 1800s, and continued to sell for nearly a century. Early on, the United States Phonograph Co. offered a section of recitation records by D.C. Bangs. They included "The Old Oaken Bucket" and "The Lock of Hair." Then there was "Casey's First Experience as Judge" by the great Russell Hunting. In the twentieth century, recitation records continued to sell at times. The 1960s saw them make a comeback. "Old Rivers" by the actor Walter Brennan became a hit. Through the 1970s, regular musical numbers often featured mini "recitations," or brief spoken passages. One included Glen Campbell's "Honey Come Back." And Barry White's sexy singles—well, who can forget his lines?

Record Business Trade Press

Newspapers and magazines covered the record industry before the publishing game became too expensive and the record industry too complex. Bill Gersh's original *Cash Box* focused on coin-operated machines, while *Billboard* covered the larger entertainment business, including circuses and nightclubs. It was called *The Billboard* then. In time, it survived by staking out the record industry as its focus. Through the 1960s, a number of smaller trades popped up and then died. Often they tried to specialize. One focused on new releases only, another on disc jockeys. Some magazines published their own charts, which were not always reliable. But some indie charts were surprisingly accurate. These record industry publications peaked in numbers and influence in the early to mid–1960s, when the indie labels provided a lot of the advertising revenue. In Nashville, music promoter Charlie Lamb operated *Music Reporter*, a slick magazine that covered the scene from a Nashville perspective. Naturally, he focused heavily on publishers and labels. His magazine competed with *Record World*, a magazine published in New York City during the 1960s and 1970s. It finished a distant third among the top-three music trade publications, after *Billboard* and *Cash Box*. The origins of *Record World* date to the mid–1950s and a smaller magazine named *Music Guild*, which eventually became *Music Vendor*. That publication evolved into *Record World*, which also absorbed a magazine called *Music Business*. *Record World* served record distributors and jukeboxes operators. When it struggled in the 1970s, the magazine was often accused of working too closely with advertisers and friendly labels. But it was always entertaining as well as informative. In the early '70s it featured a large Q&A feature called Dialogue, with the movers of the business. The magazine's importance cannot be ignored; record industry leaders read it faithfully. It ceased publication in the 1980s. When *Cash Box* went out of business over a decade later, only *Billboard* remained from the group of original record trade magazines. By then newcomers, including the *Gavin Report*, had arrived. But most of them were newsletter-style publications.

Record Catalogs

Record companies once issued annual catalogs—books, actually—containing all kinds of recordings, everything from classical to novelty. This was in the first half of the twentieth century. Under the section "Comic Monologues, Recitations, Etc.," the Victor label listed a number of novelty-type records, including "Cohen at the Telephone," backed with "Goldstein Goes in the Railroad Business" by Barney Bernard; "How High Is Up? (Parts I and II)" by Arthur Moss and Edward Frye; "In a Shoe Store," backed with "The Symphony Concert" by Marie Cahill; and "Lost Pocket Book," backed by "Old Wooden Tub," by Edgar Guest. Guest, while not exactly an actor, was described as "the newest of that domestic and humoristic school of American verse poets." He was born in 1881 in Birmingham, England, and he came to America at ten years old. He worked as a newspaper reporter and editor before turning to entertainment. For years the record companies' book catalogs, illustrated by thumbnail photographs of artists, provided a detailed look at what each company offered. By the 1950s, however, the catalog was all but replaced by seasonal booklets. Today, of course, frequently issued books are a thing of the long past.

Record Changer

A device that allows a record to be replaced with another disc automatically after it is finished playing. This started with 78-rpm phonographs and was carried over, using modern techniques, to the 45-rpm players.

Record Clubs

Sold records to people in the companies' "club." They were sent by mail. Record clubs still exist, and lately they are making a comeback in the resurgence of vinyl. But they are nothing like the industry's powerhouses of yesterday. Columbia had the big one, found in 1955. By 1966, record clubs had become so successful that the Federal Trade Commission was considering legal action against them—primarily against Columbia, which had contracts to release independent labels' recordings. After many months of deliberation, the FCC was still trying to determine if this constituted a monopoly, despite a federal hearing examiner's recommendation against breaking up the record clubs. In 1965, several record clubs grossed a total of about $110 million, which translated into fourteen percent of the entire record industry's dollar volume. By the 1990s, record club sales had dwindled with the changing times. Record clubs couldn't compete as profitably as they had in the past, and the concept was losing consumers' interest.

These days, record clubs focus on certain types of music rather than a broad base of it.

Record Jacket

The cardboard case that holds the LP. (See **Album Cover**.)

Record Librarian

Kept a library of vinyl records (and earlier, shellac) and related items on file, so they could be used by the radio station's staff whenever necessary. The exclusive job of librarian at radio stations is no more. It was eliminated by corporate radio bureaucrats during Big Radio's industry coup in the 1970s and '80s. The librarian also kept track of who checked items in and out. Some big-city stations employed full-time librarians who oversaw the record library room and sometimes a listening studio where disc jockeys could hear old or new records. Some DJs considered their stations' record library their personal playpen, in which they listened to records. At medium-size stations, the librarian job was mostly part-time. The librarian also performed one or two other station functions. Somewhere, a few librarians could still be working, but the job is not necessary in the digital age. Anything can be accessed almost instantly. If you browse the Internet, you can find a lot of vinyl 45s with radio station markings on them. They came from some station's old library that was no longer needed.

Record Manufacturers

Record companies. The old record business referred to pressing plants as record *pressers*. You'd think a presser would manufacture the records, and they did, but the industry had certain definitions that dated back to the early days of the record business.

Record Pressing Plants

Factories have returned for an encore as demand for vinyl discs increases. Some new plants have opened since 2010, and pressing companies that once made records are returning to the market. They sold or scrapped all their presses in the 1990s, when compact discs came into favor. Few people believed that vinyl would ever be in demand again. The few plants that remained stayed in business by making specialty pressings. Plastic discs are more for collectors than the everyday music fan, who wants music fast and doesn't care to "own" it. As late as the 1980s, pressing plants were all over America and the world. Their main business was manufacturing singles and LPs for record labels. Some plants were owned by large labels such as RCA and Columbia, which also did custom work for about anyone who would pay. Independent plants such as United in Nashville did excellent work, too. Then there were the small plants owned by individuals, recording studios, and a few little indie labels. As a way to generate additional income, these operations often offered pressings to their customers and musicians who lived in the area and needed a record made quickly. RCAs custom 45s were easily spotted: slimmer than usual, and high quality. Of course, a lot of the quality depended—and still does—on the mastering. Today, United in Nashville is still punching out the same good vinyl discs that it did back in the 1970s and '80s. It is a survivor, and it is expanding. (See **Pressing**.)

Record Player

In the vernacular of the American people at various times, the talking machine begat the phonograph which begat the record player which re-begat the phonograph which begat the stereo. This evolution of a disc revolution started in the 1890s and ended, loosely, in the 1990s, when many people pronounced the modern phonograph dead. Let's go back a little bit. In the early years of the last century, two trademarked names, the Gramophone and the Victrola, also came into widespread generic use, similar to the way Kleenex did as a substitute for tissues. The old Gramophone was a disc-playing machine that once competed with cylinder-playing machines. Also in that spring-powered time, the Victor Talking Machine Company made the Victrola. Because of its long-standing notoriety, the name Victrola lived on for decades. Imagine: You could still buy some RCA Victor electric phonographs in 1952 that were labeled Victrola inside their lids. Under Victrola's reign, disc records went from shellac to vinyl, from 78- to 45- and 33⅓ rpm, and from spring- to electric-powered. But back to the venerable record player. To most people, a simple record player was not for sophisticated audiophiles, who bought high-grade vinyl LPs. A record player is synonymous with the golden years of the 45-rpm single because it represented youth. When stereo records became popular with nearly everyone in the late 1960s and '70s, most people started referring to the phonograph as the stereo. "Play the record on the stereo," they'd say. Both terms were interchangeable and acceptable. In time, however, stereo seemed obvious. Now, with the resurgence of vinyl and the need for phonographs being greater than at any time in the last twenty-five years, the name has reverted back simply to *phonograph*. Most people under fifty years old must think the name record player is akin to the word ice box. (FYI: A refrigerator.) In the future, who knows what people will call a phonograph? The digital talking machine?

Record Racks

Metal record racks were made of heavy wire and used to store 40–50 of the seven- or twelve-inch discs. Their prime was the 1950s through the 1970s. At one time, they were available in just about any store. Bonds of wire or metal were used to store forty to fifty seven- or twelve-inch discs. The racks were popular in the heyday of vinyl, and were often stocked for customers by rack-jobbers—one-stops and distributors who took care of the racks in larger stores.

Record/Radio Company Promotions

They did it all, and then some. From the 1950s through the 1970s, radio stations and record companies conducted separate and joint promotions that ranged from the mundane to the wild. Today's records and radio markets don't work well for some of the crazy old promotions because now formats are too segmented and record companies think on national and international levels. In past years, however, you could hit most of the teen audience by promoting to any city's largest Top 40 station. A lot of record company promotions were set up to offer something—clothes, TVs, and other merchandise—if a young fan won a contest involving a recording star or the DJs at a station. One promotion included bringing a stagecoach to a country music station to promote a star's album. Another time-tested promotion, and a bit more lively, was the look-alike contest. Such events were held throughout the country to promote records or stations. The Beatles offered a great opportunity for look-alikes, but then so did other big-name rock stars of the era. To promote an act's upcoming performance in a city, record company promotion people used to advertise on local radio stations, which often were involved in the same campaigns. One such look-alike occurred in New York in 1973, when Dawn featuring Tony Orlando was scheduled to perform at the Copacabana. Their label, Bell Records, set up a look-alike contest. The goal was to find six kids who looked like Orlando. They were to come from area high schools, junior colleges, and universities. The winners and their dates were invited to be the singer's guests at the club. To attract interest, Bell printed and distributed 5,000 flyers to schools throughout greater New York. The label also sent forms for bio materials, photos, and other vital information. No word on how Tony felt when he saw six versions of himself—at seventeen to twenty years old. But Bell Records must have been happy. It was able to expose its act to the kids of New York.

Record Ramblings

Well-known 1960s column in *Cash Box*, written by multiple staff contributors who received no bylines. It featured music-business news items from various cities, including Philadelphia, Hollywood, Chicago, and New York. Often it carried small items that could not be used as stories in the magazine. The column was well-read by record company executives because it often mentioned them.

Record Roundup

Innovative publication from the record industry's most innovative record chief, Syd Nathan of King Records. When his independent King label in Cincinnati began hitting big with hillbilly music and some early R&B, Nathan thought of a good way to promote his country acts. They were then the strongest sellers on the label. In 1947, he founded a small magazine, *Record Roundup*, which he sent to record stores, department stores that sold records, radio stations, and individuals. The monthly magazine carried brief stories about artists, photographs, and even a chart. Naturally, Record Roundup had its share of King Records news. But Nathan had a way to make it more interesting. He wrote about country singers from other labels, and on occasion used one of their acts on the magazine's cover. In this way, the magazine was like a record one-stop. It continued for about another couple of years, when Nathan discontinued it for financial reasons.

Record Shops

They were in every town, in every big city. They serviced the young, and sometimes the older ones. Anyone over fifty years old will remember the record shop. Along with soda shops, record shops will be forever revered as true Americana. They were not stores that sold and still sell used vinyl discs, but stores that carried only new records—both singles and LPs. Such mom-and-pop shops flourished into the late 1960s, when shop owners could no longer make a living selling less profitable 45s. Some stores carried them exclusively. The small shops could be found in small towns as well as big cities. Many hung on through the '70s and some into the '80s, but by then only the last holdouts were sticking around.

Record Slips

Paper record slips that accompanied cylinder records from the late 1890s to the 1920s. An old-time version of modern liner notes, the slips contained information about recordings, artists, and sometimes the stories behind the records.

Record Success

In 1967, the record industry achieved its first billion-dollar sales year. Jukebox operators were the biggest contributors, followed by rack-jobbers. Though at 16.8 percent the singles category represented an increasingly smaller share of total record sales, the number of singles sold directly to jukebox owners went up by over five percent. In a disturbing trend, *Billboard* reported that record sales from independent retail record shops continued to decline.

Record Theaters

Innovation that never caught on in record stores outside of the East Coast. In the late 1960s, record theaters were small projectors on which three-color music films could be shown. The three-minute movies featured three individual hit songs and their performers. Customers could watch the promotional films inside the record stores. Cinova Enterprises, Inc., creator of the experimental promotional device, intended to feature records from various labels, with Buddah Records being the first. Buddah's Neil Bogart believed the disc theater was "an audio-visual breakthrough in selling records. They are designed to build traffic and create customer excitement." Buddah was the disc theater's biggest proponent. After installing the projectors—they occupied no more than three feet of store space—in five stores around New York, Buddah and Cinova planned on placing more in thirty-three stores and eventually to many larger record stores across the country. Unfortunately, the idea was rejected by store owners.

Recording Department

Equivalent of the A&R department. Record labels of the early 1900s asked people to write in care of the recording department—that is, the department that made the recordings. Edison's was at 79 Fifth Ave., New York City.

Recording Horns

Forerunner of both the electric microphone and the amplifier. They varied in length. Smaller horns, twenty-five to twenty-seven inches in circumference, were used to record the guitar, banjo, and brass instruments. In this era of acoustic recording, sound engineers used six to twelve recording machines with horns, simultaneously, to make multiple masters in the days when masters were more easily damaged. Artists stood directly in front of the horns and sang or shouted into them. The longest horn on record measured 125 feet in length. It consisted of a series of rounded brass sheets connected by 30,000 rivets. Edison donated it to a war scrap drive in 1945. Horns were also used as amplifiers for playbacks, even on home phonographs. At home, phonograph owners could record themselves by singing or talking into small horns attached to their cylinder machines. The machines recorded on blank cylinders. When finished, the owner played back the recordings, which had captured the sound and put it into grooves.

Recording Laboratories

The early name for what we now call the recording studio. The early laboratories were sparsely furnished places with pianos, chairs, and stools for musicians, and metal recording horns that protruded from eight to a dozen cylinder phonographs. (This was before durable, long-lasting masters could be cut.) The majors—the Edison, Columbia, and Victor labels—all operated their laboratories in greater New York and New Jersey. A number of independents, such as Gennett Records in Richmond, Indiana, also owned their own studios. When the new electric microphone arrived and changed the record industry in the mid–1920s, the more scientific-sounding recording laboratory name soon faded. The term recording studio didn't come into use until the 1930s, when electrical recording had become firmly established and radio arrived. Even later, indie studios were scarce because the equipment had to be custom-made. In the 1950s, a few indie studios started popping up, even in smaller communities. Studios in the 1950s and '60s became more sophisticated in appearance, equipment, and sound. (See **Recording Horns**.)

Recordists

Audio engineers, both amateur and professional. When tape recording arrived around 1948, and was still new in the early 1950s, trade magazines came up with the name recordists to describe tape enthusiasts. The name vanished for home users by the early 1960s. Every so often, you will see it used to describe a professional.

Re-Creation

An Edison Diamond Disc, patented in 1910. The name for quarter-inch thick, heavy discs came from the obvious recreation of sound ("Comparison with the living artist reveals no difference.")

Red Bullet

Introduced by *Cash Box* on February 28, 1959, the Red Bullet feature was designed to "call readers' attention in one swift glance [to] the single records which show the strongest upward movement each week." The mark was superimposed over the song's current chart number to show a "sharp jump from the position it held last week." Everyone in the record business wanted a red bullet.

Red Vinyl 78s

Issued as early as 1946 by RCA, the crimson-colored vinyl 78-rpm disc was a failure, mainly because of its higher production costs.

Red Wax

Red vinyl. Starting around the time of the Korean War, RCA shelved its standard red-vinyl singles in favor of carbon-filled black vinyl ones. The company began to use various colors, including red, to denote each genre of music.

Reference Lacquers

Original copies of a test pressing, with typed or hand-written names of songs and artists. They were meant to show the producer or artist how their soon-to-be released records would sound. (Some mastering studios and pressing plants still use them as reference tools.) In the 1950s and 1960s, publishers cut acetates—sometimes called dubs—directly from demo sessions and sent copies to interested producers and record companies. The acetates were cut on the spot, often with the writers singing their own songs. By the late 1970s, audio cassettes replaced acetates for song demos. Don't play acetates too often, or they will wear out.

Refs

Music-business slang for a reference copy, usually an acetate disc and later a reel-to-reel tape. In the late 1950s, when a label chief wanted to hear a copy of a song, he would say, "Send me a ref."

Regional Breakouts

A breakout was a record that was receiving strong radio airplay and sales in a major market. The Regional Breakout, at times called the Local Breakout, was a popular listing in *Billboard* in the 1960s. Other trade publications had their own names for the breakouts. In the early part of the decade it was placed on the magazine's cover. Many of these records went on to become national hits. For example, in one listing in March of 1962, several future hits were breaking out across the country. They included

"Soldier Boy" by the Shirelles on Scepter Records (Detroit), "Twistin' Matilda" by Jimmy Soul on SPQR Records (Philadelphia), "The One Who Really Loves You," a Motown creation by Mary Wells (Detroit), and "Uptown" by the Crystals on Philles Records (Philadelphia). Philly was a hot, important radio town for breaking soul records. Records received widespread regional airplay in other larger radio markets including Dallas-Fort Worth, New Orleans, St. Louis, etc. Radio programmers liked the records and took chances on them. Regional breakouts usually came from cities that encouraged records by new artists.

Regional Hits

Singles that hit in one large city or one region. People in the record business were obsessed with them, because they could—just might—break loose nationally. From about 1955 to 1970, radio stations across the country helped create this beautiful phenomenon. It peaked from 1960 to 1970. Every city seemed to have its share of local labels, particularly New Orleans, perhaps the most local-friendly city in the country. Plenty of labels pushed the Gulf Coast Sound. (See **Pick-Up**.)

Regional Music Centers

Cities that turned out many hit records and created their own signature sounds. They included Muscle Shoals in Alabama, as well as Cincinnati, Detroit, Norfolk, Memphis, Philadelphia, New Orleans, and other places, often less known in the business but potent forces nonetheless. A few hits from the hinterlands included "Working in a Coal Mine," Lee Dorsey, New Orleans; "Memphis" and "Wham!" Lonnie Mack, Cincinnati; "New Orleans," Gary U.S. Bonds, Norfolk; "Mustang Sally," Wilson Pickett, "Take Time to Know Her," Percy Sledge, and "Take a Letter, Maria," R.B. Greaves, all from Muscle Shoals. In today's homogenized world of recording, such a music network seems impossible—and an unlikely success story. Younger musicians would find it difficult to believe that their cities once competed with labels in New York, Nashville, and Los Angeles. But from the 1940s through the 1970s, the hits flew out of all these towns, plus out of Pittsburgh, Jackson, Mississippi, and even smaller communities that were one- or two-hit wonders. The larger cities in the group had success for long periods because they built their own recording infrastructure that included cooperative radio stations, powerful distributors, talented musicians, locally-based but national record labels, music publishers, producers—most of all—talented vocalists and songwriters. Most of regional centers had active nightclubs, radio music programs, and roadhouses to support the

Dale Wright, left, poses with singer-actress Donna Loren and Dick Clark to promote one of Clark's rock 'n' roll shows in the mid-1960s. Wright started his career as a regional recording artist in Ohio in 1958, when he hit with a moderate national hit called "She's Neat." Soon he founded Dale Wright and the Wright Guys. He became one of the nation's more successful regional recording artists even though he never had a major national hit. He continued to record for the Fraternity label of Cincinnati. Wright's group became so popular in Southwestern Ohio and Northern Kentucky that his records regularly landed in the top ten on local radio charts. He was a regular on Glenn Ryle's *Dance Party* on Cincinnati television and on Dick Clark's *American Bandstand* tours. Wright also appeared in a film with Chuck Connors. As the Beatles arrived, Wright did not stop. But by the late 1960s, his clean-cut image had worn thin. He cut a record with the Heywoods rock group and in 1968 became a disc jockey near Lexington, Kentucky.

musicians when they weren't recording. In the 1940s, Cincinnati became a country music and R&B town, with Hank Williams recording a few songs at Herzog Recording. King Records turned out dozens of R&B and country hits by Bull Moose Jackson, Cowboy Copas, Hawkshaw Hawkins, and others. Later, Detroit hit big with some local studios. What Berry Gordy, Jr., did with his Motown label is legendary. In the 1960s and early '70s, Memphis, the self-proclaimed home of the blues, was turning out hits by soul singer Al Green as well as pop vocalists B.J. Thomas,

Merillee Rush, Elvis, Dusty Springfield, and many others. Then, it all crashed. The record business became consolidated and was operated by a few large corporations. After that came the digital revolution. Suddenly, artists didn't go to Muscle Shoals for its special sound. Artists recorded at home if they wanted. But while it lasted, the regional music center was one of the most potent and productive forces in modern music history. Although local musicians are still making music in their cities, their viable record-business infrastructure no longer exists. New Orleans was once a good city for regional recordings. Its music had a strong presence in the city's clubs, and also a strong indigenous sound. A New Orleans record was recognizable by the sound that the musicians brought to the session. Perhaps more than any other city, New Orleans had—and still has—a "sound" that was peculiar to its diverse and historic background. This sound spilled over into recording sessions. Memphis was another prime example. So were Atlanta and Philadelphia. The most interesting thing about the regional centers was the competition. Regardless of size, they supported larger independent labels and producers as well as smaller ones. Take Memphis, for example. In the 1960s and '70s, soul singer Al Green emerged nationally on the Memphis-based Hi Records, while the Box Tops, a local rock band, hit big with "The Letter," recorded locally and released on Bell Records, a New York–based independent. Other communities, such as Muscle Shoals, concentrated mainly on recording, and not on distribution and labels.

Regional Recording Artists

Into the 1970s, some performers' records gained as much attention as the national labels' hits. Often this came through exposure on local television and radio. Many times the local acts had number-one hits in their regions, and often their masters were leased by larger labels for national release. But for every singer or band who went on to become national stars, there were a thousand who did not. Their records remained local or regional hits, yet their teenage radio listeners didn't mind. The nation was not so homogenized then. People were proud of their communities and their own performers. New Orleans was one of the leading cities for successful local recording artists and hits. Another was Cincinnati, where regional artist Dale Wright recorded for the national Fraternity Records for years. In the 1950s he had a moderate national hit with "She's Neat." His subsequent records were hits in Cincinnati and neighboring cities. Wright worked with Dick Clark when the *American Bandstand* mania came into Cincinnati. Though today's performers can be in demand in their own regions, they don't have support from local radio stations. When radio stopped playing local records in the 1970s, regional recording artists were all but knocked off the airwaves. Radio stations continued to tighten their play lists and dropped the smaller labels. From then on, local performers would have to rely on word-of-mouth and reputation. (See **Regional Hits**.)

Regrinding/Grinding

Labels coveted shellac so much that they recycled unwanted 78-rpm records. The labels ground up the discs in a process called regrinding. In post-war times, a few cost-conscious labels began recycling their excess singles and LPs to recover vinyl for reuse. The process was also known as regrinding, or sometimes simply as grinding. King Records of Cincinnati was a leader in this technique, thanks to its president, Syd Nathan. Unfortunately, the results were not always so positive for the quality-control department. Apparently, this was due to the age of the King presses and the quality of its vinyl.

Reissue

Companies reissued some discs that were out of print or about to go out. New pressings were made. In today's market, reissues are often older albums brought out on CD. (Not to be confused with the term re-release, which included second chances for hits such as "The Twist" by Chubby Checker on Parkway Records in the early 1960s.) Later, the term reissue came to mean discs reissued as oldies, such as those in Columbia's Hall of Fame series and RCA Victor's Gold Standard series.

Remakes

Years ago, a "remake" was simply that—the remaking of a song that had been recorded earlier and was no longer active on disc. Today the word is used interchangeably with the cover version. In the 1960s and 1970s, successful remakes seemed to hit the charts every month. They included Donnie Osmond's "Twelfth of Never," a 1973 version of the Johnny Mathis hit from 1957; Rod Stewart's "Twistin' the Night Away," a remake of the 1962 Sam Cooke hit; and "Tracks of My Tears," the 1965 Miracles hit recorded in 1967 by Johnny Rivers, in 1969 by Aretha Franklin, and in 1976 by Linda Ronstadt. Ritchie Valens' successful B-side, "La Bamba," became a prolific remake by the Tokens (1962), Trini Lopez (1966), and Los Lobos in the 1980s. But, over time, the term remake has lost favor to the term "cover." Even many record business people say a song has been covered. It is another example of changing terminology. Thus, the true cover record has become nearly a record business anachronism, while the remake still flourishes and will always do so. (See **Cover**.)

Remix

Popular with the arrival of multi-track tape recording in the 1950s, when two tracks became the norm. Remixing became even more critical with the arrival of four-track, eight-track, and more sophisticated tape recorders of the 1970s and 1980s. If record company A&R departments were dissatisfied with an initial mixing of tracks, they asked producers to remix a song. Prior to the introduction of multiple-track recording, records needed no remixing because the process used only one track on acetate disc and one-track tape. What you heard is what you got. The mix had to be done before the recording session took place, by setting up the microphones and musicians properly. This was tricky. An audio engineer had to have a keen sense of sound and balance. (See **Mix**.)

Repeaters

Continued success by recording stars. The name was used by jukebox operators and sometimes radio people in the late 1950s, when young singers such as Paul Anka and George Hamilton IV came back with hit after hit. On March 31, 1958, *Music Vendor* featured them—plus Frankie Avalon, Johnny Nash, and Danny and the Juniors—on the magazine's cover. It was the second time that they appeared there. "All these artists are teenage favorites and their repeated success proves they are not flashes in the pandemonium," the editors wrote in March of 1959. "The fact that repetition of a cover in unprecedented for *Music Vendor* affirms that the accomplishments of these young artists on the ABC-Paramount label are also unprecedented."

Reporting Stores

Music trade magazines once took weekly surveys to determine record sales and rankings for their charts. They contacted trusted record stores, radio stations, and distributors. The stores were called reporting stores. Individual magazines, including *Cash Box*, based a record's chart standings in part on these surveys. The magazines determined their best sellers, and less impressive ones, for their positions on the pop, country, and R&B charts. When the Nielsen SoundScan arrived in 1991, *Billboard*, the major trade magazine, replaced its weekly surveying with the computerized program that determined record sales much more accurately by scanning UPC bar codes. Gone was the era of laborious weekly surveying, and of course the few records that had been hyped into the low 100s.

Reproducer

Head on an early acoustic disc-playing phonograph. It contained the needle, stylus bar, and diaphragm. (See **Sound Box**.)

Re-Release

A previously released disc took an encore because the record label thought the song had a chance again. Sometimes disc jockeys would rediscover older records, those out of circulation, and play them, creating a new public demand. Sometimes record executives simply decided to give a record another chance. An example is "The Twist" by Chubby Checker, a No. 1 hit in 1960 and again in 1961, and "Light My Fire" by the Doors, a big hit in 1967 and a chart record in 1968. "Wipe Out" by the Surfaris came back too.

Reverb

A word that once meant two different things in the recording studio. On records made in the 1960s, sometimes audio engineers used reverb instead of echo. Why? It came down to money. Reverb is short for reverberation. *The Makeshift Musician* differentiates the two sounds this way: Reverb is blended repetition and echo is distinct repetition, like saying hello in the Grand Canyon. In today's world of high-tech equipment, the two terms are often used interchangeably, but years ago producers were more inclined to know reverb as the poor cousin of true echo used on recordings. Producer Phil Spector used pure, acoustic echo on his hits. The less expensive spring reverb systems were often used when studio owners couldn't afford the new artificial echo machines or an older-fashioned acoustic echo chamber. In those days, reverb was not considered as impressive as pure echo, especially when the reverb was turned up too high. That caused a hideous distortion. If it was dumped on, say, a chorus, and sounded harsh, there was no getting rid of it in the mastering phase. It was permanent. Back then a little reverb went a long way. The more sophisticated and expensive studios—and even some of the smaller ones—installed echo chambers. The results sounded smoother, longer-lasting, and pleasing—a true effect. (See **Echo Chambers**.)

Rewrite

Using parts of existing songs. In a less litigious time, some wise guy songwriters and A&R men decided to replicate hot items—hit songs. To put it bluntly, the music men rewrote the hit numbers of the day. Some people in the trade called a copied song a rewrite. The "golden days" of the rewrite came during the wild west-style R&B era of the early 1950s. Overeager A&R men sometimes jumped on major hits—"Hound Dog" is one—to create their own answer-song versions using some of the original's melodies and even lyrics. The competitors believed that if they lifted only a part of a melody and used only a few of the original's lyrics, they would be on safe ground. One of the most flagrant examples concerns "Hound Dog" by Willie Mae "Big Mama" Thornton. Teenage songwriters Jerry Leiber and Mike Stoller wrote it and produced Thornton's original version for Don Robey's Peacock label. Robey was not one to cross. He carried a gun and he wasn't afraid to use it. If this guy had the publishing rights, he intended to keep them. When Big Mama's record hit big, rewrites popped as answer songs. So many of them came out that it was difficult to track them all. Suddenly, lawsuits exploded because so many spin-off songs came from the original. In the end, the rewrite guys lost.

Riding a Record

Radio stations playing a record heavily, inserting it into the rotation. In the 1950s, they were "riding a record."

Risque Records

Gave buyers a laugh. Music-trade publications named the risqué because teenagers liked them. So-called risqué records included such provocative titles as "Big Ten Inch Record" by Bull Moose Jackson on King Records. "Risques" should not be confused with party records, which were, well, even naughtier adult fare that often featured recitations and monologues if they were recorded in clubs. All party records were generically risqué, but not all risques were party records. If you get the idea. By the 1960s, the terms party records and risqué records were used almost interchangeably. Risque records for teens were usually recorded by R&B acts in the genre's early days, from 1948 into the mid–1950s. They often featured the double entendre, a loose—pardon the pun again—story line, and an impish delivery. The fad died out when older people caught on and finally expressed their displeasure with the songs. In a story in *Variety*, a King executive had to all but apologize for ever making them and promise not to do it again. The arrival of rock further squeezed the risqué disc out of the market. Other risqué records included "I Want My Fanny Brown" by Wynonie Harris, "Work with Me Annie" and "Annie Had a Baby" by Hank Ballard, "I Want a Bow-Legged Woman" by Bull Moose Jackson, and "You Can't Keep a Good Man Down" by Billy Ward and the Dominoes. The most recognizable risqué hit was "Sixty Minute Man" by Ward and his group. It was recorded by artists of several genres. King even did a pop version. Not coincidentally, all of the aforementioned risqué records were released by King.

Ristaucrat "45"

A thirty-pound jukebox that measured only twelve inches wide, twelve and three-quarters deep, and sixteen inches high. Small wall or bar speakers could be connected easily, according to the owner, Ristaucrat, Inc. With the dawn of 1950 came the Ristaucrat "45," a breakthrough in smaller jukeboxes of the era because it played twelve 45s in succession, without requiring the owner to restack them. It was perfect for drug stores, motels, small taverns, road stands, and other small businesses. The company claimed the unit was "the only successful music box ever designed for small locations, the music box for the spot you forgot." They were passed by technology.

Rock Magazines

Followed rock 'n' roll like hound dogs on the loose in the late-1950s. Magazines already existed for country music fans, but now teens could enjoy reading new publications such as *Rock and Roll Songs*, which featured stories about the new hit-makers as well as lyrics to their songs. In one issue of *Rock and Roll Songs*, photos of Clyde McPhatter and Fats Domino were splashed on the cover with Connie Francis and the headline, "The Big Bopper's Name Is His Claim to Fame." As the 1960s arrived, more magazines proliferated. Many of them focused on rock bands. Such magazines still exist, but not in such large numbers as they did during the heyday of the 45.

Rockabilly

White rock music that lasted in its original form from about 1955 to 1964. Unlike rhythm and blues, which developed in the early 1950s and went on and has never fallen out of use, rockabilly music nearly died by the early 1960s. Since then it has enjoyed a modest revival, first re-introduced by the Beatles, who worshiped Carl Perkins. First dubbed "rockabilly" by the media, it was a mixture of the rhythm of southern country music and the beat of R&B. At times since the '60s rockabilly and semi-rockabilly records have popped up on both the country and pop charts at times, but never in such large numbers as in the '50s. Dominated early on by white Southern males (but certainly not exclusively), rockabilly music's defining sound was and still is Perkins' "Blue Suede Shoes." Sun Records in Memphis developed the sound with acts such as Perkins, Jerry Lee Lewis, Elvis Presley, and Johnny Cash. As the term rock music became popular in the late 1950s, encompassing both white and black artists, rockabilly faded and so did its stars. In more recent years the music has seen a new but more underground revival accompanied by a strong interest in the 1950s lifestyle.

ROSA

You can get it all at a one-stop, they used to say—everything but respect. This is why far-flung owners of one-stop operations joined together to help their narrow business grow. The larger one-stops enlisted the aid of the smaller operators to help build a national organization that promoted one-stops and found some solutions to problems facing the operators. One-stop owners had to compete with record distributors, who focused—well—on selling their exclusive labels' records. As a result, the one-stops formed ROSA—an acronym for the Record One-Stop Association. The group was prominent among one-stoppers in the 1960s. Sadly, today most one-stops are relics of the music business. So is ROSA. (See **One-Stop**.)

Round

A recording session. In the days before engineers developed long-wearing masters, five to fifteen talking machines had to run simultaneously to capture a performance. A "round" was an approximately two-minute performance, which the artists would have to repeat as many as forty times to build up enough original cylinders from which to press copies of a popular number. When the phonograph was in its infancy in the late 1800s, record companies paid singers and actors fifty cents to one dollar per round to make wax cylinders. This spilled over into the early 1900s. Companies had not yet learned how to manufacture large quantities of recordings without direct help from the performer. Every few weeks or months, an artist had to return to the recording laboratory and stand before a number of acoustic recording horns. This practice ended a few years later, when the industry finally developed longer-wearing masters from which hundreds and even thousands of copies could be pressed.

Royalty/Appearance Disparity

Not all bands were paid the same. Prior to the arrival of the Beatles, rock bands of all kinds—the famous, the infamous, and the obscure—didn't earn as much money for personal appearances, comparatively speaking, as groups do today. That's just the way things were then. Unfortunately, most country performers had to wait until the 1980s to earn the bigger money. The Beatles turned rock 'n' roll into a more serious business. As a result, other bands expected to be paid more, too. Appearance fees shot up. The image of rockers improved—at least as "artists." The public figured that anyone who could write something as moving as "Michelle" had to be an artist. The pay increase didn't happen overnight, and it wasn't huge for even the medium-famous, but it did gradually improve, even for local bands. Denzil "Dumpy" Rice, Lonnie Mack's long-time band member, once said that before Lonnie hit with "Memphis" in 1963, the popular Cincinnati band sometimes had to split money with others involved in a gig. "We'd end up with $15 a piece," Rice said. "But I didn't care. I just wanted to *play*." So he thought he was living large when he started *taking home* fifty dollars a night. (Uncle Sam was also happy with the musicians' newfound pay, but that's another story.) On top of that, royalties were not as much as the public imagined, either. They depended on performer's individual contract, but sometimes a singer was lucky to get three cents per record. Some got less. Making things worse, an artist had to pay recording session fees out of his and her meager royalties. This particularly hurt the singles acts because 45s didn't generate all the much income for the record company, let alone for the artist. Rockabilly and country singer Rusty York toured he South based on the strength of his modest hit single "Sugaree" in 1959. He stayed in nice hotels. "Later I realized that the company [Chess Records] was deducting the costs of my lodging from my royalties," he said. "Just about every expense came out of my royalties. I think they even charged me for my socks!" Though the larger record companies were generally more business-like and dependable with payments than the indies of the 1940s and '50s, the fates conspired to rip off songwriters and recording acts. Today, not much has changed with downloads, streaming, and other digital sales on which royalties are paid.

RPM

Originated in the early days of the phonograph, when several turntable speeds were available. By the 1920s, 78-rpms dominated. During the disc wars of the early 1950s, when two main speeds were competing against each other, revolutions per minute became a major topic of debate. The 45-rpm single or the 33⅓ LP? For a time, teenagers went for the 45. Audiophiles preferred the LP.

Rubber Records

Didn't bounce, but they did spin. Early disc records (in the late 1890s) were pressed in vulcanized rubber. The discs were promoted as "indestructible," and, compared with wax cylinders, they were. Unfortunately, the rubber records soon became flat in spots, causing them to skip. That's when Emile Berliner's phonograph company turned to a shellac type of compound made by the Durinoid Company of Newark, New Jersey.

Rube Sketch

Comedy record popular in the years before World War I and in the 1920s. One of the major rube acts was Cal "Uncle Josh" Stewart, but many other artists performed an occasional rube sketch. Its purpose: poke fun at rural people.

Rube Songs

Poked fun at rural people in America at the turn of the last century. Rube songs included the often-recorded "Turkey in the Straw" and "I'm Old but I'm Awfully Tough" by Cal "Uncle Josh" Stewart.

S

Save Our Singles

Campaign to rescue the single from financial disaster. When the singles business hit a sales slump in 1969, *Billboard* wrote an unsigned editorial urging the record business to "SOS—save our singles." The magazine called it "a campaign of the utmost gravity and merit." The writers called the singles business "a fantasy business" because it represented only a minor part of the industry's total dollar volume. Yet the social impact—the single was the main choice of young people—had just the opposite effect.

Scrap Drives

Reached their apex in 1942–1943. During World War II, when shellac was scarce and needed for the war effort, groups of celebrities backed record scrap drives. The idea behind them was to solicit 78-rpm records from donors. Thousands of records were collected at the drives and then sent out to be recycled for their shellac. Frank Sinatra was but one star who backed the scrap drives and appeared at rallies where records—both old and new—were donated by the public.

Second Pressing

Pressing that followed the first one. Some later pressings looked different. Larger labels often pressed 5,000 copies at first. If the record started selling in various markets, additional pressings were ordered as needed. Often they were pressed in different plants across the country, so they felt different to the touch. Usually, second pressings aren't worth as much to collectors.

Select-O-Matic

One of the more modern jukeboxes from the mid–1950s. Its contemporary design is easily recognized today, with a large glass top and chrome front. Looking down into the machine, the customer could watch the discs move onto the playing surface. Built by Seeberg, the Select-O-Matic was "the most widely publicized mechanism for the playing of recorded music," according to the company.

Self-Service Deluxe

Records placed conveniently on wall racks and "islands" for the convenience of customers, who either wanted to browse or select a record that they knew they wanted when they entered the store. Before the employee shortage brought on by World War II, America's larger record stores were like shoe stores. "Can I help you?" and a smile greeted the customer. Then came what the trades called self-service deluxe. The Lazarus stores' record departments put up a sign saying, "Every record at your fingertips." Of course, if someone wanted to ask a question, he asked for the manager or a clerk. The new sales technique also helped radio and appliance dealers who had taken on records to help boost profits in a time when their usual products were hard to order. Smaller record shops continued to greet their customers with the personal approach, but by then self-service was here to stay.

Sepia

Category that described music made by African Americans. Record labels also used the name Race music, which the music business seemed to prefer by the late 1940s. Like hillbilly, sepia was another marketing term used by record labels in the early days of electrical recording. One of the all-time biggest sepia acts, if not the biggest, was Louis Jordan and his Tympany Five. They pioneered the small band in the day of big bands. Their music was the forerunner of rock 'n' roll. These days Jordan is known mainly by historians and fans of older music, which places him lost in the twilight between the big bands and rock and soul bands of the early 1960s. Only twenty years earlier, Decca Records promoted Jordan heavily, taking out double-truck ads in *Billboard* and other trade publications. By 1944, the company claimed he had sold 5 million records. They climbed *Billboard's* pop chart as well as the Harlem Hit Parade chart, the top sepia jukebox chart. A decade before Alan Freed promoted R&B groups in his teen shows, Jordan was selling records to both teens and adults of all races. A 1944 photo shows a long line of teens (many of them white) entering the popular

Trocadero Club in Los Angeles. Decca ads touted Jordan as the "founder of teen age concerts," "the King of the Bobby Soxers," and "the No. 1 Sepia Artist." (See **Race Records**.)

Seven-Inchers

Jukebox operator slang for 45s. Actually, the early 45s were six and seven-eighths inches in diameter. (See **Forty-Five** and **Singles**.)

Sheets

Slang for sheet music. In the nineteenth century, sheet music was popular for decades. This carried over to first half of the twentieth century, when people stayed at home more often and entertainment options were limited. They tended to gather around the piano, playing the sheet music they bought at the sheet music stores. But as more records became popular there was less demand for sheets. Single sheets devoted to one song are still made, but not in the vast quantities of the earlier years. In those days, sheet music publishers were so strong that they could publish sheets on songs that were not popular on records. Then into the 1930s and '40s, sheet music remained popular and featured movie songs such as "White Christmas." In sheer numbers, fewer pieces of diverse sheet music were produced in the 1950s, although through the 1960s single sheets were still popular. You could find them in record shops and music stores. Single sheets were based on the record of the same name, and often included the artists' photographs on the cover. In the 1960s, many sheets were issued on records that were not major hits. Even records that reached the eighties on the trade magazine charts often had accompanying sheets. But sheets were usually designed for piano use. When the guitar became the more popular instrument among young people, sheet music sales declined in favor of songbooks (folios), which remain popular. They are also often arranged for the guitar. Today, sheets have become a tiny niche business.

Shellac

The female lac bug's secretions. Her passion prompted some enterprising soul to harvest the bug's resin, turn it into flakes, and dissolve it. This happened primarily in India, Thailand, and various other nations in Southeast Asia. The substance was used to coat many products in the nineteenth century, including wood and even some specialty food items. By late 1800s, the record business had already discovered shellac to make its new 78-rpm discs. This manufacturing process was disrupted for a few years during World War II, when the government rationed hard-to-get shellac. It was needed for various war uses, and it had to be obtained from territories threatened by Japanese armies. So the U.S. government slapped controls on the use of shellac and many other materials needed for the war effort. As a result, records became more difficult to obtain. Suddenly record-pressing companies were forced to turn to alternate and less effective manufacturing methods. But shellac became more widely available again after the war, and for years it continued to be used as a vital compound on 78s. The disadvantage of using shellac was that as time passed it left the discs "breakable," as people described it at the time. Brittle might be a better word. Actually, shellac was only a part of the mixture used to seal disc records, but it became the universally known ingredient. When the war ended, restrictions were lifted.

Shotgun Producer

Took the jobs that no other staff producer wanted. The name was used during the 1960s and 1970s. Billy Sherrill, the head of Epic/Columbia Records in Nashville, once called himself the shotgun producer of the label's staff in the early 1960s, when he was first hired. How the term originated is unknown.

Show Songs

Known as trade or show songs in the early to mid–1960s. The idea was simple. Great songs from past Broadway productions and other well-known movies and off-Broadway plays could be recycled—to use a less-than-flattering word—as singles. It had been done before, but no one realized that it could be turned into a trend, and introduce well-known adult-audience songs to the younger audience. For example, Jay and the Americans did it with "Some Enchanted Evening," from *South Pacific*, which opened on Broadway in 1949. In the fall of 1965, at the peak of the British Invasion of rock bands, Jay Black and the group went to number thirteen with the song. Most kids didn't even know it was old as them.

Side Thrust

Tone arm and stylus moving slightly to one side caused problems on some transcription players and early record players.

Sides

The word side (or sides) is still used, but not nearly as often as it was in the mid-twentieth century. It means a recorded song. As a headline in *Music Vendor* proclaimed in 1960, "Ten Sides Enter *MV* Top 100

This Week." A couple of them were listed: "Devil or Angel" by Bobby Vee and "My Heart Has a Mind of Its Own" by Connie Francis. No B-sides were given. Many of today's younger record-industry people prefer the term tracks to describe their recorded songs. Cuts is also applicable; it is perhaps the oldest term of the three. All these names are acceptable. But in the 1960s and '70s, more often a record chief or performer would say, "How many sides do you have?" Or, "That side you cut for Mercury is terrific." Many veteran record executives and performers used the word sides. Decca Records cut 256 *sides* on Brenda Lee before she turned thirteen. Most likely, the term side, singular, and sides, plural, originated in the early days of the phonograph disc. They came from a shellac record's side—some early 78-rpm discs had only one recorded side—and sides, with both sides being used. When multi-track recording became dominant in early 1960s, the word tracks began to refer to a recorded song. But at that time and even some years later the veterans still dominated the business, and they preferred to say sides. By the 1990s, the newcomers were saying tracks.

Silent Salesman

Cardboard holding cases used in record shops in the 1960s. Individual record companies usually offered one preferred LP for sale in the cases. Some boxes were a little larger than LPs and held about fifteen of the records. Others were stand-up units that allowed the records to be stacked on end. These units often came with signs on top, providing the name of the record company, such as Verve. One sign said, "Hear! Here!"

Silver Record

In the vein of the gold record, and just as good. In the late 1950s, Steve Sholes, chief of pop A&R at RCA Victor Records, wanted to start honoring the producers of RCA's gold records, so he came up with the idea of giving them silver records. In those days, gold records weren't given to everyone involved in recording a hit song. Sholes wanted to recognize the musical director, as he or she was known at the time, for shaping a recording. Perry Como's "Catch a Falling Star" on RCA happened to be the first official gold record awarded by the Recording Industry Association of America. Como got the gold. Joe Reisman got the silver. Sholes presented it to Reisman for producing "Catch a Falling Star." Perhaps Sholes wasn't aware that in 1937 the Regal Zonophone label gave a silver disc to George Formby for selling 100,000 copies of his hit "The Window Cleaner." There was no official gold record in those days. To Regal Zonophone, silver was gold.

Simulreleases

Simultaneous releases of American recordings in Europe and the United States.

Single-Face Records

Once, gramophone record companies issued disc recordings with only one side used. The public didn't question the policy, for consumers were desperate for records. Known as one-siders in the trade of the early 1900s, these discs were just what they were called—phonograph records with one recorded side. Usually, the flip side was smooth and blank, with no grooves or paper label. Sometimes the records came with a piece of paper adhered to the smooth side. It explained the record's series and the artist. In the fall of 1908, Columbia Records discontinued its single-face discs in favor of double-side records. By the end of the year, Victor began eliminating some of its single-side records, and the Zonophone label also brought out the new double-face discs. Although Victor finally stopped pressing all single-side records in 1923, it did make them available on some of its older recordings until the 1930s. In fact, a new RCA Victor long-playing series—on one side only—came out in the early 1930s. In modern times, a few single-face 45s (mainly promotion copies) were issued.

Single Thirty-Three

Introduced by Columbia Records in 1960. The Single 33, as it was officially called, was intended to compete with the Compact 33 issued by RCA Victor. The seven-inch disc played at 33⅓ speed, like a long-playing record, but contained fewer selections and was aimed at boosting single sales to the jukebox industry. Ironically, a spokesman for the juke operators criticized the 33, saying it was just another name for the old jukebox mini album. The man preferred 45-rpm singles. Without unified support, the Single 33 became just another name on the market. It was issued to the trade August 1, 1960, and was simultaneously available with the 45-rpm version. The stereo version was called the Stereo Seven.

Singles

The 45-rpm vinyl disc. (Later known as a compact disc with one important song accompanied by one to three others.) But the term's historic reference will always be the 45. Actually, the term single is more of a concept. When 78-rpm discs flourished, the single most often came with one song on each side. In those days there was no other real alternative, except for a few sets of records that made up the "album," mostly in classical music. The idea carried over to the new 45-rpm disc in 1949. It is no exaggeration that the 45—about seven inches in diameter; average running time in the late 1970s, three minutes—helped establish rock music. It supplanted the 78, even though the 78 manufacturers switched to an "unbreakable" material in the mid- to late 1950s. A part of the 45 single's popularity was its portability and toughness. Kids liked it. According to *Billboard*, the single was saved twice. The first time was in the mid-1930s, during the darkest period of the Depression. Legendary music executive Jack Kapp, of American Decca, lowered the single's price to 35 cents and three for one dollar. Other companies followed his lead, and the single survived. The second time came in the early 1950s, when the new 45-rpm disc pumped new interest into the single concept and prepared the public for the single's golden age—1956 to 1976. But the little disc hit some hard times in the 1960s. Then in August of 1964—thanks largely to the Beatles—the single saw one of its best sales months of all time. Over the next few years, singles sales went up and down. By 1969, it represented only about fourteen per cent of the record-sales market. Today, the concept of the single is practically dead, having declined with the 45 in the 1980s. Although the larger music stores often carried a rack of "singles" on compact disc (many of them carry with two to four songs), they were often considered little more than promotional tools for the record companies. Generally speaking, buyers aren't excited about the single anymore, unless they're downloading or streaming a single track online.

Singles Surveys

Free lists of the week's Top 40 (or whatever number) singles in the 1960s. They were issued by local radio stations. In the late 1970s, the practice died out. Customers could pick up the free lists at record shops and discount stores. Today, the old surveys are collectibles that reflect an era when programming differed from city to city.

Sixteen-Fifty Broadway

An address that spelled music. Its sister was 1619. They were at the epicenter of the American music scene. In the 1960s, 1650 Broadway was one the most important easily recognized record-business center in the nation. It received less attention than its counterpart, 1619 Broadway, known as the Brill Building. The Brill was the home of Aldon Music and some of the best commercial songwriters in the nation, including Carole King, Barry Mann, and others who wrote long-lived songs that are still recognized by the public, 1650 had perhaps a greater variety of record industry operatives who were financial and artistic leaders on the nation's music scene. If not more, than an equal amount. Songwriters, publishers, agents, managers, record labels—1650 had them all, and more. Hot indies such as Musicor Records operated there, as well as the under-appreciated Allegro Sound Studios, a hit-making machine where Tommy James and the Shondells cut most of their big records. Allegro turned out a lot of Top 40 singles—very commercial ones such as "Yummy Yummy Yummy" by the Ohio Express. The studio had an older, custom-made board then and a great echo system. The staff engineer, Bruce Staple, was a magician with sound. Other hits That came out of Allegro include "Younger Girl" by the Critters, "The Worst that Could Happen" by the Brooklyn Bridge, and "Mony, Mony" and "I Think We're Alone Now" by Tommy James and the Shondells. About 1975, the name of the studio changed to Generation Sound. By the 1980s, the shine wore off the music businesses located in the two buildings.

Skidding

A grating sound made on transcription players and phonographs when the tone arm and its stylus ran wildly across the record. The abrasive action caused a horrible scratching sound and damaged the grooves and the stylus. Today, the term skidding is nearly forgotten but the awful sound continues.

Skiffle

An early form of English rock 'n' roll that came out of traditional jazz. It has been compared to America's rockabilly. According to Billy Bragg's *Roots, Radicals and Rockers: How Skiffle Changed the World*, the new brand of music arrived in the early 1950s, when British teenagers discovered American folk and blues. Suddenly, guitar sales increased from 5,000 a year to 250,000. In 1956, a Scot named Lonnie Donegan was a major skiffle star whose hit "Rock Island Line" landed in the top ten in America and England. Like rockabilly, skiffle featured a rhythmic beat, strong vocals, and intense feeling. Most people in the States had never heard of skiffle, even when they were buying a skiffle record.

Slapback

Gave a special sound to the records of Elvis Presley, Johnny Cash, Jerry Lee Lewis, and other Sun stars. Charlie Feathers, one of the original Sun rockabilly artists, once claimed that slapback made the Sun Sound. In the mid-1950s, Sun's founder and crack recording engineer Sam Phillips arranged his two newly acquired Ampex 350 tape recorders to create slapback echo delay. In short, Phillips used the tape heads to slightly delay the tape. While recording a performance on one of the Ampex machines, he also recorded the playback on the other machine. It created a weird and creative echo effect, which he often used on the vocals. You can hear it on "Whole Lotta Shakin' Goin' On" by Jerry Lee Lewis and other Sun hits. Because there was "actual physical space between the heads of the machines," as *Popular Mechanics* explains it, there was "an audible delay and echo, a unique and iconic sound best heard on tracks like Elvis' 'Blue Moon of Kentucky.'" When Elvis wanted to use slapback on "Heartbreak Hotel" for RCA Victor in 1956, Phillips declined to give RCA engineers his method. To no avail, they put Elvis in a restroom and turned on the echo. Over the years other Nashville recording engineers tried to duplicate Sun's slapback by drenching their tapes with tons of echo, but they also didn't succeed. Slapback was too distinctive. Oddly enough, Phillips first tried it because he lacked an echo chamber. Slapback was born from necessity.

Sleepers

Records, either albums or singles, that weren't expected to become hits. The name became popular in the 1960s in radio and recording. To use a cliché, they came out of left field and onto turntables across America. The word could be used in two ways: a hit record that had received no promotion and was acquired somewhat as an afterthought by label management. Surprise best-sellers, as they were called in this industry lingo. Then there was the album version, which had been on the market for some time and suddenly caught on with the public. A few briefly became solid sellers, while others were long-term sellers. But all of them had risen from the ocean floor of "product." Sleepers ranged from rock to classical. In the late 1960s and early '70s, *Record World* devoted space to unheralded discs called "Sleeper Picks of the Week." Most of its predicted sleepers remained that way—asleep. But those that did sell were often label-savers. The classical field became a good place for sleepers. Columbia did particularly well with them. So did RCA Victor and London.

Sleepersville

Where sleepers were reborn and lived a second, charmed life straight out of the companies' back lists. Bored music trade writers at *Record World* came up with the term that expounded upon another term. It wasn't a town. It wasn't even a physical place.

Sleeve

A paper envelope in which a 45-rpm single and an LP are kept. The term, still in use today, dates back to the turn of the twentieth century, when fragile records were placed in company sleeves. Company sleeves are printed with the record company's name and sometimes other information. For old 78s, record companies often printed lists of other records and various advertising slogans. Company sleeves continued in use when the 45 disc arrived in the late 1940s, and today they are an up-and-coming collectible. Colorful sleeves of the 45-rpm era (from about 1949 to the late 1980s) are fascinating artifacts of the music business. Many labels did not use company sleeves, however, because of the additional printing cost. They simply used factory sleeves—plain sleeves with no printing. Most often they were white, and sometimes tan.

Small Spindle Hole

Usually found on EPs and LPs, as opposed to the large hole on the 45. In time a dual spindle hole for singles gained advocates in the United States, and in 1973 *Record World* devoted a story to this idea. Meeting at a retailing conference late that winter, retailers, rack jobbers, and distributors asked record companies to manufacture singles with a plug that could be punched out, so that record players could accommodate both the large-hole and small-hole single. "This idea, which has been lauded in recent weeks, would make the single compatible with small and large hole machines," reporter Gary Cohen wrote. Unfortunately for advocates of the dual spindle hole, support from record companies never came. The large-hole single continued to dominate. (See **Punch-Out Hole**.)

Smash

The big ones. Though recordings sell well today, the "smash" that people experienced in the 1950s through the 1970s no longer exist in the immediacy and form of old. Neither does the "high" that its makers felt. And if they occasionally do arrive, they hardly cause the commotion they once did. Yet you can still hear the word "smash" used today, though not as often and certainly not with the intensity and fervor of years past. This is because of multi-genre national charts, many variations of radio, the Internet, streaming, and whatever else has neutered a recording's impact on the market. Now, songs are focused on a demographic group. In the days when most medium-size radio markets had one dominant station, a smash was easier to ascertain because it hit with the force of a hurricane. Kids who listened to Top 40 heard the smash because they all listened to the same big station. In cities with a number of big stations, the same song was playing incessantly as well. In 1960s recording lingo, a smash was the quintessential biggie. "It's a smash!" said the producer, the record executive, the DJ, and everyone else. The word was almost always said with an exclamation point. Often the word hit followed smash, as in "a smash hit," although the redundancy is obvious. A smash would remain at the top of the charts longer than a "mere" hit. Smash meant a mega radio hit, which was also known interchangeably as a "monster." One trade magazine ad exclaimed: "No. 1 Monster of the Year!" The record? "I'm So Lonesome I Could Cry" by B.J. Thomas and the Triumphs on the Scepter label. Having a smash or a monster became the goal of every record producer and every record company. A really good monster was called, in 1960s lingo, a stone smash. Stone fabulous, a groovy thing, baby. Enamored by the sound and image of the smash hit, Mercury Records named one of its subsidiaries Smash Records. The label had a number of them, including "Hey, Baby" by Bruce Chanel in 1962 and "Walk Away Renee" by the Left Banke in 1966.

Smathers Bill

Introduced in the U.S. Senate in 1958 to try to prohibit broadcasters from getting involved in any music interests. It was named after the colorful U.S. Senator George Smathers, a Florida lawyer and moderate Democrat known for his strong anti-communist views. At the time, some federal officials were concerned that Hollywood film companies, broadcasting networks, and individual broadcasters were seeking entry into the music business through record labels and various other music portals. It appeared to Smathers that this could be a conflict of interest, or at least would put some music industry firms at a disadvantage. At the time, Hollywood wanted vehicles to release its movie soundtracks, and broadcasting companies wanted to spin off record companies to take full advantage of talent pools available to them. Smathers believed the motive of individual broadcasters was to get richer. Once the Senate started debating the Smathers Bill in May of '58, however, the whole chamber rocked with disagreement. Senators debated with their colleagues, indie label owners either protested the bill or welcomed it, and lawyers earned a fortune. Soon, it was learned that individual film producers would be exempt. Continuing the debate, Senate lawyers called in witnesses to testify, including Lew Chudd, whom *Billboard* described as the "major domo" of Imperial Records. Apparently he wasn't worried about networks or anyone else owning labels. He said times had never been better for the independents. Archie Bleyer of Cadence Records, another indie, agreed. A smug Chudd told the Senate that he was perfectly satisfied with the $5 million he had grossed the previous year. A senator—possibly hinting at payola—responded by asking Chudd how he managed to get so much airplay for an independent label. Chudd replied, "I work hard." As the debate continued, the Senate expanded its initial inquiry into other music business matters, including the day-to-day operations of both song-publisher licensing agencies and independent labels. Senator John O. Pastore, a Rhode Island Democrat, said he was "disturbed by testimony from many witnesses that songwriters could not get into ASCAP." One of them was country songwriter Mae Axton, a co-writer of Elvis Presley's "Heartbreak Hotel." She testified on the matter before a Senate committee. At the time BMI was doing most of the business in the rock publishing world. ASCAP, the upper crust of music, looked down on BMI. The older group was concerned about swirling rumors of payola in the rock business. Because of ASCAP's reluctance to admit rock 'n' roll songwriters, "young talent couldn't connect," according to Senator Pastore. "This is of tremendous significance for the record [industry]." Of course ASCAP soon came around; the money generated by rock songs was too big to ignore. Hearings and testimony on the Smathers Bill soon turned into a free-for-all. But it did have one interesting result. Prosecutors began looking into reports of a few powerful DJs being given part ownership of independent record companies and others receiving payola. By the time debate had ended on the Smathers legislation, the Senate was more interested in *talking* about problems in the broadcasting-recording industries than doing something about them. Soon various attorneys general, including those on the federal and state levels, began to investigate claims that specific broadcasters were taking payola. The famous rock DJ Alan Freed went to jail, and payola itself was driven even deeper into the underground. (See **Payola**.)

Society of Record Dealers (SORD)

Founded as a trade association in 1959 to promote and represent record store owners. Its members participated in a co-operative buying plan with members of a second group, the Association of Record Dealers. SORD's position in the industry was significant because it represented store owners—the backbone of the record business. At the time, record stores were still a potent force in the business, although they faced increasing competition from increasing strong rack-jobbers and one-stops. Naturally, SORD battled big-label record clubs, and sued Capitol's club for what members considered unfair competition. To members' surprise, Stan Gortikov, Capitol's general manager of record distributing, attended the group's summer meeting in Chicago in 1961 to reassure members that Capitol took the group seriously and wanted to have a good relationship store owners. His appearance reassured members that the large company took them seriously. At the group's meeting that summer, several big-name record executives attended. They included Randy Wood, president of Dot Records. He assured them that Dot would not, as rumored, start its own record club.

Art Talmadge, a label chief and president of the American Record Manufacturers and Distributors Association (ARMADA), told SORD members that they should do something about competition from rack-jobbers and one-stops instead of complaining about them. He offered to work more closely with SORD members but noted: "The only way for a bootlegger record to reach the public is through the dealer." At its peak in the vinyl era of the early 1960s, SORD was guided by president Howard Judkins and vice president Dan Winograd. In a 1961 editorial, *Music Vendor* claimed SORD provided "a noticeably aggressive check against the very many excesses" which were often committed in the record industry's race for quick profits. As record stores dwindled in number, SORD's membership dwindled as well.

Song Plugger

Sheet music firms' song pluggers were the equivalent of record promotion men. This was when New York sheet music companies flourished and dominated the music business. The term plugger had another meaning then. From the 1890s to the 1950s, the hardworking song plugger—the publisher's representative—promoted his company's latest songs to entertainers of all kinds in hopes of convincing them to sing his company's latest compositions on stage. If a plugger got lucky, he would find a big-name entertainer to adopt a piece as his theme song. The idea was to introduce a song to the public, who would then buy it as a piece of sheet music to sing and play at home. Scores of pluggers combed the cities and the countryside, offering new songs to band leaders, vocalists, and musicians. Pluggers worked day and night, going to beer halls, brothels, vaudeville houses, department stores—any place where entertainers performed. A requirement of the job was versatility. A plugger had to sing and play the piano to demonstrate the songs in the days before audio tape. After rock music and vinyl records eclipsed Tin Pin Alley's sheet music, song pluggers began working for a growing number of song publishers, who held the broadcast rights to most songs. These publishers were not sheet music people. They were "rights" people. Their pluggers did pretty much the same job that the old-timers did, except they didn't have to enter brothels—at least not on the job. Their goal: find performers who would agree to sing the pluggers' songs and record them. Meanwhile, the trades began to refer to the pluggers as song promoters when in greater numbers they began to move over to record labels. They promoted discs to radio stations, record producers, TV talent, and talent agencies. By the early 1960s, the two terms were practically interchangeable. Tony Orlando became a plugger for a song publisher when he briefly stopped singing on the road in the early 1960s. He worked his way up into song-publishing management. One day a familiar record producer spotted him in an elevator at a music-business building in New York. After exchanging greetings, the producer asked Tony to do a free-lance singing job in the studio. Reluctant at first because he might be fired, Tony thought it over, then agreed. The result? "Candida" by Dawn—and a revival of Tony's singing career. He no longer had to plug other people's songs. He was a singer of songs again.

Song Title Strips

Red and white title strips with black letters showed the names of songs on jukeboxes and wall boxes. The heyday of the title strip was through the mid–1950s and even into the 1960s—the heyday of the jukebox. They're still around, but not as obvious.

Sound Alikes

Peaked in the mid–1950s, when some new record labels decided to record singers who sounded like those who sang on the hits. The sound-alike labels could operate on low budgets because they recorded hit songs with unknown singers. Today this sounds strange, but in that era people were willing to buy a cheaper version of the hit just to get a copy of a particular song. This general concept was a carryover from the days of sheet music sales, when people enjoyed the song, regardless of who was singing it. A national label, Bell Records in New York, specialized in this unusual record genre. But many other labels, including regional ones, also recorded sound-alikes. At the time, sound-alikes had their relatively small but dedicated group of buyers. National and regional sound-alike labels, such as Bell and Big G in Cincinnati, did not attempt to compete on the charts with original versions. That was not the purpose of the sound-alike anyway. Though the sound-alike had to be recorded note for note like the original, it sometimes was released weeks after the hit version was already on the charts.

Sound Box

Another word for the reproducer on the early disc-playing phonographs, many of which were spring-powered. The sound box transmits the sound from the record to the metal horn. This is called the acoustic recording method. The box includes a thin piece of mica about one inch in diameter. Mica sends the sound waves to the horn by vibrations. A good sound box can create an unusually loud sound.

Sound Effects

On singles, often dubbed from sound-effects albums, were once considered cool. They were even used on album cuts. They usually appeared at the beginning of a record, and sometimes at the end. They included the sounds of car crashes, squealing brakes, buses, and anything else related to the song. Most singles didn't feature the effects, but at one point in the early 1960s sound effects were popular and acceptable. Listen to the rocket on "Telstar." It starts and ends the record and gives it a space-age feel. Other sound effects on various records included jet planes flying, cars crashing, doors creaking and slamming, buses pulling out, rain falling on tin roofs, thunder clapping, and whatever you can imagine that fit with the song and set a mood. One of the more interesting examples of the sound effect is in "The Letter" by the Box Tops, recorded in Memphis by producer Dan Penn. He told me that he liked the song by Wayne Carson Thompson, and envisioned the roar of a jet airplane at the end. So Penn borrowed a jet sound from an effects record, then added it at the end of his new record. He mixed the recording and proudly played it for ace producer Chips Moman, who operated the studio and production company where Penn was working. Moman heard the tape and liked the production but suggested that Penn remove the jet. He simply didn't like it. An angry Penn threatened to pick up a razor blade and cut the master tape into pieces before he would eliminate the jet noise. Moman told him to relax. He said he was only suggesting. But sound effects did work well on other songs, including "The Monster Mash," "Walkin' in the Rain," and a number of singer-songwriter Mickey Newbury's beautiful songs. Sound effects are still used occasionally, but their heyday has passed. Today they are considered corny.

Sound Fidelity

Audio quality in the late 1950s. The higher the better, at least in the record manufacturers' minds. To catch the public's attention, record companies championed hyperbole. They offered more infidelity than fidelity to the cause of recorded sound. Some of them started printing paper sleeves for singles with boasts such as: "Dynamic High Fidelity," Roulette Records; "Full Color Fidelity," ABC-Paramount; "Ultra High Fidelity," Dot; "A New 'High' in Ultra-Sound," Duke; "Super High Fidelity," Tops. Coral offered a simple and by this time anti-climactic "High Fidelity." By the time the '60s arrived, most of the colorful boasts were unceremoniously dropped.

Sound Lathe

A recording studio or mastering studio used a sapphire-tipped stylus mounted on a sound lathe to cut sound grooves into a blank lacquer disc.

When the engineer played sounds into the lathe, the vibration cut grooves into the blank disc.

Souvenir Record

A disc given away or sold cheaply, usually by companies as premiums. They ranged from souvenir records of WLW radio's 45-rpm recording of the Apollo moon landing to Tony Bennett's "Autographed Edition of Hits," a six-side Columbia record made for Coca-Cola.

Special Pressing

A specialty pressing was one designed specifically for radio stations. For example, in 1971 Sussex Records, a label distributed by Buddah Records, released Bill Withers' single "Grandma's Hands" in two forms: a two-minute disc for retailers and one-stops and a special 2:59 minute version for radio. The longer disc featured a recitation by Withers. Special pressings were common.

Speed Control

A device that controls the speed of a turntable revolution. Acoustic talking machines employed a simple brake method whereby the listener pushed a small leather-tipped or felt piece of metal, which slowed or stopped the turntable. Electric phonographs used a more sophisticated but similar method that controlled the revolutions at 16, 33, 45, 78 or some other speed. An interesting device called the Cobra-Matic arrived about 1950 from Zenith. Advertisements claimed: "The first and only changer that plays any speed record now made or yet to come, 10 RPM to 85 … with two simple controls a six-year-old can operate."

Speeds

The number of revolutions that a turntable turned. The most popular were 78-rpm, 45-rpm, and 33⅓-rpm.

Spindle

The spindle held discs and dropped them onto the turntable to be played. In the 1980s, the most recognizable spindles were heavy plastic ones made to play 45s. Made of metal or plastic, the spindle stood in the middle of the turntable.

Spindle Hole

Stamped in the center of the record to accommodate the spindle.

Spinner

A trade magazine name for a disc jockey in the 1940s.

Spinning the Groove

Playing a record, usually a 45-rpm disc. The turntable was responsible for spinning the record's grooves.

Spins

The number of times a record was played on the radio. In 1964, Kapp Records chief Dave Kapp told *Music Business* magazine that a new Jack Jones record, "Where Love Has Gone," would have to receive 10,000 to 12,000 spins per day on radio stations to be successful. He meant stations across the nation.

Split Play

Radio program directors and disc jockeys of the 1950s often turned a single over and played the flip side if they liked it. Music insiders called this act "split play," because it split the airplay between A- and B-sides.

Spoken Word Records

Recordings that included speeches of all kinds, readings of literature, recreations of events, and longer soundbites from important events, such as astronauts talking to the world during the moonwalk of 1969. Typically, the genre excluded the comedy record. By the 1960s spoken-word discs were a genre of their own. Usually the material appeared on LPs, but sometimes on EPs and occasionally even on 45-rpm discs. But mainly the spoken record was reserved for LPs, which had the space to devote to larger chunks of speeches and other spoken material in the 1950s and 1960s. The spoken-word record hit its prime in the early 1960s. In those days, spoken-word albums carried speeches by important political, social, and creative-field leaders. The Rev. Dr. Martin Luther King, Jr., President John F. Kennedy, and business leaders had parts of their speeches turned into albums. Other recordings featured famous actors reciting works of famous creative people and whatever else the spoken-word labels believed was of interest to the public. This included poets and authors reading their own works. One interesting spoken-word LP was called *The World of Sound, 1965*. It featured a black-and-white cover and short but relevant events as they were reported on radio in that turbulent time. Cuts included "A Walk in Space," "Casey Stengel's Farewell," and "U.S. Steps Up War in Vietnam." Another 1960s album, consisting of two discs, featured excerpts from the Army-McCarthy hearings, held a decade earlier. In the grooves Wisconsin Senator Joseph McCarthy sparred with high-ranking government officials over his claim of communist infiltration inside the federal government and military. The decline of the spoken-word LP was noticed as early as 1971, when Dr. Arthur Klein, president of Spoken Arts Records in New Rochelle, New York, complained to *Billboard* that major American distributors showed no interest in his catalog. He sold albums to schools, libraries, bookstores, and direct accounts. He admitted that his catalog was not exactly a "hot product," but there was some consumer interest in it. He added that the spoken-word LPs served an educational need. He told the magazine, "The major distributors have never showed great interest but recently they have even stopped replying to correspondence." In an effort to sell more recordings, he expanded into audio cassettes to attract younger consumers. At that time, he estimated his catalog contained about 400 items, including about fifty spoken-word cassettes in publication, but they had a combined sales of only 8,000. He said when it came to major distributors, "I have washed my hands of them." If only he had been able to stick around long enough to enjoy the revival of popular books that are read on CDs. They are popular with today's commuters. The genre has become a large market, with Barnes and Noble stores dedicating several racks to audio books.

Spool

Hollow plastic center piece on which a reel of audio tape was wound.

Spring-Driven

Heavy springs powered early phonographs. They had to be rewound after a few records had been played. The springs were encased in heavy metal canisters. When they broke (making a loud thud), they had to be replaced. Often children wound the phonograph crank too tightly, causing the spring to break. Spring-driven phonographs were phased out over a long period as more homes became wired with electrical outlets. However, a few new ones can be found, made for campers and emergencies.

Stacks of Wax

Another 1950s term for records, but it originated much earlier, in the days of wax cylinders of the early 1900s. The famous Edison Records two-minute molded black wax cylinders thrived from 1901 to about 1912, when Edison concentrated production on its more durable Blue Amberol cylinders. But even after 1912, the firm continued to make some wax cylinder records. In early 1914, a fire destroyed the cylinder pressing plant. For dictation machines, wax cylinders continued in production until the 1950s by Thomas A. Edison, Inc.

Staff Writer

Songwriters signed exclusively to one publishing company. Some of the greatest hits of all time came from staff writers. But certainly not all hits. Through the 1970s, the larger- and medium-sized song publishers kept a number of writers on the payroll. Usually they received a weekly salary—not a lot of money, but enough to help them pay their bills. They received the money as an advance on royalties, which they also received periodically. Though the staff-writer system is still in use today, fewer writers are involved and songwriters are having a difficult time earning a living strictly from their songs. In the heyday of the new rock 'n' roll phenomenon and even in country music, staff writers flourished. They included Carole King and Gerry Goffin, Barry Mann and Cynthia Weil, Neil Diamond, and Chip "Wild Thing" Taylor. These days, the writers are scrambling for jobs. "We've lost more than half of America's professional songwriters over the past decade," Bart Herbison, executive director of the Nashville Songwriters Association International, told the Associated Press in 2004. "The ones staying alive have really had to adapt." He blamed radio consolidation, which the AP described as "a narrow variety of artists, fewer songs, and relying on cookie-cutter programming." Because of mergers, only five major music companies exist as of this writing. And most of the important independent labels that once turned out many hit records have decreased in power and scope.

Stamper

Metal mold that acts as a reverse imprint of a lacquer. It's the device from which vinyl records are pressed. Often made from the mother. It moves only 1½ inches but exerts one hundred tons of pressure per square inch.

Standard Artist

Established middle-of-the-road vocalists such as Andy Williams, Patti Page, Johnny Mathis, and others, plus instrumentalists such as Roger Williams and Al Hirt.

Starting Groove

The first groove of a disc that pushes the stylus or needle into the recorded grooves. In the early 1970s, during a particularly poor time of record pressings, jukebox operators complained of bad starting grooves.

Static Charges

A common phenomenon on records, which generated considerable charges, especially in winter. When records were played, static showed up as popping and cracking when the tone arm was placed upon the disc. In a research project conducted by Shure Brothers, scientists rubbed cat hair on electrified records while they were on turntables. This resulted in negative charges of between 2,000 and 4,000 volts. When scientists lifted the discs off the turntable, the charge went as high as 30,000 volts. The electrostatic field was mainly between the underside of the disc and the top of the turntable. Lesson: Do not pet your feline while playing "Blue Suede Shoes."

Stereo Records

Sound coming from more than once source, as opposed to single-source monaural. With the introduction of microgroove technology on long-playing albums in 1948, stereo became feasible. On stereo records, sound came from two points of view on two speakers, providing a three-dimensional effect. "The stereo record," Capitol copywriters explained, "re-creates the needed perspective." In 1958, the record industry introduced stereophonic LPs. This did not impress William T. Thomas, president of James B. Lansing Sound, Inc. "If you stayed up 100 days and 100 nights," Thomas said, "you couldn't think of a better sales gimmick than stereo, but it has no place in the mass market. Stereo belongs to the audiophiles." Two years later, labels reaped some additional income from the new albums. By the early 1960s, stereo albums gained sales, but they were released concurrently with their monaural brothers. According to statistics collected by *Billboard* in 1969, mono album sales dominated stereo until 1967, the pivotal year when stereo bested mono. In 1968, a giant crash occurred, and mono was nearly swept away. It happened in two major LP categories—popular and classical.

Stereo Round

A patented system that involved a matrix connection to improve play on 45-rpm singles. The system was started by Rowe International, the jukebox company, in 1968 to help in stereo reproduction. At the time, Rowe and other jukebox companies had trouble finding stereo singles, and "little

LPs," or extended play records, were the best stereo records for jukebox operators.

Stereo Singles

They were late in coming, and they weren't always appreciated. Nonetheless, stereo 45-rpm singles began to appear in the late 1960s, although monaural 45s continued to be widely distributed throughout the early 1970s. Monument Records, the Nashville-based independent, began by releasing stereo singles in 1968, and increased their production in 1969. Jack Kirby, the company's vice president, said, "This will be for the benefit of both jukebox operators and FM stations, because we feel stereo singles increase our airplay." Other companies jumped on the stereo single wagon as well, even as many producers continued to provide mono master mixes to record label chiefs, who didn't hesitate to release mono singles. By releasing in stereo, record companies faced additional expenses because they had to maintain separate inventories for stereo and mono. So for the time being, mono singles remained available. Often labels' promotional singles for radio in this period featured a mono version on one side and the stereo version on the other. This satisfied both AM and FM radio stations. Although stereo 45s became a major breakthrough in the late 1960s, they were actually pioneered in the mid–1950s by a small Los Angeles label named Bel Canto Records. It just took the majors and everyone else a little while longer to catch up because they had to satisfy radio stations and jukebox operators. Bel Canto was so small that it catered to jazz fans. (See **Bel Canto**.)

Stiff

In 1960s lingo, a stiff was a record that failed to sell. The term was often used as a noun, such as a record was a stiff; also as a verb, adjective, you name it. Billy Joe Royal once told me, "My first few records stiffed. I knew things had to get better." And they did. He had a string of live ones.

Story Record

Known colloquially as the story song, the story record usually recounts an incident, situation, or personal experience in story form. The story record is specific. Like all good stories, usually it has a beginning, a middle, and an end. A good example is "Ode to Billy Joe." Composer-singer Bobby Gentry told an intriguing story in her song. It hit in 1967, and some years later spawned a film by the same name. "Ode" is a good example of how a story record does not simply provide emotion and information set to melody, as many songs do. The story song creates a mini world in less than three minutes. The Top 40 story record remained popular with radio audiences for years. It never has died out completely. Story records reached their peak in the 1960s and early 1970s. Nowadays, Top 40 radio rarely touches them. They seem old-fashioned. Country stations are still open to them, although a new crop of Nashville writers don't care about them so much. Examples of story records in the 1970s include "The Night the Lights Went Out in Georgia," written by Nashville songwriter Bobby Russell for his television star wife, Vicki Lawrence; "The Wreck of the Edmund Fitzgerald," written and performed by Gordon Lightfoot after the real ship sank on Lake Superior in 1975; and another fictional song called "The Gambler," written by Don Schlitz and recorded by Kenny Rogers. Story records were done in all the major radio genres, with country being the most popular. R&B story records were also somewhat popular through the years. A good one that hit in R&B and Top 40 radio was "Patches," written and performed by Clarence Carter. What a story.

Strange Phonographs

Phonographs were installed in clocks, windmills, and hearses. But by far the strangest phonograph was the Jumbo, made by the Gramophone Co. of Great Britain about 1910. J.E. Hughes, a big-game hunter and record enthusiast, traveled to Africa and found a job in Rhodesia (Zimbabwe today). He took his records with him and introduced them to Africans. He later became a safari leader. In 1909, Hughes set out to kill a gigantic elephant named Wungwa, which on rampages had killed a number of natives. After tracking Wungwa for six weeks and killing the animal, Hughes cut off its foot and sent it to the British phonograph company. Engineers equipped the top of the foot with a Senior Monarch phonograph turntable, crank, and horn. Soon a Jumbo Records label appeared, using this promotion: "Jumbo Records—not cheap and nasty, but cheap and good."

Strings

Considering the shrinking profit margin on rock singles in the late 1960s, labels justified spending less money on recording unless the acts were big-time or potentially big. Nonetheless, often singles featured strings, horns, background vocalists, and professional studio musicians who received union scale—and sometimes double and even triple scale. In those days, strings—real ones—were common on singles and albums. They were a part of most recordings unless they were straight-out rock 'n' roll, and then some of them also had strings. Even records by unknown or unproven artists with previous releases used strings when the producers and labels concurred that songs called for them. Today, new musical tastes and digital equipment rule. People hear a track and don't even imagine strings on it, unless it's an obvious piece like a Tony Bennett record or one that screams out, "Strings here!" Unfortunately, rock bands back then did not always appreciate strings because they had to try to replicate the sounds live with four- or five-piece bands. Listen to the Left Banke's "Desiree," a major production with a big-string sound and horns. Sadly, the record—one of the Banke's better ones—hit only number ninety-eight toward the end of 1967. The group seemed to have trouble overcoming the loss of the baroque sound used on their hits "Walk Away Renee" and "Pretty Ballerina." Of course, in those days there were no digital keyboard instruments that could replicate the sound of strings with authority. Nowadays, if a track needs strings, a keyboard instrument can and does replicate them. Real strings are still used, but not nearly so much. Times have changed.

Studio Bands

They picked on sessions that produced million-selling records. Regional studio bands flourished in recording centers such as Memphis, Muscle Shoals, Norfolk, and other cities. From the 1940s to the 1980s, they brought a stamp of personality to the music and the records. In other words, they each had a special sound provided by musicians who had often lived and worked in their regional music centers. In Memphis, Chips Moman's American Group Productions players cut more than one hundred hit singles for major artists such as Dionne Warwick and Dusty Springfield in the late 1960s and early 1970s.

In those heady times of the professional sideman, some expert players could earn a good living by playing exclusively on records in regional music towns such as New Orleans, Detroit, Cincinnati, Muscle Shoals, Memphis, and other cities, not to mention the musicians who did it regularly in New York, Nashville, and Los Angeles. One famous group—actually a pool of musicians in L.A. known as the Wrecking Crew—played on hundred major hits in the '60s and '70s. They would do a Carpenters pop session in the morning, and a Grass Roots rocker that afternoon. They finish a song on a couple of takes. Versatility was another strong point they brought to sessions. The Crew included a woman bassist, Carole Kaye, one of the best in the business. The guys who played on records in the smaller cities could also make a national name for themselves and never step foot on the coasts. Their hometowns gave these musicians a certain funky mystique that was impossible to get by playing in New York. Today, however, most professional studio players—those who do it for a living or for good money—have dwindled while their towns have declined as hit-making capitals. The super pickers were all over the map back then, laying down some of the hottest tracks in the industry. Who can forget Tommy Cogbill's lively, thumping electric bass on Dusty Springfield's "Son of a Preacher Man"? The record may have said Atlantic Records, New York, but the sound was pure Memphis. Sidemen gave each town a sound of their own, an identity that is overlooked by present-day record labels. A few of the super sidemen were guitarist Reggie Young of Memphis, who played the sitar on "Cry Like a Baby" by the Box Tops in 1968; the Swampers, a group of Alabama boys who owned their own place, the Muscle Shoals Sound Studio, and usually played on all the records made there; and David Hood, the white bass player who performed on many soul hits at Fame Recording in Florence, Alabama. But this doesn't diminish the contributions of studio players in New York, Nashville, and L.A., where sidemen were grouped as the A teams, the B teams, and others. Even the B teams were fantastic.

Studio Web

A late-1960s term used by trade magazine writers and record company executives to describe a label's affiliation with independent studios and often their house bands. As these studios began to cut hit records for labels, especially those based in New York, record executives wanted to repeat the sounds that created their hits. So they signed deals with the studio owners. Bell and Atlantic were forerunners in the trend. If necessary, the labels would become partners with studio owners, but often this wasn't the case. Some of the regional studios favored by New York labels for "web" deals included American Studios in Memphis, where producer Chips Moman had cut many hits for Bell, Scepter, and other labels; Papa Don Schroeder Studios in Pensacola, Florida, which was in an ownership deal with Bell; FAME Recording and the Muscle Shoals Sound Studio in Alabama; and Buzz Cason's studio in Nashville. Bell's Larry Uttal said such deals were not aimed at saving money, because hit records made cost a relatively minor issue. He said the reason was creativity: Independent producers could be more creative in their own studios. The concept of web studios declined in the 1980s with the rise of electronic instruments and the trend toward a more homogeneous sound.

Stylus

On early hand-cranked phonographs, there were three main types: a steel needle, a sapphire ball, and a diamond point. Other materials were used from time to time, including wooden needles, but the big three dominated for years. When hi-fi electric phonographs came into vogue years later, the stylus was still made from diamond and other hard-surface materials. By then there were the cutting stylus, which made the grooves in the original master disc, and the reproducing stylus, which played recorded sound in the grooves.

Subsidiary Labels

Offshoots of the parent record company, and, later, independent labels distributed by larger companies. Atlantic had ATCO. Columbia had Epic. They were true subsidiary labels—another division of the company. In today's view, however, the name subsidiary is used interchangeably with the distribution deal. Originally, distribution deals came when indies needed better market penetration. A larger label would sign a deal with the smaller label to distribute in exchange for a cut on the royalties. OK Records was Columbia's R&B subsidiary. Another subsidiary was Harmony, Columbia's budget line. By the late '60s, the trades were loaded with stories and ads touting new and older indies receiving distribution deals with larger labels. As the trend continued, more producers, songwriters, and other heavy hitters with new labels sought distribution deals. Chips Moman of Memphis went to Capitol with his new Chips Records. The thinking was: If a producer or a successful sales agent was turning out hit records, he might be able to do it for the larger parent company. Even smaller labels found homes with larger indies. Moderate-size independents such as the Pittsburgh-based World Artists Records had subsidiary labels. Most of them did not work out. But the few that did, such as producer Jeff Barry's Steed Records, were lucrative businesses. (See **Distribution Deal**.)

Suitcase Phonographs

The rage in the early 1920s. They enabled music lovers to take their phonographs to the beach or anywhere else. They were heavy things; the old spring-powered phonographs were loaded with real wood and metal guts. But they were portable and therefore handy. The convenience factor remained throughout the twentieth century, and suitcase phonograph became synonymous with portable phonograph. The suitcase name was misleading, however, for only the strongest of muscle men could lug around a heavy phonograph as large as a suitcase. Most people who owned a suitcase also owned a large, for-the-home phonograph. Today, the suitcase models are back, but now they are more the size of a thick briefcase.

Summer Hits

Meant money and memories, particularly if they were romantic records. In the late 1950s and 1960s, teens could buy records from limited sources, including record shops and stores such as K-Mart. Only one or two important rock stations operated in each moderately large city, so most kids heard the summer hits. If a record company landed a big summer hit, it could put them in the black for the rest of the year while providing teens with sounds they would remember for the rest of their lives. In the summer of 1962, one of the best summer for singles in memory, rack-jobbers reported a twenty-four percent increase in business over the previous year. Store sales increased five per cent—not bad for a store. Some summer hits from August of 1965: "I Got You Babe," by Sonny and Cher; "Help!" by the Beatles, "California Girls," the Beach Boys, and "Unchained Melody," the Righteous Brothers. The trades didn't discount the importance of the summer hit. As *Record World* noted in its Single Picks on the magazine's cover on July 11, 1970: "Make it three in a row for the Gentrys. 'He'll Never Love

Interest in summertime hits came at a time when many kids had three months off—to swim, dance, and listen to 45-rpm singles. In 1961, the Valmore and Empress labels of New York took advantage of the youth market by offering four new records for summertime listening.

You' (Knox [Music], BMI) is a Jimmy Hart song with a perfect summer sound and it's nice and short (1:59.)" Today the words summer hit means just that—a hit in the summer. There is no special feeling in it, no romance. There we have it. The record business still valued the summer hit as well as any record that was under three minutes.

Summer Slump

Despite the popularity of summer hits, American record companies usually experienced downturns. Sales dropped, presumably because young people were out of school. They had more outdoor entertainment options, including swimming, camping, and exploring the opposite sex. As a result, the sale of 45s decreased. Album sales often held up better, but even they declined as parents spent more time taking the kids on vacation. Interestingly, the traditional summer slump stopped in 1958, and it didn't return until 1963. Labels executives were perplexed. They attributed it to the newness of rock 'n' roll records, and then the arrival of the Beatles and other English combo bands into the mid-'60s.

Sure-Spins

Inserts made to fit into the large holes of 45-rpm singles so that the listener could play them on phonographs with small spindles usually reserved for LPs and EPs. Sure-Spins—they came five to a pack for thirty-nine cents in 1968—were distributed exclusively by Fine Tone Audio Products, Inc., of Brooklyn.

Surface Noise

Any annoying noise coming from the surface of a vinyl record. Pressing plant people were highly sensitive to this "dirty" word. So were record chiefs. The noise came from a variety of sources, including the manufacturing process and from worn-out records or those close to being worn out. In the 1960s, Betty Solomon wrote a column called "Surface Noise" for *Music Vendor* magazine. But it wasn't about surface noise. It was filled with industry chitchat about the stars. In it, Solomon used lines like "folklauded at the fete were the Limelighters, Theodore Bikel." No surface noise here, unless the stars and their "waxings" were considered the real surface noise.

Surprise Hit

A record that no one, including the record company and disc jockeys, expected to become a big hit. The term was used most often in the 1960s, when surprise hits had more of a chance.

Sweetheart Records

Nickname for songs featuring girls' names. Some record producers on the coasts were known to use the name sarcastically, but the sweetheart record had its place in Top 40 radio from the late 1950s into the 1980s. In the day of the sweetheart sound, some romantics were flattered to know that a boy would sing about someone with their first name, or with any girl's name. It was romantic. The sweetheart record had to have two constants: the song *must* be named after a girl, and it must be a tribute to her or at least express a longing for her. Songwriters used names of wives, girlfriends, and anyone whose name rhymed with love. Sweetheart hits included "Peggy Sue" by Buddy Holly, "Denise" by Randy and the Rainbows, "Walk Away Renee" by The Left Banke, and "Mandy" by Barry Manilow. Sadly, the sweetheart record ended with the rise of the women's movement, although there was no official connection. Time just moved on. The high-school dating scene changed along with cultural mores. As for contemporary music, the sweetheart record is all but irrelevant. Men don't often write songs emphasizing women's names, and if they did, women would probably complain that it's sexist. Long live "Denise"!

T

Tabletops

Developed for those people who wanted a phonograph that took up less space than the full-size models that dominated the phonograph market in the first half of the twentieth century. Early tabletops were spring-powered, with a crank. Many customers still preferred the stand-alone phonographs, but tabletop sales grew steadily. They were manufactured by a number of companies, including Columbia and Edison. Edison's earlier tabletops played cylinders; Columbia's played 78-rpm discs. The problem was that most of the space-saving tabletops were often made of solid oak or some other real wood, which made them too large and heavy to carry from room to room. As electric models arrived for good in the 1920s, tabletops became more user-friendly, requiring less arm strength to start. By the mid-1940s, tabletops were constructed somewhat smaller and lighter, but many were still made of wood. They continued to play 78-rpm discs. Tabletops were nothing new when the vinyl 45-rpm single and the LP were born in 1949. (Tabletops should not be mistaken for suitcase-style portables, which also had been around for decades.) The seven-inch vinyl 45 seemed perfect for a small tabletop. RCA Victor led the way in making and marketing them. By the mid-'50s, the smaller tabletops had become hot sales items. RCA Victor, Admiral, and other companies started making them with lighter-weight plastic, and smaller bodies. Suddenly, the one-speaker tabletop was the perfect music machine for pre-teens and teenagers, who put them in their bedrooms, took them to slumber parties, and went off to college with them. The venerable tabletop had finally emerged as cool. Today, with the rebirth of vinyl records, tabletops are made again, but they look nothing like the front-speaker ones that once served the 1950s boppers. They are dominated by portable, and colorful, models.

Take-Off

It used a part of another record to expound on a new subject. Not nearly as prevalent as the answer record in the 1950s and early 1960s, the take-off record was nonetheless another fascinating side of the old record industry. While the answer record directly answered another, the take-off record used another record's style or signature sound to expound upon another subject. For example, the Beach Boys' 1960s hit "Barbara Ann" turned into a take-off when "Bomb Iran" came out during the Iranian hostage crisis of the 1970s. More recently, "Weird Al" Yankovic has turned his parodies of popular songs into a long career. His songs could be considered take-offs.

Talking Machine World

This magazine, a forerunner of the modern record-business magazines, was aimed at people who were interested in music, recorded sound, and talking machines in the early 1900s. It covered the industry as an early trade publication.

Tape Clubs

In the 1950s, tape recorders for home use became popular with teens and adults. Teens started school tape clubs while their parents did the same thing through tape pen pal groups around the world. Their purpose was to promote tape recording, encourage friendships, and receive technical tips from fellow enthusiasts. *Magnetic Film and Tape Recording* magazine ran a monthly column called Teen Tapers. The writer, a high school senior named Jerry Heisler, provided information about recording and put taped-out teens in touch with one another. He described his column as "the new hangout for teen-age recordists." Both kids and adults lugged heavy portable tape machines around to record audio for family slide shows and home movies. By 1955, many teen tapers were recording rock 'n' roll off the radio and giving the reels of tape to their tape fiend friends. Suddenly, and briefly, reel-to-reel taping for teens was cool.

Tape Op

Larger recording studios hired tape operators to operate the tape machines, place new reels on spindles, and perform other tasks related to the tape recorders. This freed the sound engineer from those duties. Tape ops often graduated to engineering jobs. Today, the magazine *Tape Op* is one of the nation's best publications for people interested in recording and audio engineering. Editor Larry Crane is also a studio owner and audio engineer.

Tape Pirates

A record industry term for rogues who illegally duplicated tapes of all kinds, but mainly audio cassettes and eight-track cassettes in the 1960s and 1970s. Duplicating tapes was easier than copying vinyl records. Bootleggers, as they were also called, didn't have to bother with mastering and pressing. They simply copied an existing tape onto another tape. Tape bootleggers were all over the country. They could do their work about anywhere, including right under the noses of record companies in Nashville or in New York or in small towns. Their most relentless opponent was Capitol Records, which in 1970 filed a court action against forty-four companies and individuals. A judge granted a temporary restraining order. Capitol pursued the matter further. "We are determined to stamp out illegal duplication of our product," said Sal Iannucci, president of Capitol. Of course, Capitol couldn't catch them all. The pirates continued to make tapes in large numbers until tapes were no longer relevant.

Tape Worms

A grotesque term used in the early 1950s to describe amateur tape-recording fans who recorded and collected sounds such as birds chirping, people talking in various languages, big dirt-diggers, and other mundane sonic subjects. A tape company even published a little fanzine called *The Tape Worm*. One recorder magazine published a story about a man who lugged a heavy-but-portable recorder wherever he went, just to capture sounds that he could play for his friends. When this fan traveled by airplane, he picked out someone who spoke in a foreign language and asked to record him or her. A picture showed him talking to an Indian woman dressed in that nation's garb. Obviously, the luster of recording everyday noises wore off by the mid- to late 1950s, when many people owned tape recorders.

Tearjerkers

Teenage Top 40 songs that evoked sadness or crying. The tearjerker (aka the weeper) hit its stride in the late 1950s and 1960s. Today they are called teenage tragedy songs. Because of their depressing nature, some producers refused to record them. Many studio and record personnel were older, often anywhere from forty to sixty, so they were jaded when it came to emotional outbursts from or about teens. Yet the record-makers knew that such songs would sell. Some of them were well-written and -performed. Girlfriends and boyfriends drowned, were shot, killed in car crashes, and lost in wars. Theoretically, a tearjerker could recount the death of a teenager due to any cause, natural or accidental. But a lot of these hits concerned girlfriends being killed in car crashes, and the boyfriend storyteller feeling overwhelmingly sad. Distributors kept track of most record sales in small and medium markets. If a distributor was selling 10,000 copies of any over-the-top teen death single, a far-away label's head A&R man might growl to his staff, "Don't forget to check on that weeper in San Antonio!" This type of record began when rock 'n' roll developed and all but ended with the arrival of the Beatles and the more serious songs in the mid–1960s. Yet tearjerkers persisted in various degrees of sadness. They included "Billy and Sue" by B.J. Thomas, the previously mentioned "Patches" by Dickey Lee, and "Teen Angel" by Mark Dinning. "Tell Laura I Love Her" by Ray Peterson was a tearjerker *and* a cover, by Johnny T. Angel. The quintessential tearjerker hit was "Last Kiss" by J. Frank Wilson and the Cavaliers. A co-producer of the record, Major Bill Smith of Fort Worth, is said to have despised teen tragedy songs, but he managed to suck up his pride and helped in the making of the record anyway. It was a car-wreck tragedy, written by Wayne Cochran of the C.C. Riders fame. When the tearjerker died, it died unceremoniously and without mourning. Either the young audience just grew up fast with the Beatles or else the teen-death record wore itself out from boredom.

Teen Set

Largest teen-oriented merchandising and promotion campaign in the history of Capitol Records. In 1965, *Teen Set* magazine, a thirty-two-page fan publication that featured exclusively on the Beach Boys. It was launched with a print run of 750,000 copies. They were given free with the purchase of one Capitol teen album. The magazine generated so much interest that the label printed 500,000 copies of the fifty-two-page *Teen Set*, Volume 2, which was also given away free with the purchase of a Capitol LP. This time, the company set aside 350,000 copies for this purpose. The remaining 150,000 were sold for thirty-five cents each. The powerful promotion demonstrated to the record industry how a big-name label should promote its top-selling acts. The second *Teen Set* included stories about Capitol artists, including the Beatles, Dick Dale, Bobby Rydell, the Kingston Trio, Cilla Black, the Lettermen, and Peter and Gordon. Capitol spent heavily on the merchandising, setting up six-foot high display stands that held fifty album copies and 100 magazines. The project also included a Teen Set Fan Club, which cost one dollar to join. Nearly 20,000 teenagers had signed up by March of 1965.

Teen TV Rock Programs

Veteran *Music Business* columnist June Bundy was using the term years before she left *Billboard*, and she didn't stop after she arrived at her new employer. She had a number of shows to write about back in the mid-1960s: *Shindig, Hullabaloo, Upbeat*, and others, not to mention the local teen rock shows broadcast in nearly every large and medium market. Bundy had an opinion that must have disturbed the producers of such programs. She believed the kids cared more about the bands and vocalists than the "elaborate production numbers and special camera effects." She also maintained that the big-name hosts of the national rock shows didn't mean much to the kids who bought records. She wrote, "They [the kids] prefer shy Brian Epstein, who emcees the only black and white (and comparatively unpolished) version of *Hullabaloo*." She claimed the full-time record magnate had "wistful appeal." Regardless of any host's reputation or lack of one, teen rock shows were hot in the late '50s and into the 1970s. Local versions of *American Bandstand* gave teens the chance to show off dance skills honed at their weekly dances back home, when girls mostly danced with their girlfriends and shy boys would only venture onto the floor for slow dances.

Tent Cards

Promotional items from the 1960s that were inserted onto jukeboxes to alert the public to a new or favorite older record available for play.

Test Pressing

When producers or record companies wanted to hear how their newly mastered record would sound, the pressing plant would send them a test pressing made from the original master lacquer, which was used to make a metal stamper for pressing records. Sometimes these test pressings show up in record auctions. They usually come with typed or hand-written labels. Today, test pressing is making a comeback due the resurgence of vinyl discs. (See **Acetate**.)

Thirty-Three Single

A 33⅓-rpm, seven-inch single introduced by Columbia in 1960. The company had unrealistically high expectations of the new record, which was meant to serve both the jukebox and radio industries. In *Cash Box*, an editorial reminded the record business that 1960 was "the year which gave birth to the 33-rpm single—a factor which will have an important bearing on the record business to come." When industry insiders used the term "the thirty-three," what they really meant was a record that turned at 33⅓-rpm. It could hold six minutes of playing time, which supposedly would make it better for jukeboxes and radio stations. Despite being highly touted in its early days, the thirty-three pleased neither business. Both made money on *shorter* singles. Many innovations of the vinyl disc attempted to unseat the humble 45 over the years, but most failed.

The Three-Sixty

It arrived in 1952, about three years after Columbia Records introduced its ground-breaking 33⅓ long-playing record. The company realized it was going to need a new phonograph on which to play the LP. The company soon announced the arrival of Columbia's famed 360, which would become one of the most successful and popular phonographs in the last half of the twentieth century. At first, the company offered only a new attachment for $29.95. It enabled the record-buying public to play LPs on their existing phonographs. The attachment helped the company establish the LP during a time when other record companies were introducing competing records, including the 45-rpm single issued by RCA Victor. Then came the 360. It was known as "the hi-fi in a hat box." *Music Business* magazine would later note, "The '360' had an almost unbelievable effect on phonograph merchandising and design. It proved, first of all, that a mass market for a good high-priced phonograph existed." The 360 sold for $139.95, which at the time one could also buy a nice radio-phonograph unit. But the small yet powerful 360 had powerful side speakers that boomed out high-quality sounds. Its success "was so strong that the firm couldn't make the units fast enough to supply the demand," the magazine went on. Columbia had designed a phonograph that set the standards for other companies' new units. In 1964, coincidentally when the Beatles arrived, Columbia began selling its *Stereo-360*. Now all the new 360 needed was for the primarily mono record industry to catch up with it.

Three-Track

One of the record industry's more short-lived innovations. Confined to two tracks by the mid- to late 1950s, recording engineers and producers needed more. Then came the three-track machine. Vocals could be placed on a separate track, reducing the amount of sound bleed-through from other tracks. But the three-track's reign was relatively brief. Surprisingly, some engineers didn't like it. They kept their two-tracks. Soon Ampex and other recorder manufacturers let it be known that they intended to introduce the four-track as soon as possible. By the mid–1960s the four-track recorder began to find its way into studios nationally. It seemed perfect. Engineers who didn't obtain the three-track went wild over the four. Who could ever need more than four? Still, some studios in secondary markets kept their three-trackers. In 1970, when sixteen-track recorders were just coming in, "Rumble" guitarist Link Wray rebelled by opening Wray's Shack Three Track in Accokeek, Maryland. In 1971 he recorded an album for Polydor Records in his little studio. Later, he hauled the small Wray's Shack on a flatbed truck to his new home in Tucson, Arizona.

Tin Ears

Used by recording executives and producers to describe colleagues who were unable to pick hit songs. Also, high-fidelity fans used the term to describe many radio-phonograph manufacturers, which the hi-fi people claimed operated years behind the times as far as sound reproduction.

Tin Pan Alley

Once concentrated along West Twenty-Eighth Street, between Broadway and Sixth Avenue in Manhattan. Its nickname was universal. To the public, Tin Pan Alley meant any song publisher anywhere. The Alley's reign lasted from the 1890s to around 1956, when Elvis changed the way people looked at sheet music. At the peak of its influence, from the early 1900s to the 1940s, the Alley boomed with music publishers, lyricists, composers, and tireless numbers of song pluggers whose job was to convince performers to record their publishing companies' songs. In those days, the business worked this way: the public heard performers sing songs. This led music lovers to buy the sheets, which they played on parlor pianos and sung at home and in various public performances. In his book *Tin Pan Alley*, David A. Jasen noted that before Presley's arrival, "a song's popularity was determined not by the number of records it sold but by the number of copies of sheet music it sold." This changed with the arrival of rock 'n' roll. Slowly, the name pluggers gave way to promoters, but the name pluggers still wouldn't die. Though sheet music was widely available through the 1970s, its sales gradually declined. Records, mainly singles, dominated. Interestingly, a bastion of Tin Pan Alley was the Brill Building. When the new vinyl craze hit, the old, established sheet-music publishers started moving out and record people started moving in. The changeover was complete by the 1960s. The Brill became known as the focal point of pop—or rock—music. Rock 'n' roll killed Tin Pan Alley.

Title Strips

Narrow, rectangular title strips were used in jukeboxes for decades, and in some cases they still are made. Two manufacturers were Stop Record Services in Kansas City, and the Sterling Title Strip Company in Newark. The strips featured the names of both sides of the 45-rpm disc.

Tone Arm

Originated at the turn of the twentieth century, when acoustic disc talking machines used hollow-tube tone arms to carry the sound from the reproducer to the horn. When electric-powered phonographs came into favor years later, the tone arm kept the same name but delivered sounds through electricity. Columbia developed a lighter-weight tone arm in the late 1940s to play the LP without wearing out the records so quickly.

Tone Test

A popular event in the late 1800s, when the phonograph was still a novelty, especially in rural areas. Phonograph companies or record entrepreneurs used to book churches and small-town theaters to stage tone tests for the public. When sponsors brought in popular performers who made records, they hid the entertainers behind a curtain and asked them to sing live or announce or perform whatever it was they had recorded on the record. Then the sponsor would play the record and ask the audience: which was the real sound of the performer? Surprisingly, people often did not know the real from the recreated. It was an early version of the commercial, "Is it real or is it Memorex?"

Top Forty

Top Forty, a radio term for a format of commercial 45-rpm singles, had its heyday from the late 1950s to the late 1970s, and was responsible for breaking many of the industry's greatest hits. At the time, there were fewer musical genres and less competition. As the Top Forty hits gradually dwindled to nothing more than the top twenty or twenty-five, radio moved in another direction—fragmented formats that we hear today. Top Forty's beauty was that it allowed room for many kinds of records, including country, R&B, and pop.

Topical Records

Connected to current newsmaker, a political event, a product, or any topic on the lips of Americans. They were either serious or funny. The topical, as it was known, was a relic of the early 1900s, when President Theodore Roosevelt made a cylinder record. After the introduction of vinyl records in the late 1940s, topicals were often made as LPs. In the early 1950s, Freedom Discs of New York issued *I Speak for Freedom, Excerpts from the Testimony of William Mandel Before the McCarthy Committee*. Before the late '40s, the problem with many topicals was that they had to be issued on 78-rpm discs. When the 45-rpm single arrived, and the LP, the topical had more options. *Cash Box* listed Topical Singles. They were a mixture of serious and humorous recordings. The topical novelty single had an advantage over its humorless counterpart. It could entertain in a couple of minutes. These novelties went for radio airplay, so most of them were humorous—either recitations or songs. Most big-name producers wouldn't touch them for obvious reasons. A delay of two months—weeks, even—could make the material old news. The best topical novelties were based on popular crazes, scandals, and political gaffes. Nixon and Watergate worked. Another example was Ray Stevens' "The Streak," which poked fun at the so-called streakers who ran naked on college campuses and in other public places in the early 1970s. Other topicals were news-related or national fads. (See **Novelty Record, Radio Era**.)

Track

Tape recorders are known by the number of tracks they offer. They include one track, two tracks, three tracks, eight tracks, sixteen tracks, and twenty-four tracks, and more. They are all used on different kinds of recorders. The word track has several meanings, one of which is old and simple: Track is the sound that comes from one source. Like the term "side," a track can also refer to a cut on an album. Ten songs on an album would be called ten tracks, or sides. Used as a verb, track means the act of recording. "We're tracking the song right now," a producer would say.

Tracking Force

Weight of the reproducer on the vinyl groove.

Trades

When someone in the record business mentioned "the trades," he or she meant *Billboard*, *Cash Box*, and *Record World*, plus a number of small magazines that operated in the 1960s, such as *Music Business*.

Train Songs

Songwriters have written about many subjects since the beginning of mankind. From the 1920s to the 1960s, so-called train songs were prevalent. A train song is what it seems, a song related in some way to trains, freight or passenger. Their popularity rose alongside the arrival of the train in the nineteenth century. Train songs were known by this name at radio stations, record labels, and music trade magazines. Train song crossed genres, too. One of the earlier and hugely successful train songs was "Wreck of the Old 97," cut in 1924 by country singer Vernon Dalhart. So many train songs were cut over the years, especially in country music, that they developed into a musical subgenre. In 1963, country star Hank Snow cut an album of train songs. In the late 1969s, the Box Tops rock band recorded the soulful "Choo-Choo Train." As train traffic faded in the 1970s, the trucking song rose to take its place.

Transcriptions

Radio programs that were recorded on large black discs. Stations could buy these prerecorded programs and commercials or record their own transcription onto blank discs that looked like records with no grooves. They were recorded on machines that looked like record players. They inscribed grooves into the blanks, which could then be played. The transcription method remained popular until tape took over in the 1950s. Despite tape's convenience, the transcription method continued to hold on at various stations and studios for years.

Transistor Radios

Arrived in 1954, just as the 45-rpm single was winning the battle of the speeds, and when rock music and Elvis were emerging. Suddenly, kids had a portable music system. Its impact on the development of rock music is overlooked.

Triangle Records

In England, records looked different. They were known as triangle-center records. They were usually seven-inch singles that came with a triangle inserted in the 45 hole. The center of the triangle contained a smaller hole for playing the disc on an LP spindle. You don't see many of these records in the United States. The English Decca label made most of them during the mid–1950s, when the LP and 45 were battling for supremacy.

Triple-Play

An automatic record changer made by Admiral in 1949 that cost $69.95 and up. One tone arm could play the three formats—78s, 45s, and LPs.

Trucker Records

In the heyday of the vinyl single, songwriters liked to write about transportation, the romance of the road. Songs about truckers and trucking became popular in the late 1960s and into the 1970s. They were issued on 45-rpm singles for radio. Entire albums were devoted to trucker songs. Some of them became radio hits, mainly on country stations. The independent Starday and King labels catered to this demographic group by selling discs and audio cassettes at truck stops. King released albums with nothing but trucking-related songs. One of its LPs was titled *Radar Blues*. Red Sovine became known for his trucker-friendly records. Sovine managed to combine the trucker record with the topical and the tear-jerker. It was a successful formula. After having a career cold spell, veteran country singer Red Sovine returned to the charts in the late-1960s and the 1970s with some topical hits called "Phantom 309" and "Teddy Bear" on the Starday label out of Nashville. Red, born Woodrow W. Sovine, almost single-handedly made the recitation disc popular with his country audience. "Phantom 309," which charted in 1967, told the story of a hitchhiker who was picked up by a spectral big rig. "Teddy Bear," which reportedly sold a million copies over a period of years, was another big country hit that also did moderately well on the pop charts in 1976. "Teddy" was a real weeper about a boy who was no longer able to walk, and wanted companionship after the death of his father. "Teddy" was big—and it kept selling to truckers, who bought tapes in truck stops in a time when a country hit was lucky to sell 75,000 copies. To modern country fans, records like "Teddy Bear" and "Phantom 309" must seem like something from the 1800s.

Tune Categories

From the 1950s through the 1970s, before varied so many categories of music emerged and changed the music industry, jukeboxes carried a special identification grouping. It featured what were commonly known as "tune categories." From today's perspective, they were simple. Here is a 1970 music category list from Wurlitzer: hit tunes, top forty, golden oldies, rhythm and blues, hot country, polkas, novelty, and waltzes.

Tunesmith

A music trade magazine alternative name for songwriter. Popular in the 1940s through the 1960s, and still in use occasionally.

Turntable

A revolving circular piece on which a record lays. Its rotation propels the needle through the grooves. At the beginning of the twentieth century, turntables were usually made of pot metal or heavier-grade metal and covered with felt to prevent records from being scratched. Turntables continued to be made of metal for years. In the 1960s, some less expensive models switched to plastic. FYI: In the mid-1960s a guy by the name of Mike Turntable wrote feature stories for *Music Business* and edited *Behind the Scenes*, which *MB* described as "the most outspoken of all weekly [music] newsletters." Apparently Mr. Turntable's life revolved around 45s, phonographs, radio shows, and rock 'n' roll.

Turntable Hit

A record that failed to sell up to expectations, no matter its chart position. Producer Dan Penn has said his 1967 hit "Neon Rainbow" by the Box Tops became a turntable hit, providing disappointing sales despite ranking fairly high on the national charts. This probably happened because the record was so different from the band's previous hit, "The Letter." But then just about any record that followed "The Letter" was likely to have a tough time. "Turntable hits just didn't sell as well as they should have, despite their individual rankings on the charts," Cincinnati producer Carl Edmondson said. His turntable "hit" was "Hey-Da-Da-Dow" by the Dolphins on Fraternity Records in the 1960s.

Turntable Rumble

A hum heard from vibrations in the motor and drive assembly of the phonograph. Some 1950s audiophiles went so far as to make "rumble filters." Radio stations went to a lot of trouble to prevent turntable rumble.

Turntable Tom

Anyone who added sound effects to records and was obsessed with doing it. In television, the Turntable Tom preferred his audio effects over the visual.

Twelve-Inch Single

In the mid–1970s, during America's disco affair, record promoter Tom Moulton pressed an unusual single. It was not an average one. When engineer Jose Rodriquez ran out of seven-inch blanks at Media Sound Studios, he tried a twelve-inch test pressing. The disc looked odd with its tight band of grooves. So the engineer spread the grooves to make the disc look fuller to the eye. That meant that he also had to increase the level on the transfer. As a result, the record sounded louder and fuller. Moulton loved it. He later made his first purposeful twelve-inch single: "So Much for Love," a funk song by Moment of Truth on Salsoul Records. Moulton launched a studio career in disco, mixing for major acts and producing. He was careful to always make seven-inch discs for radio and twelve-inch ones for clubs. The big discs are still being pressed, mostly for hip-hop acts. Moulton's name will always be associated with the LP-size single, and for his ability to mix a great dance track.

Twelve-Incher

Collector slang for the LP.

Twin Labels

Term used by disc manufacturers when they inadvertently glued two labels on records. Sometimes they were directly on top of each other, but other times they were not.

Twin Spin

A radio term that meant playing two records with no commercial interruptions. Twin spins were most popular in the 1960s. They gave radio stations something to keep their listeners from changing stations.

Twist Instrumentals

People who worked in the record and music industries in the 1960s referred to instrumental versions of "The Twist" simply as twist instrumentals. They had limited success on the radio, but the owners of jukebox outlets appreciated them. The twist became so widespread that it became as imprinted on the public consciousness. Twist instrumentals were recorded by big-name acts as well as by nobodies. Organist Bill Doggett got into them; so did saxophonist King Curtis. The large number of twist instrumentals reflected the public's obsession with Chubby Checker's record in 1960. No dance will ever be as popular because radio formats are so

236 Twist Instrumentals

In 1955, bassist Bill Black, vocalist Elvis Presley, and guitarist Scotty Moore were at the epicenter of the rock 'n' roll quake. While Presley moved on into icon status, Black formed a musical group and Moore began producing for Fernwood Records in Memphis. Black's band had a number of nationally charted records, including one that latched on to the Twist craze. "Twist-Her" was promoted as "The Untouchable Sound," referring of course to one of the early dance-by-yourself dances.

fragmented now that most people listen solely to one kind of music. Then, the records appeared on major labels, minor labels, and ultra-minor ones. One record producer must have been dismayed that Checker's record lasted less than three minutes, so he recorded a twist instrumental that ran for twenty minutes. It should have been billed as "Twist Cardio." "The Chicken Twist," as it was called, appeared on a LP of the same name. Its cover read, "Chicken-Flickin'-Cotton-Pickin' Twenty-Minute Twist. If you quit before this record (is over)—you're CHICKEN!" Other instrumental twists on singles were named "Stick Shift Twist," "Big Twist," "Raunchy Twist," "Blues Twist," "Organ Grinder's Twist," "Pickwick Twist," "Afro Twist," "Bandstand Twist," "Twist Along," "Hully Gully Twist," "Candy Stick Twist," "Honky Tonk Twist," and "Soul Twist." For the early globalists in America, there was "The Israeli Twist," "Hava Nagila Twist," and "Chinese Twist" by the Popcorns. Oddly enough, it was recorded in Sweden.

Two-Sided Hit

Both sides of a 45-rpm single became hits. Two-siders occurred when disc jockeys and radio program directors had the authority to play what they liked. When they received a record with a designated A side, they couldn't resist listening to the flip. Sometimes they liked what they

Two-sided smashes were not rare in the golden age of vinyl, but they were not common, either. If a band had a two-sided smash on the charts, the group—and the disc—was red hot in the company's sales department. Usually, however, one side won out over the other. The smash side left its companion behind, to remain an unmemorable moderate national hit. So it was with Brenda Lee's smash A side, "Fool # 1," which peaked at number three on November 13, 1961. Its B side, "Anybody but Me," which Decca claimed would become a smash as well, reached a predictable number thirty-one on October 23, 1961.

heard and played it instead of the A side. On rarer occasions they played both sides. Most of the time, however, the recording artist was competing against himself or herself for airplay on two sides, so one song might hit the top ten while the other ended up in the forties or fifties. Occasionally, both sides were equally successful. Though the major stars (Elvis, the Beatles, etc.) were more likely to achieve a two-sided hit, the feat happened often enough to be anything but a freak accident. The Beatles were the kings of the two-sider. Imagine the delight of teenagers in January 1964 when Capitol Records pushed "I Want to Hold Your Hand," backed with "I Saw Her Standing There," onto *Billboard's* Hot 100. While "Hold Your Hand" was peaking at number one, the flip side was cresting at number fourteen. Between them, the sides remained on the chart for twenty-fix weeks. That April, while the Beatles were still new and red hot in the States, Tollie Records promoted itself into another two-sider: "Love Me Do," landing at number one, and its flip side, "P.S. I Love You," at number ten. No doubt the boys over at Capitol wept. They had turned down these Beatles masters as well as several others.

U

Unbreakable

The records were tough, when stacked up against shellac 78s. Right there on the label, "unbreakable" came printed for all to see. Compared with the delicate 78s, 45s did seem "unbreakable." But as owners of those records sadly discovered, the new discs were not. Still, the vinyl technology had made a huge leap forward, for both radio station personnel and eager teenagers who mostly bought 45s.

Underground

Radio stations that broadcast to the United States from another country, usually Mexico. Some DJs called them the Underground, or the Underground Air, to describe the renegade stations. In 1950s, when R&B and country music first collided to create primitive rock 'n' roll, a renegade, a clear-channel radio station called XERF blared its 50,000 watts of big-beat music from its location in Mexico, just across the border from Del Rio, Texas. At night, when the ionosphere helped bounce the station's signal for thousands of miles, Louisiana and Texas were at ground zero for a sonic boom. Night disc jockey Wolfman Jack, born with the generic name of Robert Smith, became known for his gig at XERF. For the most part the Underground died out as the 1970s and FM radio arrived.

Universal Reproducer

Enabled the listener to play both hill-and-dale records (Edison) and lateral-cut records (Victor, Columbia, etc.) in the early part of the twentieth century.

Upbeat

Television continued to boost rock 'n' roll in the 1960s and '70s. *Upbeat* was a Cleveland rock television show, representative of others produced in cities across the country in the 1960s. But this one was different—it was syndicated nationally, to be shown on TV stations who subscribed to it. The popular program was produced by Herman Spero. One of his more memorable shows came in 1969, when he saluted Super K Records and producers Jeff Katz and Jerry Kasenetz. They flew their entire staff and ten of their major bubblegum bands into Cleveland for the show. *Upbeat* was shown in a number of major markets of the period.

Upright Bass

It thumped its way into rock 'n' roll. The big upright bass—known affectionately as the bass fiddle—was an important instrument for both public performances and recording sessions in the days before the electric bass began to dominate in the 1950s. They shared the same purpose but not the same sound. The upright was acoustic. It was used extensively by the early country and rockabilly bands. You can see it in action in some old film clips. The bass player had to slap the strings and practically make love to the instrument, which stood as tall as some of the musicians. Gene Vincent's band, the Blue Caps, used an upright on "Be-Bop-A-Lula" in 1956, and Marcus Van Story used one on many of the Sun Records sessions. When he first started playing on sessions at Sun in Memphis, he had to provide both the bass lines and the drum sound. "We didn't have drums then," he said, "so I had to compensate. I had to slap the strings against the neck real hard. That's how we came up with the slappin' bass." The old rockabilly records had a special sound, and it came from the upright bass.

V

Variable-Speed Turntable

It could handle records from sixteen to eighty-three rpm. In the 1950s, turntables that used continuously variable speeds could accommodate almost every disc on the market, past and present.

V-Discs

By the end of World War II, the government had sent four million records and 125,000 spring-wound phonographs to troops in Europe and the Pacific Theater. There were no electrical outlets in the field, so the old crank phonograph technology had to be revived. The discs, courtesy the Armed Forces Radio Service, featured all sorts of entertainment, including performances by famous singers and other stars. AFRS pressed the famous V-discs at RCA Victor's Camden, New Jersey, plant.

Vertical Cut

The "vertical-cut" records included Pathes and Edison Diamond Discs. Some were played with a sapphire ball stylus. Vertically cut is the hill-and-dale method of grooving, in which the groove length is varied. A special reproducer was needed to play these discs properly.

Victorgroove

In January of 1949, *Time* magazine came up with a catchy nickname for RCA Victor's new microgroove 45-rpm single. "Victorgroove" was more of a pithy little name than a serious one, for by this time the magazine's writers—and everyone else—were becoming a little confused by all the new record technology that was entering the market so rapidly. For years the venerable 78-rpm disc had reigned as king of the industry. Twenty-five years earlier it defeated its only viable challenger, the cylinder record, which had died in a slow spiral. Then in June of 1948, seemingly without warning to record buyers, the powerful Columbia Records, Inc. introduced its new Microgroove long-playing album. Not to be outdone, RCA Victor proudly demonstrated for reporters its 45-rpm disc. *Time* blurted out its slightly sarcastic "Victorgroove" term. The magazine called the situation an "out-of-the-groove battle." Victorgroove was Microgroove, the tightly packed grooves of the new technology, but RCA's seven-incher came with a larger hole and required—at least at that time—a special record player to accommodate the new disc. By the middle of the following decade, *Time's* Victorgroove would change the lives of teens across the world. The single was coming on strong.

Victrola

Familiar name used on phonographs made by RCA Victor in the early 1950s, when the company's new 45-rpm records arrived on the market. But the name was not new. It had been used for decades on spring-powered talking machines manufactured and sold by the original Victor Talking

Machine Company of Camden, New Jersey. The company used the name on external horn phonographs until the larger living-room models arrived. Obviously, Victor Records had done a great job of marketing its product. In the first thirty years of the twentieth century, spring-wound Victrolas were known for their superb sound (for acoustic players) and fine furniture appearance. To the public, the Victrola even became a generic name for the phonograph. The Victrola name continued in use into the electric era.

Vinyl

The name is ubiquitous, entwined with the word record. The word vinyl is spoken more today than it was in its proudest moments, when everyone took it for granted. Who dared question the longevity of a dynasty? The story began with the start of the War of Speeds, which in the late 1940s pitted the new 45 against the LP and the outdated but still-surviving 78-rpm disc. When the speed war ended, vinyl was the real winner. Formats were incidental. Vinyl was available in almost every record shop, department store, library, five-and-dime store, and in any kind of store in between. From the arrival of rhythm and blues to the coming of psychedelia and then disco, vinyl reigned without question. For baby boomers, the 45 was an all-consuming glory. On their way to slumber parties, high school girls grabbed cases filled with 45s, to which they danced the Twist and the Pony; the boys retired to their rooms to play the hottest singles until the grooves wore down as smoothly as their young faces. They were ready to embark on a wonderful journey to the land of vinyl. When baby boomers reached their late teens and early twenties, they began to appreciate their parents' preferred format, the LP. It allowed them to enjoy multiple and longer tracks for playing more "serious" rock 'n' roll. By then, vinyl was the vehicle of record in the record business. When it sunk into oblivion in the 1990s, it went fast, disappearing in an ocean of new media. Today, young buyers have renewed the spirit of the 45s *and* LPs. With the help of a new generation, demand for them has returned. Sony's decision to resume vinyl pressing came about thirty years after the company dropped its vinyl production. At that time, most people believed the venerable disc was dead. Then suddenly, quite unexpectedly, vinyl re-emerged. The King of Sound was back, this time possibly to stay.

Vinylite

RCA used the word to describe its new non-breakable vinyl discs in 1949. Promised to wear 10 times longer than conventional shellac discs, Vinylite was a derivative of vinyl. Vinylite was the optimum in record pressing for a time.

Vinyls

Record industry slang for a seven-inch disc inserted into national magazines to promote record labels' artists and new singles. The first "vinyls" appeared in 1969 when several labels, including Apple, inserted the records into high-circulation publications, such as the popular *Holiday* magazine. *The Saturday Evening Post* carried a vinyl by comedians Dick Martin and Dan Rowan, and in another issue a vinyl single by singer Mary Hopkins was glued into a special folder. *Billboard* noted, "The unusual aspect of this new involvement with magazines is that the products are a regular record," and not a .004 or .006 mil plastic sampler so often seen in magazines. Some vinyls became after-market records, and some chart records. Unfortunately, vinyls proved too expensive and awkward to insert, and soon they were gone.

Vitaphone

An external-horn phonograph and a record label. In the early 1900s, American Vitaphone claimed it made its seven-inch discs from a mixture of paper and shellac. Vitaphone was a forerunner of the indie labels of the 1940s.

Viva-Tonal

The Columbia Phonograph Company's improved acoustic phonograph could play electrically recorded discs in the mid–1920s. By 1927, the machine had gained popularity. Its fancier model, the 810, sold for $300—a sizeable sum in those days.

Vocal Version

Vocal interpretations of popular instrumental hits in the 1960s and early 1970s. When adult contemporary instrumental singles began falling out of favor on Top 40 radio, listeners often heard what was called the vocal version. In many cases the lyrics were written after the instrumental had been released. For example, after the film *Mary, Queen of Scots* came out in the early 1970s, with a lush score by John Barry, Johnny Mathis recorded a vocal version of the title theme, called "This Way, Mary," for Columbia. Anita Bryant also recorded a vocal version of the instrumental "Wonderland by Night" for Carlton Records about 1960. Vocal versions were yet another way to bring home a hit record in the eras of vinyl and shellac.

Vogue Records

Highly artistic and colorful picture records, which today are prized by collectors for their artwork of various people and scenes. In the 1940s, the Vogue Record Company issued them. They were the fancier forerunners of the picture records of the 1970s and 1980s. Now highly collectible, they can be found at antiques shops and on-line. (See **Picture Disc**.)

W

Wall Box

Ubiquitous little jukebox units that sat on the end of tabletops in restaurants and malt-shop booths. They are now an anachronism, but in their day they were popular. Kids loved to read the song titles and pop nickels into the slots. The boxes were connected to the main jukebox in the restaurant. At their peak in the early 1960s, before chain restaurants and fast-food dragons consumed the nation, wall boxes flourished in the most unlikely places. Customers could play one song for ten cents and three songs for a quarter.

Wall of Sound

The name of producer Phil Spector's mighty combination of vocals and music in the 1960s. His sound was imitated by other producers, but only Spector himself could make it his signature product. It consisted of large rhythm sections, horns, strings, and background vocals. Spector used multiple rhythm players—as many as five pianists at times, and several guitarists. First, he cut the massive rhythm-section instruments and horns together, and then recorded strings and horns. Though other producers used these ingredients on their records, they couldn't duplicate the Wall of Sound concept. As Los Angeles producer Denny Bruce once said, "The Wall of Sound was Spector's idea, but [arranger] Jack [Nitzsche] was the architect." Nitzsche wrote the charts and arranged the symphonic sound that hit listeners like a tsunami. Supposedly, he earned only fifty dollars per song. The Wall was powerful for various reasons. It was recorded on limited-track recorders—no more than two or three tracks at first, which gave the many instruments and vocals a tight, locked-in feeling. Also, many of Spector's earlier records were done in monaural, which tended to give the sound an even larger presence when coming through speakers. The Wall was designed to be big, as heard on "Ebb Tide" by the Righteous Brothers and "Be My Baby" by the Ronettes. An unsung hero in the making of Spector's sound was pure echo from a real echo chamber—especially the excellent one at Gold Star Recording in Los Angeles, where the team often recorded. The Wall's—and Spector's—glory days ended with the arrival of the British Invasion in the mid–1960s.

War of the Speeds

Trade magazines and the news press called the battle between RCA and Columbia the War of the Speeds. Columbia fired the first shot by introducing the 33⅓ LP in 1948. The next year, RCA brought out its 45-rpm disc. Temporarily confused, the public did not know how to respond. For a time, the two new formats competed with the 78-rpm disc, but soon its sales began to fade, leaving the two new formats to coexist and complement each other. In 1950, RCA declared that the war of the speeds was finally over, and that 78s would continue to be made until there was no longer any demand for them.

Warping

Occurred accidentally for various reasons, often starting with the manufacturer. Sometimes warping was so bad that the tone arm appeared to be riding a wave. Warping problems spiked in the early 1970s, when disc manufacturers pressed extremely thin records. Though more aesthetically pleasing and comfortable to hold, thin records—mainly singles—often became cupped in jukeboxes and popped out of the jukebox record holder arms. But singles of this era where not the sole victims of warping. During World War II, some independent pressing plants made records with poor-quality shellac substitutes. As a result, the records were often warped. Syd Nathan, founder of King Records, once said of his first pressings in 1943: "They looked like soup bowls."

Watter

Referred to a radio station's power. This radio term, from the 1950s and '60s, described a station's output. Example: a 50,000-watter. Watts were all-import, for they represented the station's far-reaching power. For radio and teens, everything was about power.

Wax

Originated in the early days of the cylinder phonograph. When wax was used to manufacture cylinder recordings, the word became popular in the record industry, and spilled into the public's vocabulary. As the word was commonly used, a wax was a copy of a recorded work. Soon after, discs used a similar yet different version of the process. Hot wax was poured onto

"Dynamite on wax!" could be the slogan of rock 'n' roll, for the word wax continues in usage long after record companies stopped making records with wax masters in the early 1900s. Radio programmers just can't resist saying "black stacks of wax" and "hot wax weekend." This advertisement, from the independent King Records in the late 1940s, promotes the firm's shellac records from the time when vinyl records were about ready to invade the world. Even then, advertisers knew that wax sounded catchier than shellac. Hot shellac weekend just doesn't excite anyone, nor does hot vinyl weekend. This is why wax is embedded in the public's consciousness and will remain there, comfortably, so long as people have something to slap onto a turntable. To millions of people who enjoy vinyl records, wax will be synonymous with the 45-rpm single.

a hot plate to create a master. A needle or stylus cut grooves into the wax as a performance was recorded. Through the years the word wax refused to leave the public's consciousness. Subsequently, use of the name continued long after the substance had been replaced in record pressing. When someone in the studio tells Glenn Miller (in *The Glenn Miller Story*) that "a wax" will be ready shortly, the man means an acetate copy of the day's session. Today, the word wax is often used to describe records made in the 1950s, although by then the manufacturing process had changed. So when you hear DJs on the oldies stations promoting their music as "black stacks of wax" and "a hot wax weekend," they are talking history.

Waxer

Through the 1950s, the trade-magazine word described everything from a record man to the singer or the performer on a record. The singer *waxed*—or sang or played on the record. The term is not used today.

Waxeries

A trade magazine term for record companies. By the 1960s, the name had all but vanished. Reporters had become hipper.

Waxing

Synonymous with recording. Used by trade magazine and entertainment writers.

Wax World

A term used in the late 1950s by those who were on the outside looking in at the record business. Trade and entertainment writers of the era sometimes described the business as wax world. By 1961, Sam Cooke was the king of wax world, according to *Rock and Roll Songs* magazine.

Wire Recording

Sound machine that used a thin wire on which to record. Before tape dominated, wire recorders were popular for several years for mostly home recording. Radio stations used wire at times and sometimes even record labels tried to make records on wire recorders. Unfortunately, the wire was inferior to tape for recording music. Both types used the magnetic method of storing sound. The most well-known seller of wire recorders was Webster-Chicago. It advertised heavily, particularly in local newspapers. Wire recorders for the public got the jump on tape recorders, starting in earnest as World War II was ending in 1945. When commercial tape recorders finally arrived on the market around 1948, they received most of the attention in the newspapers. The arrival of tape was similar to the arrival of the talking machine. People were genuinely excited. As a result, sales of wire recorders declined steadily. By the mid–1950s wire machines were definitely on the way out. It was like the duel between BETA and VHS, the two types of video recording tape in the 1980s. Once it was clear that VHS had won that war, BETA's days were clearly numbered. So it was with wire.

Wood Shed

An appropriate name used by musicians and studio engineers to describe tedious and exhausting rehearsals in the days of acetate-disk recording and one-track tape recording in the early 1950s. This is when studio personnel had to do everything right—in one take—or else try it again. And again. And again. It must have been a boring and repetitive routine straight out of the film *Groundhog Day*. As a result, engineers borrowed the name wood shed from their childhood experiences, when the name "wood shed" meant receiving physical punishment, apparently in the wood shed at home.

Wurlitzer 1015

This 1940s jukebox is the most collectible and famous music machine because of amber bubble tubes that use a special liquid with a low boiling point. When people think of the classic jukebox, they think of the 1015. Paul M. Fuller designed it—one of thirteen full-size jukeboxes he created in eleven years. In the process he earned a reputation as "the Vincent Van Gogh of jukebox art," according to writer Joseph Gustaitis. Fuller's Model 850, with revolving polarized-light acetate discs inserted behind a peacock glass front, has captivated collectors since it was made in 1941.

Y

Youth Unrest

The record business was spinning along nicely until it hit a small snag. Label chiefs and everyone else referred to the issue as youth unrest. Protest songs had been around for some years, but they were mainly confined to folk music. Then Top 40 and the album crowd started putting a beat to it, and a white counterculture edge. First came the Buffalo Springfield's single "For What It's Worth (Stop, Hey What's That Sound)," a catchy protest song that hit the top ten in 1967. Soon others followed, inspired by anti-war protests, civil-rights turmoil, and rebellion against the status quo of parents. The unrest came on strong in 1970 when riots and demonstrations broke out on campuses across the nation. More hit records reflected the turmoil with their anti-war messages. As a result, record store managers in college towns and on campuses saw a temporary decline in sales to students. It was so noticeable that *Billboard* assigned a reporter to write a top-of-the-cover story about it. He spoke with store managers and others who gave their take on what was called "widespread student political activity." At Harvard, a man identified only as the manager of the Co-op Record Department told the magazine that student protests had definitely hurt his sales. He had an interesting way of looking at it: "They are living the lyrics of some of the records which we sell. Why should they buy them?"

Z

Zilch

To jaded recording engineers in the 1950s, a zilch was any unknown performer who came into the studio to make a record. Every star began as a zilch until he or she proved otherwise. Sadly, most singers remained a Big Z forever. Interestingly, a 1970s Nashville club featured a guitar-strumming singer with black plastic glasses and a sense of humor. His name? Zilch Fletcher.

Bibliography

Sources: Some terms used in this book came from the backs of old records, advertisements of the period, numerous trade magazine stories, documents and books in the author's collection, and interviews with many people involved in the record business from the 1940s through the 1980s. Primarily, the author drew on his thirty years in (and out) of the record business as a songwriter, producer, and label owner. Also useful for the early years: stories in *Antique Phonograph Monthly* (later simply *APM*), published by Allen Koenigsberg in Brooklyn, New York, and *The New Amberola Graphic*, once published by Martin F. Bryan in St. Johnsbury, Vermont; and *Blue Suede News*, issued in Duvall, Washington, by publishers Marc Bristol and Gabby Maag-Bristol. I highly recommend it if you enjoy rockabilly and other old music. The magazine has been published for years and it is the last word on roots music. In addition, *Goldmine*, another long-running music publication, has been a good source of information as well as an employer of many free-lance writers over the years, including this writer.

Books

Abott, Kinsley, editor. *Little Symphonies: A Phil Spector Reader*. London: Helter Skelter Publishing, 2011.
Amburn, Ellis. *Buddy Holly: A Biography*. New York: St. Martin's Press, 1995.
Broven, John. *Record Breakers and Makers: Voices of the Independent Rock 'n' Roll Pioneers*. Chicago: University of Illinois Press, 2009.
Copeland, Peter. *Sound Recordings*. London: The British Library, 1991.
Dawson, Steve, and Jim Dawson. *45 RPM: The History, Heroes & Villains of a Pop Music Revolution*. San Francisco: Backbeat Books, 2003.
Dethlefson, Ronald. *Edison Blue Amberol Recordings, 1912–1914*. New York: APM Press, 1980.
Fiegel, Eddi. *John Barry: A Sixties Theme*. London: Constable and Co., 1998.
Gelatt, Roland. *The Fabulous Phonograph, 1877–1977*. New York: Collier Books, 1977.
Hoover, Cynthia A. *Music Machines—American Style: A Catalog of the Exhibition*. Washington, D.C.: Smithsonian Institution Press, 1971.
Kennedy, Rick. *Jelly Roll, Bix, and Hoagy: Gennett Studios and the Birth of Recorded Jazz*. Bloomington: Indiana University Press, 1994.
Kennedy, Rick, and Randy McNutt. *Little Labels—Big Sound: Small Record Companies and the Rise of American Music*. Bloomington: Indiana University Press, 1999.

McNutt, Randy. *Cal Stewart: Your Uncle Josh.* Hamilton, Ohio: Weathervane Books, 1981.
_____. *Guitar Towns: A Journey to the Crossroads of Rock 'n' Roll.* Bloomington: Indiana University Press, 2002.
_____. *Too Hot to Handle: An Illustrated Encyclopedia of American Recording Studios of the Twentieth Century.* Hamilton, Ohio: HHP Books, 2001.
_____. *We Wanna Boogie: An Illustrated History of the American Rockabilly Movement.* Hamilton, Ohio: HHP Books, 1988.
Millard, Andre. *America on Record: A History of Recorded Sound.* New York: Cambridge University Press, 1996.
Moore, Scotty, as told to James Dickerson. *That's All Right, Elvis: The Untold Story of Elvis's First Guitarist and Manager, Scotty Moore.* New York: Schirmer Books, 1997.
Norman, Phillip. *Rave On: The Biography of Buddy Holly.* New York: Simon & Schuster, 1996.
O'Shea, Shad. *Just for the Record.* Cincinnati: Positive Feedback Communications, 1989.
Otfinoski, Steve. *The Golden Age of Rock Instrumentals.* New York: Billboard Books, 1997.
Powell, Austin. *Bubbling Under the American Charts, 1959–1963.* Booklet, Fantastic Voyage Records. London, 2015.
Rapaport, Diane Sward. *How to Make and Sell Your Own Recording: The Complete Guide to Independent Recording.* New York: Prentice-Hall, 1999.
Ribowsky, Mark. *He's A Rebel: The Truth about Phil Spector, Rock and Roll's Legendary Madman.* New York: Dutton, 1989.
Swenson, John. *Bill Haley: The Daddy of Rock 'n' Roll.* New York: Stein & Day, 1983.
True, Herbert. *Television Dictionary/Handbook for Sponsors.* New York: Sponsor Services, 1955.
Van Ryzin, Lani. *Cutting a Record in Nashville.* New York: Franklin Watts, 1980.
Whitburn, Joel. *Joel Whitburn's Top Pop, 1955–1982.* Menomonee Falls, Wisconsin: Record Research, 1983.
White, Glenn D. *The Audio Dictionary.* Seattle: University of Washington Press, 1987.

Periodical Articles

Allen, Bob. "Billy Sherrill: Nashville's Sharp-Tongued Studio Genius." *Country Music,* May 1979.
"Allied Record Company: A History of Firsts." *Record World,* April 26, 1969.
"Answer Discs Gain Momentum." *Music Vendor,* August 15, 1960.
"Answer Records." *Rockin' '50s,* August 1989.
Becker, James F. "Selecting Your High-Fidelity System." *Radio & Television News,* November 1950.
"Bell Inks Team in Studio Build-Up." *Billboard,* July 13, 1968.
Biro, Nick. "Hi-Fi 'Platter Turners' Make Juke Box Ops Edgy." *Billboard,* February 16, 1963.
"Blackburn, Blonstein in Epic, Custom Promotions." *Record World,* June 21, 1969.
Blevins, Brian. "Orient Pirate 'Playground.'" *Billboard,* March 14, 1970.
Blitz, Matt. "How Sam Phillips Invented the Sound of Rock and Roll." *Popular Mechanics,* August 15, 2016.
Brooks, Tim. "Book Review: Jukebox Saturday Night." *Antique Phonograph Monthly,* August 1979.
"Buddah Bowing 'Disk Theater' Merchandiser." *Billboard,* September 21, 1968.
Bundy, June. "Film-Theme Singles Were Hot Then." *Billboard,* November 14, 1960.
_____. "Kids Dig Wistfulness." *Music Business,* March 13, 1965.
_____. "New DJ Radio Look Causes Concern to Personality Jocks." *Billboard,* May 12, 1958.
_____. "Panicsville Again." *Music Business,* December 12, 1964.
"Business Roundup." *Fortune,* January 1950.
"California State Anti-Piracy Law Constitutional: Judges." *Record World,* August 15, 1970.

Bibliography 251

"Capitol Launches Greatest Promotion on 'Teen Set' No. II." *Music Business,* March 13, 1965.
"Cap's Historical Attack on Piracy." *Billboard,* March 14, 1970.
Caviness, Jim. "Spotlight on Buddy Knox." *Rockin' '50s,* August 1989.
"Charting the Hits ... " *Music Vendor,* August 15, 1960.
Cohen, Gary. "Retailers Favor Small Holes for Singles." *Record World,* March 24, 1973.
"Columbia's Challenge." *Newsweek,* June 28, 1948.
"Cover Record Waste—Says Janus Chief." *Billboard,* July 11, 1970.
"Crosby Back in the Groove." *Billboard,* November 30, 1968.
Daily, H.W. Letter to record business in *Cashbox* advertisement, November 27, 1976.
"A Dastardly Act." *Music Business,* March 13, 1965.
"Defective 45's 'Crisis.'" *Billboard,* March 11, 1972.
Dezzettel, L.M. "The Auditioner." *Radio & Television News,* November 1950.
"Disc-O-Mat Is Eyed as a Promotion Tool." *Billboard,* February 15, 1969.
"Diskin' Data: Bright 'Twilight' For Platters." *Music Vendor,* March 31, 1958.
"Does Life Begin or End with 'Top 40'?" *Music Vendor,* March 31, 1958.
"Douglas Releases a Book-Pkg. on Guevara's Life." *Billboard,* June 15, 1968.
"Down Twice, Saved Twice." *Billboard,* July 12, 1969.
"Fast Pace Set for Phonograph Makers." *Music Business,* December 12, 1964.
Faye, Christopher. "No One's Going to Emancipate ME." *High Fidelity,* August 1955.
Feinstein, Robert. "Footnotes on a Phonographic Wonder." *Antique Phonograph Monthly,* Vol. VII, No. 1, 1981.
Feldman, Len. "Ambient Sound." *Modern Recording,* June 1978.
Finkle, Dave. "It's Where the Girls Are With 'Happening' Groups." *Record World,* March 2, 1968.
"Firms Circulate Vinyls As Promos in Magazines." *Billboard,* undated clipping from 1969.
"Forty-five-rpm Single Fading Away." *Country Music Reporter,* June/July 1989.
Fulton, Ken. "Beware of Pirates." *Boy's Life,* November 1980
"Future of Low-Priced Field in $1.98" Record World, March 12, 1966.
Gerome, John. "Country Songwriters Face Woes." *The Cincinnati Enquirer,* April 1, 2004.
Glassenberg, Bob. "Youth Unrest Cuts Disk Sales, Dates." *Billboard,* May 23, 1970.
Good, Dave. "Fifty Years of 'Wipe Out.'" *San Diego Reader,* July 16, 2012.
Grein, Paul. "Disco Contributions Impressive." *Billboard,* July 24, 1976.
Grendysa, Peter. "The 45 Turns 45." *Discoveries,* May 1994.
Grevatt, Ben. "Competition Trends Cue Even Gladder Rags for '58 Albums." *Billboard,* January 27, 1958.
_____. "Indies Success on Single Records Draws Many Entrants into Field." *Billboard,* December 3, 1955.
Griggs, Bill. "'B' Side Hits." *Rockin' '50s,* December 1988.
_____. "Big Bopper's Record Broken." *Rockin' '50s,* December 1988.
"Group Efforts." *Music Vendor,* June 5, 1961.
Gustaitis, Joseph. "The Jukebox: America's Music Machine." *American History Illustrated.* November/December 1989.
Hall, Claude. "Music Director: Fading Job." *Billboard,* June 15, 1968.
_____. "You-Asked-for-It Radio Booming Across Nation." *Billboard,* May 7, 1966.
Herrera, Clara G. "Classic Vinyls Hard to Find; Harder Still to Find Machine That Will Play Them." *Fort Worth Star-Telegram,* February 3, 1994.
"Instrumental Hits: Some Patterns Emerge." *Cash Box,* June 2, 1973.
"Is Number Up for 4-Track? Tape Executives Say Yes." *Billboard,* March 14, 1970.
"Is Standard Acts' Switch to 'NOW' Music Aiding Jukebox?" *Billboard,* January 4, 1969.
"Is Stereo Too Successful?" *Music Vendor,* September 22, 1958.
"Jukebox a Happy Part of 1967 Singles Sales Picture." *Billboard,* September 21, 1968.
Kirby, Fred. "Classical 45's Enter as Film Doors Open." *Billboard,* August 24, 1968.

Bibliography

Klee, Joe. "From the Golden Age: In the Beginning ... From Berliner to WWI." *Antique Phonograph Monthly,* Issue No. 83, Vol. IX, No. 3, 1990.
Knemeyer, George. "45s Taking Their Time (Longer): Poll." *Billboard,* August 1, 1970.
_____. "Oldies $pur Jukeboxes." *Billboard,* February 20, 1971.
Kuntz, Phil. "Surf-Rock Classic 'Wipe Out' Inspires Puzzling Wave of Counterfeit Surfaris." *The Wall Street Journal,* August 15, 2001.
"Labels Are Lifeline of Independent Distribs; Strong Have Survived." *Cashbox,* November 27, 1976.
Lang, Roy B. "Reducing Turntable Rumble." *Radio & Television News,* September 1954.
"Live vs. Tape Test Set for Chicago Trade Fair." *The Music Reporter,* April 21, 1962.
"Mainline: Indie Faces Oblivion." *Billboard,* September 13, 1969.
Mayo, E.W. "A Phonographic Studio." *Antique Phonograph Monthly,* June 1980.
Mierisch, Fred. "Did You Ever Write a Song?" *Illustrated World,* January 1923.
"Mini-Mini on White Whale." *Billboard,* August 31, 1968.
Moulton, Tom. Disco Mix column. *Billboard,* July 24, 1976.
Muller, Marion. "Jukebox: Extinct but Not Forgotten." Undated *Billboard* supplement.
"Music for the Home." *Fortune,* October 1946.
"New Co-op Offers Records at Above 'Distributor' Bottom Cost'—CORD." *Record World,* March 12, 1966.
"The New 600." *Radio & Television News,* September 1954.
"Newcomers Hit Spotlight Overnight as Folk Invades 'Pop.'" *Folk World,* November 1963.
"Ops Applaud Singles Push." *Music Vendor,* July 24, 1961.
"Out of the Groove." *Time,* January 17, 1949.
Paige, Earl. "Box Oldies Promo Clicks." *Billboard,* May 29, 1971.
_____. "'Hey, Jude' Irks Programmers." *Billboard,* September 21, 1968.
"Patriotic Stickers Make Good PR on Les Montooth's Jukebox Route." *Cash Box,* October 11, 1969.
Paul, George F. "The Core of the Problem." *Antique Phonograph Monthly,* Vol. VII, Vol. 1, 1981.
"Pirates Run Rampant...: Fogel." *Billboard,* January 24, 1970.
"Playtape Plans 99c Cartridge Youth-Grabber Market." *Billboard,* June 21, 1969.
"Pop Stars Clicking on Flicks." *Music Vendor,* September 18, 1961.
"Promo Gambit Spreads to East." *Music Vendor,* August 28, 1961.
"Purple, Man, Purple." *Time,* July 7, 1958.
"RCA Gets into the Battle of the Discs." *Business Week,* January 22, 1949.
"Repeaters." *Music Vendor,* March 31, 1958.
Richbourg, John. "Striving for Better R&B in Sophisticated Market." *Record World,* March 12, 1966.
Rodriquez, Stephanie. "An Unforgettable Laugh." *Sacramento News Review,* March 3, 2010.
Rosemont, Dick. "Originals: The Earliest Records of Hits and Classic Songs." *Discoveries,* September 1998.
"RPMs Gone Mad." *Newsweek,* February 21, 1949.
Schlachter, Ron. "Key 'Indie' Record Firms Split on Dual Distribution." *Billboard,* September 13, 1969.
_____. "Monument Believes in Stereo Singles." *Billboard,* January 4, 1969.
"Should You Run for Cover?" *Music Guild,* March 7, 1955.
Sobel, Robert. "MONY Urges Shedding 'Long' Single; Vows Legal Step-Up." *Billboard,* May 29, 1971.
"Sock Sales Stimulate." *Billboard,* 1944 Music Year Book.
"SORD Parley Ends on High Note." *Music Vendor,* July 24, 1961.
"Spoken Arts President Raps Distributors' Lack of Interest." *Billboard,* November 13, 1971.
Sternfield, Aaron. "Record Clubs Take: $110 Million in 1965." *Billboard,* May 7, 1966.
Stevenson, Philip. "Roll, Jordan, Roll." *Tape Op: The Book,* 2007.
"Super K to Be Saluted on 'Upbeat' Show." *Billboard,* February 15, 1969.

"Thoughts on Watkins Glen." *Record World,* September 1, 1973.
Tiegel, Eliot. "Costs Skyrocket in Cutting Hip Sound." *Billboard.* Undated.
_____. "4-in-1 Single to be Bowed by Capitol." *Billboard,* September 12, 1964.
Weber, Bruce. "Vending Firms Gobble up Jukebox Routes." *Billboard,* September 21, 1968.
Wilkins, James "Rick." The Origins of the Victor Paper Record Label." *Antique Phonograph Monthly,* August 1979.
Willey, Day Allen. "Making a Talking Machine." *Technical World,* November 1979.
Williams, Bill. "60 Label Services By 2 Indie Distribs." Billboard, March 22, 1975.
"WINS Surprised at Freed Walk." *Billboard,* May 12, 1958.
"You Can't See the Profits for the Squeeze." *Record World,* March 2, 1968.

Major Interviews

Burgess, Sonny. February 10, 1987.
Carlson, Harry. April 18, 1980.
Edmondson, Carl. June 21, 2016.
Ford, Frankie. July 21, 1980.
Griffin, Herman. November 2, 1981.
Hawkins, Dale. July 18, 1987.
Hood, David. June 9, 1999.
Jones, Grandpa. February 2, 1991.
Knox, Buddy. April 7, 1988.
Lee, Dickey. July 18, 1986.
Mack, Lonnie. June 6, 2015.
Matassa, Cosimo. June 13, 1995.
Meyers, David. June 5, 2020.

Neal, Gordon. September 1, 1973.
O'Shea, Shad. September 12, 1994.
Pash, Jim. August 6, 1993.
Penn, Dan. August 19, 2000;.
Reynolds, Allen. August 18, 2000.
Royal, Billy Joe. May 11, 1992.
Samuels, Jerry. April 30, 1992.
Van Story, Marcus. June 15, 1989.
Vincent, Johnny. June 18, 1995.
Wallace, Slim. June 14, 1986.
Watkins, Bill. April 18, 2001.
Wright, Dale. October 18, 1986.
York, Rusty. September 10, 1999.

Index

Numbers in **_bold italics_** indicate pages with illustrations

A-One Distributors 103
Abnak Records 116
Accurate Sound Studio 32
Ace Records 1, 104, 115
Acoustic Sound Research 119
Aerrie Records 101
African Markets Exports 60
Alamo, Tony 56
Alexander, Arthur 134
Alexander Street Records 101
All-State Distributing 103
Allied Radio Corporation 16–17, 95
Allied Record Company 75
American Bandstand 54–55, 88, 89, 154
American Federations of Musicians 20, 162, 164
American Graphophone Company 91–92
American Sound Studios 18, 126–128
Americom Corporation 165
AMI Inc. 10
Ampex Electric and Manufacturing Company 10, 74, 141–142, 150
Amy Records 140
Anita Kerr Singers 17
Ann-Margret 37, 150
anti-war movement 33, 41, 56
Apple Records 242
Applebaum, Stan 14
The Archies 30
Arista Records 15
Armed Forces Radio Service 240
ASCAP 59
The Association 96
Astro Records 105
Atco Records 51
Atkins, Chet 15

Atlantic Records 10, 50–51, 52
Atlee, John Yorke 143
Automated Music Instrument Company 87
Average White Band 99–100

Babbitt, Bob 60
Bacharach, Burt 25, 77
Backyard Studios 105
Baekeland, Leo Hendrik 18–19
Baez, Joan 41–42, 82
Bagdasarian, Ross 144–146; *see also* Seville, David
Baker, LaVerne 45
Bakersfield, California 19
"The Ballad of Davey Crockett" 49–50
Bally Manufacturing 112
Bally Records 112
Banner Records 16, 62
Barry, Jeff 30, 161
Barry, John 80, 89–90, 242
Bartholomew, Dave 140
Beach Boys 32, 85
Beacon Record Distribution 150
Beatles 25–26, 33, 37, 42, 44, 99, 166–167, 169
Beckenbaugh, W.O. 143
Beckett, Barry 134
Bee Gees 78
Bell Records 62, 127–128
Bell Telephone Laboratories 152
Belltone Records **_66_**
Bennett, Tony 69, 73
Berliner, Emile 91–92, 116, 159, 168
Berliner phonograph 155
Bernard, Berney 177

256 Index

Berry, Chuck 45
Big Bopper 27
Big Brother and the Holding Company 88
Big State Distributors 103
Bikel, Theodore 82
Billboard 30, 49–50, 63, 68–69, 75, 76, 79–80, 85, 102, 135, 169–170, 247–248
Bill Haley and the Comets 19; *see also* Haley, Bill
Billy Ward and the Dominoes 62
Black, Jeanne 13
Blaine, Jerry 102
Bleyer, Archie 206
Blood, Sweat and Tears 47, 99
Blue Caps 239
BMI 59
Bob Seger System 60; *see also* Seger, Bo
Bobby B. Sox and the Blue Jeans 169
Bobby "Boris" Pickett and the Crypt Kickers 146; *see also* Pickett, Bobby
Bogart, Neil 28, 161
Bond, Johnny 33
Booker T. and the M.G.s 126; *see also* Jones, Booker T.
Boone, Pat 37
Bopper, Big 105
Border City Sales 173
Boston, Massachusetts 7
Bowen, Jimmy 15
Bowery Records 21
The Box Tops 83, *127*, 140
Boyce, Tommy 20
Boyd Records 101
Braun, Bob 154
Brent Records 58
Brians, Robin Hood 106
Broccoli, Cubby 89–90
Brothers Four 82
Broven, John 104
Brown, James 35–36, 53–54, 56, 90, 94
Brubeck, Dave 51
Bruce, Denny 243
Brunswick-Balke-Collender 15
Bryant, Anita 242
Buchannan, Bill 24, 145
The Buckinghams 24
Buckley, William F., Jr. 42
Buckner, Jerry 146
Buddha Records 28, 69
Buena Vista Records 68; *see also* Disney
Buffalo Springfield 247
Buie, Buddy 176
Bullet Records 99

Bullock, Wayne 94
Burgess, Sonny 56
Burns and Schreiber 166
Burton, Robert 59
Butler, Artie 14

C. Company 143–144
Cadence Records 166
Cahill, Marie 178
Calello, Charles 14
Calloway, Cab 48
Cameo Records 56, 69, 124, 161
Campbell, Glen 51, 126
Capital Records 15, 32, 33, 70, 83, 85, 123, 132, 148, 166
Carlson, Harry 1, 35, 43, 93, 135
Carlton Records 242
Cash, Johnny 104, 140, 193
Cashbox 9, 11, 31, 68, 135, 142
Castle Recording Laboratory 150
"Catch a Falling Star" 90
CBS Records 123
C.C. Rider 99
Chad Mitchell Trio 82
Challenge Records 62
The Champs 52
Chandler, Gene 93
Chantico Records 42
Charters, Sam 176
Checker, Chubby 37, 55–56, 69
Chelsea Records 99
Chicago (musical group) 99
Chicago, Illinois 16, 20, 27, 46, 137, 139, 163–164
The Chiffons 50
The Chipmunks 144, 145–146
Christian Anti-Communist Crusade 42
Christian Music 109
Christie, Lou 78
Chrysler automobiles 95
Chudd, Lou 206
Cincinnati, Ohio 1–3, 21, 23, 35–36, 42, 53, 62, 147–148, 154
Cinderella Sound Studio 73
Cinova Enterprises 183
Clanton, Jimmy 37
Clark, Dick 54, 89
Clark, Petula 25, *26*, 32, 126
Cliff Nobles and Company 57
Clooney, Rosemary 89
Cochran, Wayne 32, 99
Coe, David Allen 166
Coffey, Dennis 60
Cogbill, Tommy 18

Index

Colder, Ben 11, 146; *see also* Wooley, Sheb
Colgems 36
Colter, Jessi 101
Columbia Broadcasting System 129
Columbia Records 8, 15, 16–17, 36, 52, 58, 61, 68, 69, 73, 76, 83–84, 92, 94, 121–122, 123, 129, 138–139, 143, 151, 167, 240, 242–243
Columbus, Ohio 20–21, 42
Command Records 65
Como, Perry 49, 84, 90–91
Concord Radio Corporation 95
The Confederacy 58
Copas, Cowboy 81, 104
Costa, Don 67–68
Cothar, Ed 170–171
Cott, Tom 158–159
Counterpart Records 2
Crazy Cajun 105
Crazy Elephant **29**, 30, 88
Cream 165
Credit, Joni 13
Creedence Clearwater Revival 149
Crewe, Bob 72
The Cricketts 27
Crosby, Bing 15
Crown Records 62
The Crystals 169

"D" Records 105
Daily, H.W. 103, 174
Dalhart, Vernon 76, 81
Dalhart and Robinson 16
Danny and the Juniors 82
The Dapps 35
Darin, Bobby 17, 37
David, Hal 25, 77
Davis, Clive 15
Davis, Sammy, Jr. 121
Davis, Skeeter 13
Decca Records 15, 123, 149–151, 167
Dees, Rick 146
DeHaven, Penny 101
DeShannon, Jackie 89
Detroit, Michigan 10, 60
Deutsche Grammophon 36
Dezettel, L. M. 95
Diamond, Neil 126
Diamond Records 81
Dibango, Mana 50
"Disco Mix" 63
Discotheque Vol. II 65
Disney 8, 19, 68, 84; *see also* Buena Vista Records

Dixie Records 52
Dixon, Paul 158
D'Lugoff, Art 64
Dollar, Beau 35, 94
Domino, Fats 139
Door Knob Records 101
Dooto Records 156
Dorsey, Lee **140**, 141
Dot Records 12
Downs, Hugh 40
The Drifters 14, 129
Duke Records 54, 57
Durinoid Co., 195
Duroff, Nate 21
Dylan, Bob 41–42
Dyno Voice Records 72

echo 17–18, 73
Eddy, Duane 93, 125
Ediphone dictation machine 125
Edison, Thomas Alva 54, 61, 76, 95, 123, 159
Edison Amberola phonograph 125
Edison Diamond Disc phonograph 61, 74, 155, 240
Edison Lighthouse 28
Edison Recording 183
Edison Records 103
Elliot, Don 144
Ellis, Bob 173
Ellis, Shirley 36
Enoch Light and the Light Brigade 65
Ertegun, Ahmet 10, 50–51
Everly Brothers 30–31
The Exiles 88
The Express 28

Fabian 37
Faith, Percy 79
FAME Recording Studio 5, 134–135, 169–170; *see also* Hall, Rick
Famous Flames 36
Fardon, Don 152
Farrell, Wes 99
Fenster, Zoot 101
Fenway Distributors 103
Fernwood Records 128–129
Ferrante & Teicher **80**
Fidelitone 139
Fiesta Records 50–51
Fine-Tone 139
Fletcher, Zilch 248
Flood, Joe 158
Foley, Red 49

Index

Ford, Art 159
Ford, Frankie 139–140
Ford, "Tennessee" Ernie 49
Ford Motor Company 96
The Fortunes 49
Foster, Fred 104, 125
Fotine, Larry 21
The Four Seasons 82
4 Star Records 33
Four Store Records 66
Foxx, Red 156
Francis, Connie 13–14
Frankie Valli and the Four Seasons 78
Franklin, Aretha 134, 165, 169–170
Fraternity Records 1, 35, 43, 93, 135
Freed, Alan 6–7, 24, 45, 157, 158–159, 165
Fuller, Jerry 104
Fuller, Paul M. 247
Funicello, Annette 37, 68

Gale, Jack 77
Garcia, Gary 146
Garrett, Snuff 105
Gary Lewis and the Playboys 73
Gaye, Marvin 97–98
Gaynor, Gloria 64
Gennett Records 123
Gersh, Bill 177
GFS Records 13
Gibson, Joel 101
Gladys Knight and the Pipa 88
Go 63
Goffin, Gerry 25
Gold, Jack 42
Gold Distributors 103
Gold Star Studios 73, 243–244
Golden, Billy 43
Golden Age of Jukebox 110
Golden Records 34–35
Goldman, Ilene 156–157; *see also* Warren, Rusty
Goldmark, Dr. Peter 129
Goodman, Dickie 24, 53, 80–81, 145, 166
Gordy, Berry, Jr. 60; *see also* Motown Records
Gorwitz, David T. 63
Gramophone 116, 180
Grand Funk Railroad 6
Grand Rapids, Michigan 10
Green, Al 126
Greenbaum, Norman 109
Greene, Janet 42
Greenwich, Ellie 161

Griffin, Herman 60
Gross, Mike 106
Guest, Edgar 178
GWP Records 7

Haggard, Merle 19
Haley, Bill 149, 152; *see also* Bill Haley and the Comets
Hall, Rick 134–135, 169–170; *see also* FAME Recording Studio
Hall, Tom T. 47
Handleman Brothers 173
Hank Ballard and the Midnighters 27
Hanners, Doug 171
Harmony Records 31
Harms Brothers 25
Harris, Barbara 88
Harris, Emmylou 101
Harris, Phil 145
Harris, Richard 117
Harris, Rolf 146
Harry Fox Agency 162
Hart, Bobby 20
Haskell, Jimmie 14
Hatch, Tony 26
Hawkins, Roger 134
Hawkshaw, Hawkins 104
Haynes, Bill 49
Haynes, Dick 159
Hazelwood, Lee 73
Head, Roy 47
Heatwave 169
Heilicher Brothers Distributors 103
Hershey, Pennsylvania 7
Hilltop Records 121
Hirt, Al 6
Hit Kit 137
Holladay, Ginger 18
Holladay, Mary 18
Holloway, Brenda 47
Holly, Buddy 44–45
Hollywood Argyles 146
Holman, Eddie 78
Holzer Audio 51
Homer and Jethro 11, 146
Hood, David 134
Hopkins, Mary 241
Horton, Johnny 33
Hotwax 125
Houston, Texas 57
Howard, Chris 13
Hummingbird Records 101
Hunting, Russell 143
Hyland, Brian 146

Ian and Sylvia 41
Ides of March 99
Imus, Don 166
International Records Distributors 107

J & S Company 150
J. Frank Wilson and the Cavaliers 32–33
Jackson, Bull Moose 21
Jackson, Mississippi 1
James, Tommy 28, 161
Jan and Dean 32
Janus Records 49
Jay and the Americans 67
Jay and the Techniques 28
Jefferson Airplane 88, 96–97, 169
Jesus Rock 109
The Jewels 82
J.K. & Co. 130
Johnson, Eldridge 168
Johnson, Jimmy 134
Jolson, Al 15
Jones, Booker T. 94; *see also* Booker T. and the M.G.s
Jones, Grandpa 104
Jones, Jack 77
Jones, Tom 97
Jook 110
Joplin, Janis 88
JRLA 9
Jubilee Records 147, 156
Juilliard School of Music 80
Juke Records 113
Jukebox Wars 112–113
Jukeboxes 10, 30, 34, 36, 49, 57–58, 67, 68–69, **71**, 76, 87, 131, 136, 149, 151, 244, 247
Justice, Bill 107

K-Doe, Ernie 140–141
Kapp, Jack 15, 200
Kapp Records 77
Kasenetz, Jerry 28, **29**, 88, 239
Katsakis, George 60, 88
Katz, Jeff 28, **29**, 239
KDEO 9
Kelly, Dan 143
Kennedy, Gene 101
Kiddie Company 166
King, Ben E. 14
King, Carole 25, 58
King, Clydie "Brown Sugar" 99
King Records 15, 21, 23, 35–36, 44–46, 52, 62, 66, 67, 90, 96, 123, 147, 149, 150, **245**; *see also* Nathan, Syd

Kingston Trio 129, 152
KLAC 159
The Knickerbockers 88
Knight, Terry 6
Knox, Buddy 106
Kop, Bunny 42
KROY 9
KTRM 174

L-7 55
Lacey, Jack 45
Lamb, Charlie 72, 135, 137
Lambert Company 46
Laurie Records 104
Lee, Leapy 143–144
Leka, Paul 28, 69
Lemon Pipers 28, 69
Lenhoff, Ron 90
The Lettermen 126
Levine, Hank 101
Levine, Joey 28
Lewis, Barbara 88
Lewis, Bobby 66
Lewis, Jerry Lee 104, 128, 140
Lewis, Stan 1
Liberty Records 145
Little Mark Records 56
Locklin, Hank 13
London, Julie 13
London Records 31
Los Angeles, California 8, 14, 21, 24, 32, 63, 66, 73, 75
Lowery, Bill 176
Lubinsky, Herman 128
Lulu 169
Lundberg, Victor 143
Lynyrd Skynyrd 170

Macaluso, Dorothy "Dotty" 154–155
Mack, Lonnie **35**, 36, 93, 99, 135
Madigan, Betty 13
Mainline Distributors 102
Mala Records 60
Mann, Barry 25
Marteric, Ralph 67
Martin, Bobby 47–48
Martin and Rowan 242
Martin & Snyder 150
Mary Kaye Trio 130
Matassa, Cosimo 62, 140
Mathis, Johnny 67, 132, 242
Maverick Records 101
MC 5 60
McCall, C. W. 146

260 Index

McClinton, Delbert 134
McCoy, Van 14
The McCoys 88
McCrory's 5 & 10 Cent Store 62
McDaniel, Earl 159
McDonald, Skeets 49
McFarland, Elaine "Spanky" 88
McIntyre, Neil 142
McRae, Meredith 11
Meader, Vaughan 166
Meaux, Huey 105
Melanie 28
Memphis, Tennessee 10, 18, 38, 126–129
Mercuri, Melina 67
Mercury Records 8, 123
Mercury Scientific Products Corp. 63
MGM Records 146
Michaels, Marilyn 11
Miller, Roger 13
Mills, Haley 68
The Mindbenders 93
Mitchell, Joni 82
Mitchell, Willie 126
Molloy, Russ 21
Moman, Chips 18, 48, 126–127
Monarch Record Manufacturing Corp. 21
Monkees 20
Monument Might Master 125
Monument Records 125
Moody, Clyde 40
Moore, Scotty 128
Moss, Wayne 73
Motown Records 60, 69; *see also* Gordy, Berry, Jr.
Moulton, Tom 63–64
Mrs. Miller 150
Muir, Jean 133
Murray, Anne 126
Murray, Billy 39
Murray the "K" International Fan Club 79
Muscle Shoals, Alabama 134–135, 169–170
Muscle Shoals Sound Studio 134, 170
Music Business 148, 165
Music Reporter 72, 137
Music Vendor 10, 11, 36, 37, 66, 67, 75, 76, 136, 138, 151
Musical Sales 150
Musicor Records 77

Nashville, Tennessee 6, 14–15, 19, 31, 125, 137, 150, 170
Nathan, Syd 23, 45, 96, 128, 149, 150, 163, 244; *see also* King Records

National Association of Broadcast Engineers and Technicians 164
National Association of Record Merchandisers 86, 162
National Labor Relations Board 144
Nelson, Terry 143–144
Never Can Say Goodbye 64
Neville, Aaron 140
New Christy Minstrels 10, 82
New Colony Six 93
New Deal Record Service 150
New Jersey Labeling Machine Company 17
New Orleans, Louisiana 2, 6, 47, 62, 139–141
New Thresholds in Sound Dynagroove 72
New York, New York 6–7, 13–15, 25, 35, 50, 58, 59, 63, 66, 73, 139, 148, 164
Newberry, Mickey 73
Newsweek 152–153
1910 Fruitgum Company 28, 29, 165
Nipper 93, 142
Nitzsche, Jack 14–15, 243–244
Norman, Gene 159
Norman Petty Studios 106
Norton, Duke 159
Nutty Squirrels *144*

Odetta 82
Ohio Express 28–29, 88
Ohio Phonograph Company 143
Oklahoma 90
Oldham, Spooner 127–128
One-Stop Record Service 150
Onyx Records 101
Original Nairobi Afro Band 50
Oriole Records 62
Orlando, Tony 181
Orsattis, Don 63
Osborne, Jimmy 9–10, 81
O'Shea, Shad 1–3, 143
Owens, Buck 19
Owens, Gary 24

Pa-Go-Go Records 124, 161
The Pacers 56
Page, Patty 89
Page, Ricky 47–48
Paramount Records 103
Parker, Fess 49
Parker, Robert 140
Parsons, Ray 159
Parton, Stella 101

Index 261

Pathe Records 9, 240
Paul Revere and the Raiders 152, 175
Paula Records 1
Paxton, Gary 146
payola 23, 157, 165
Peacock Records 57
Pearl, Minnie 48
Penguins 45
Penn, Dan 5, 127–128
Percy Faith and His Orchestra 79
Perkins, Carl 128, 193
Perry, Richard 105
Peter, Paul and Mary 40, 42, 82, 129
Peterson, Ray 11
Peterson, Walter 81
Petrillo, James C. 20
Pfanstiehl 139
Philco 16–17, 96
Philips Phonographic Industries 33
Philips Records 83, 167
Phillips, Sam 128, 150; *see also* Sun Records
Pickett, Bobby 146; *see also* Bobby "Boris" Pickett and the Crypt Kickers
Pickett, Wilson 134, 169
Pickettywitch 49
Pickwick Records 8
Pitney, Gene 77
Plantation Records 47–48
The Platters 163
Plaza Music Company 62
Polygram Records 155
Popular Tunes 150
Porter, Peter 159
Posey, Sandy 127
Powers, Joey 18, 97–98
Presley, Elvis 12, 14, 18, 36–37, 61, 68, 140, 158, 166–167, 206
Presto Recording Corporation 168
Price, Ray 49, 149
protest music 33, 41, 56, 75–76, 82, 129, 247–248
Puckett, Gary 105

Quad 172
Question Mark and the Mysterians 88, 124, 161

Race Catalog 173
Rainwater, Marvin 152
Randy and the Rainbows 97–98
The Rascals 93, 165
RCA Victor 8, 18–19, 36, 39, 41, 52, 57, 67, 72, 75, 84–85, 91, 93, 122, 123, 130, 142, 149, 167, 240–241, 243; *see also* Victor Talking Machine Company
Reagan, Ronald 42
Real Record One Stop 150
Rebounds 20
Record Industry Association of America 90–91
Record Roundup 182
Record World 43, 46, 88–89, 131, 135, 149
Reeves, Jim 13
Regal Zonophone 200
Reisman, Joe 200
Remley Distributors 102
Resco Records 105
Rhythm Orchids 106
Rice, Dumpy 99
Rich, Charlie 51
Rich, Don 19
Richard, Reynauld 141
Riddle, Nelson 121
Righteous Brothers 27, 169, 243
Riley, Jeannie C. 47–48
The Ripcords 32
Robbins, Marty 101
Roberts, Cal 69
Roberts, Peter 45
Roberts Distributing 103
Robison, Carson 81
Roby, Don 54, 57
Roe, Tommy 5
Rogers, Roy 9–10
Rolling Stones 26
Ronee Records 101
Ronettes 57, 169, 243
Ronstadt, Linda 88
Rooftop Singers 82
Rose, Irving "Slim" 148
Rothstein, Nate 21
Roulette Records 124, 161
Round Table Music 42
Rouse, Sonley 32
Royal, Billy Joe 47
Royal Plastics 52
Royal Theater Studio 126
Royaltones 60
Rudman, Kal 131
Rundgren, Todd 10
Rush, Merilee 127
Ryan, Charlie 32–33, 66

Sainte-Marie, Buffy 41–42
Sakamoto, Kya 83
Sam the Sham and the Pharaohs **55**; *see also* Samudio, Domingo

Index

Samudio, Domingo 55; *see also* Sam the Sham and the Pharaohs
Samuels, Jerry 146
Sands, Tommy 37, 68
Santo and Johnny 108
Savoy Records 123
Scepter Records 38, 70
Schlachter, Marvin 19
Schwarz, Dr. Fred 42
Scott, Ed 158
Scott, Jack 27
Seals, Troy 35
Sears and Roebuck Company 62, 74, 166–177
Sedaka, Neil 25
Seeburg Corporation 70, 197
Seger, Bob 134; *see also* Bob Seger System
Serendipity Singers 82
Seville, David 145–146; *see also* Bagdasarian, Ross
Shadd, Bobby 58
sheet music 49
Sheperd, Mike 101
Sherrill, Billy 15
Shirelles 50
Silvertone Records 62, 74
Simon, Paul 134
Sinatra, Frank 89, 152
Sinatra, Nancy 89–90
The Singing Nun 83
Singleton, Shelby 47–48
Sir Douglas Quintet 27
Smash Records 105
Smith, Bob 45
Smith, Major Bill 105
Smothers Brothers 82
Snap Records 124, 161
Sonny Dae and His Knights 152
"Soul Makossa" 50–51
Sousa, John Phillip 110
South, Joe 176
Souvenir Records 33
Spanky and Our Gang 73; *see also* McFarland, Elaine "Spanky"
Spar Records 47–48
Specialty Records 123
Spector, Phil 15, 57, 73; *see also* Wall of Sound
Spenser, Len 143
Spero, Herman 239
Springfield, Dusty 126–127
S.S. Kresge Company 62
Stampers 108
The Stamps 18

Standard Radio Transcription Services, Inc. 16
Starcher, Bobby 48
Starday Records 149
Starr Piano Co. 103
Stax Records 94, 126
Steinberg, David 66, 138
Steinberg, D.M. 49
Sterling Title Strip Company 75
Stevens, April 171
Stevens, Dodie 12
Stevens, Ray 146
Stewart, Cal 76, 81, 123, 166
Stidham, Larry 11–12
Stone Ponys 88
Streisand, Barbra 88, 105
Sun Records 10, 131, 132, 150, 239; *see also* Phillips, Sam
Super K Productions 28, 239
Surfaris 27, 52, 81, 93
The Swampers 134–135, 170
Sweet Inspirations 17
Swenson, John 176
Swinging Blue Jeans 25

Talmadge, Art 10
Tamla Records 47
Taylor, Chip 214
Terrell, Tammi 97–98
"The Theme from *A Summer* Place" 79
Thomas, B.J. 18, 38, 140
Thomas Wayne and the DeLons 128
Thornton, Big Mama 11
Times Square Records 148
Tin Pan Alley 59, 208
Tina and Merle 13
Tom Duffy Orchestra 152
Tone Distributors 103
Tony Orlando and Dawn 13
Toussaint, Allen 140–141
Tower Records 8, 20
Town Hall One Stop Records 50
Trent, Jackie 26
20th Century-Fox Records *22*
Twirl Records 60
The Twist [dance] 55–56, 241
Twitty, Conway 47

The Union 58
United Artists Records 67–68, 80, 151
United Recording Artists 10, 47–48, 67–68
United States Gramophone Company 163, 176

Index 263

U.S. House Un-American Activities Committee 133
United States Phonograph Company 123
U. S. Senate 59

Vale, Jerry 132
Valens, Ritchie 27
Valli, Frankie 78
Vanderlaan, Vero 42
Vanilla Fudge 51
Van Story, Marcus 239
Vaughan, Billy 45
Vaughan, Stevie Ray 35
Vee, Bobby 17, 37
Verne, Larry 146
Victor Orthophonic Credenza 152
Victor Records 103
Victor Talking Machine Company 76, 98, 123, 142, 159–160, 168, 240–241; *see also* RCA Victor Victrola 180
Village Gate discotheque 64
Vincent, Gene 239
Vincent, Johnny 1
Vinylite 129
The Virtues 93
Viva Tonal phonograph 152, 242
Vocalion Records 15
Vogue Records 161, 243

Walker, Robin 86
Wall of Sound 15, 169, 243–244; *see also* Spector, Phil
Wallace, Jerry 175–176
Wallace, Slim 128–129
Wallis, Ruth 156
Ward, Billy 62
Ward, Joe 114
Warner Brothers 96
Warner-Elektra-Asylum 8
Warren, Rusty 156–157; *see also* Goldman, Ilene
Warwick Records 60
Watts, Ceil 5
Wax, 125
WCPO 2, 154, 158
Webb, Jimmy 117
Webcors Magic Wand Disc Changer 63
Webster-Chicago Co. 246
Wegner, Jack 17
Weil, Cynthia 25

Wells, Mary **22**, 69
Western Electric Company 152
Wheat Records 101
White, Barry 177
White, Bergen 14
White, Glenn 172
White, Josh 133
White, Tony Joe 14
White Whale Records 130
Wild Man Steve 156
Willet, Slim 49
Willett Records 49
Williams, Andy 42, 69, 132
Williams, Hank 150
Williams, Roger 45
Williams Manufacturing Company 137
Wills, Tommy 112
Wilson, Frank 32–33
Wilson, Meri 146
WINS 7, 45–46, 159
WIRL 86
Wisner, Jimmy 14
Witherspoon, Bill 28
WKLO 174
WLS 86
WNEW 158
WNIL 161
Wolfman Jack 238
WONE 2
Wooley, Sheb 146; *see also* Colder, Ben
World Pacific Records 49
World War II 86, 91
WPIX 142
Wray, Link 93–94
Wright, Dale 188
Wright, Ruby 13
WSRS 77
W.T. Grant Woolworth Stores 62
Wurlitzer 30, 81, 110, 247
WYSL 9

XERF 238

Ya-Ya Band 140
Yankovic, Weird Al 11
York, Rusty 44–45

Zodiac 81
The Zombies 25, 32
Zucker, Irwin 170 27

www.ingramcontent.com/pod-product-compliance
Lightning Source LLC
Chambersburg PA
CBHW032035300426
44117CB00009B/1065